"When they hate you, don't hate back.

When they talk bad about you, don't talk bad back.

If I lose it all in a roll of the dice, I'll never mention it,

but I will try again twice. May we all develop

the compassion and capacity to love well."

PAPA:
The Story of Papa John's Pizza

By John H. Schnatter

ISBN 978-1-63393-386-6

Published by

◤ köehlerbooks™

210 60th Street
Virginia Beach, VA 23451
800-435-4811
www.koehlerbooks.com

in association with

ML Publishing, LLC

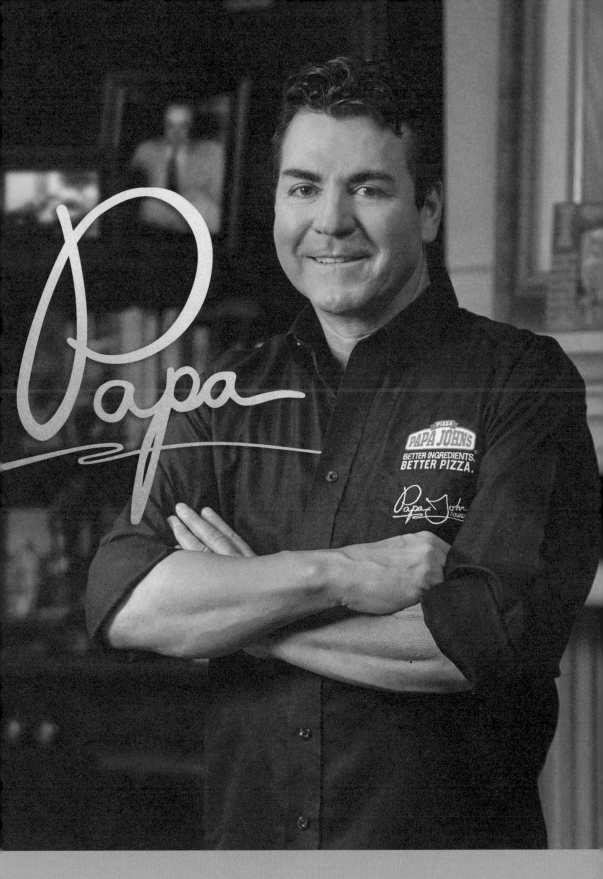

THE STORY OF PAPA JOHN'S PIZZA

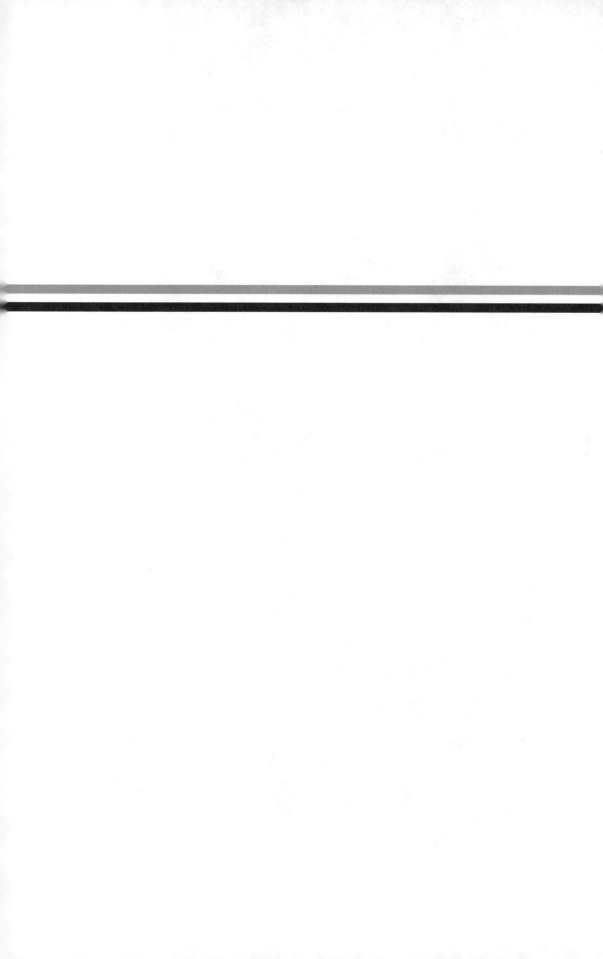

DEDICATION

For my children: Kristine, Danielle and Beau, and grandson Grayson. I love you. This book is to tell them what we did; but more importantly, it is for every young person out there, to show them what they can do if they dream big and work hard.

And to every member of the Papa John's team—past, present, and future. Together, we've built something incredible. Thank you.

TABLE OF CONTENTS

ACKNOWLEDGMENTS

Papa John's is a great American success story. A lot of people have helped get us to where we are today. I'd like to briefly thank some of the most important.

The biggest thanks goes to my Dad, Robert Louis Schnatter, and my Papaw, Louis Erman Ackerson. Papa John's wouldn't exist if they hadn't taught me so many life lessons, especially how to run a good business. The same goes for Martin G. Schnatterer, who came to America with just the shirt on his back and a work ethic like none other. I wish the three of you had the chance to read this book.

My mother, Beth Ackerson, also deserves the highest praise. She always demanded the best from her kids—pretty good never cut it. Work hard and be honest were my Mom's two guiding principles. Now I expect the same thing of my own kids, as well as my company. I have always been afraid of letting my mother down. I hope she's proud of what I've accomplished.

Beyond my family, there are plenty of others who have influenced my own approach to business. Chris Karamesines and the Fondrisi brothers showed me that pizza-making isn't a job—it's an art. In their own different ways, they taught me how to make traditional, superior-quality pizzas and run a business that benefits your community. And our suppliers, who continuously work with us to help deliver on our 'Better Ingredients' promise.

I would name the entire Papa John's team if I could, but there aren't enough trees in the world to make that much paper. The only one I'll mention here is Denise Robinson, who has been with Papa John's since before we even existed. She and I are the two longest-serving Papa John's team members—that's how steadfast and loyal she is. I name a few dozen other team members who I love and respect in Chapter Six. Again, I wish I could name everyone, but I can't. Just know that I am grateful for all of you—it is an honor to work with such talented and principled men and women.

As far as the book itself goes, it took me years of searching before I found a team that could bring my story to life. Stephen Ford writes the way I talk. Andrew Llewellyn helped me gather my thoughts. Melody Ann Weber made the book itself beautiful. Coach John Calipari frequently offered me insights into the book writing process. Aaron Thompson helped get it across the finish line. And plenty of others gave me feedback, edits, and suggestions that took what you're reading to another level.

Finally, I'd like to thank my wife, Annette. She's the only person in the world who can run a Papa John's store better than I can. Maybe someday I'll catch up to her. After all, as H.L. Mencken said, "a man may be a fool and not know it, but not if he's married."

INTRODUCTION: BETTER BUSINESS, BETTER WORLD

Before Papa John's was ever a reality, it was an idea.

The idea was that we could use better ingredients to make a better pizza. This realization came to me as a 15-year-old washing dishes in the back of a local pizzeria. Seven years later, this idea inspired me to knock down a wall in a broom closet in the back of my father's bar so that I could start making my own traditional, superior-quality pizzas. The idea worked well enough that I built a stand-alone pizzeria only a year later. Then I built a second, a tenth, a hundredth, a thousandth, and kept going. Papa John's hasn't stopped since. It never will.

My story is one of the American Dream. I didn't know what to expect when I made my first Papa John's pizza in that broom closet 32 years ago. But I did know that a principled business built on a solid foundation could achieve great things and improve people's lives. I believed we could create a popular pizzeria that kept my family well-taken care of, my team members well-paid and my community well-fed. I believed we could build a win-win-win relationship that left everyone better off. My goal was always to make a real and lasting difference in my hometown of Jeffersonville, Indiana.

What I didn't realize was that a principled business could do so much more—that it could make the world a better place for millions of people far beyond my hometown.

That's what we've done over the past three decades. Today, Papa John's International, Inc. is one of the largest pizza companies in the world. As of December 2016, we operate 5,000 stores in over 40 countries and territories, with nearly 100,000 team members at franchise stores and 21,000 at corporate stores and had global system-wide sales of $3.7 billion, with 260 million pizzas sold every year. Every day, 600,000 people walk through the doors of a Papa John's store or open their front door to find a Papa John's pizza waiting for them.

But these numbers are only a reflection of what truly makes a difference in the world around us. Papa John's has succeeded because we make something that people want—something that benefits our team members, our customers, our shareholders, our suppliers, our franchisees and many more. Through innovation, respect for others and personal sacrifice, we have created a company that has brought people together and benefited millions throughout the world.

That is what truly matters. The proper role of business is to create jobs, grow wages and give people opportunities they otherwise would not have had.

Any business can do this, big or small. I have a particular fondness for small businesses—Papa John's started in a broom closet, after all. I believe the little guy is at the heart of our entire economic system. Some small businesses turn into larger businesses because they bring tremendous value into people's lives. Even the ones that stay small continue to provide jobs and joy in their local communities. No matter what form they take, entrepreneurship and innovation are the catalyst of human progress. And anyone—no matter who they are or where they came from—can contribute to this process if they're willing to try.

Ultimately, progress is what every entrepreneur should aspire to achieve—indeed, I believe every entrepreneur *can* achieve it, no matter what industry they're in or what product or service they sell. Human ingenuity and innovation are boundless. Anyone, regardless of their socioeconomic status or station in life, has the potential to find a new way to make the world a better place. It doesn't matter where they start or how small their first experiment is. It *does* matter that they remember that they can only help themselves by first helping others.

Fortunately, some business leaders are already engaged in this noble mission, which I call "good business." Yet many others—in fact, I believe that most others—are not. Instead, they engage in "bad business."

By this I mean the type of business where they put their own self-interest above society's interests. They focus on short-term profits while neglecting long-term investments. They forgo quality in favor of mediocrity. They get bogged down by size or by bureaucracy or by falling into old habits that are hard to change. They "go to sleep," as I call it, and find it easier to break the rules or use unethical business practices. They take advantage of their people and treat them as objects of self-gain. They seek to handicap their competitors by using government to tilt the playing field in their own favor, using nefarious and devious business practices to benefit themselves at others' expense. You need only look at the latest headlines to see just how rampant these problems are.

That's why I wrote this book. I hope to remind my fellow entrepreneurs of our real calling: to make the world around us a better place. That comes from my heart. I've seen firsthand how to do this—through innovation, respect for people and focus on quality. Just as Papa John's motto is "Better Ingredients. Better Pizza," so I believe that every company, big or small, should have the unofficial motto of "Better Business, Better World."

It doesn't matter what words they use, so long as business leaders understand that their highest calling is to help themselves by first helping others.

I hope this book will help people understand how to do that. I have learned many lessons over the past four decades. I'm still learning lessons on a daily basis, and I don't expect that will ever change. There are always new and better ways to run a good business that makes other people's lives better.

For my part, I'm focused on finding out how to continue improving the quality of our traditional, superior-quality Papa John's pizzas. Even more importantly, I want to continue helping Papa John's team members achieve their own personal potential. They truly put dignity into their labor. I hope to continue finding ways to reward them and help them find fulfillment in their lives. At the end of the day, Papa John's is in the people business more than it is in the pizza business.

I have many examples of what works and how to think about situations and problems that businesses often confront. I have just as many examples—and probably more—of what doesn't work and how *not* to think. Over the course of this book, I'll introduce you to many of the concepts I've developed and adopted over the years. I hope that every chapter is filled with nuggets that will make you laugh, make you think and make you wonder how you can apply them—or improve them—in your own life.

Some of the concepts are crucial to Papa John's history and success. Chapter Two focuses on "Go Left"—a simple phrase that captures the essence of Papa John's culture of entrepreneurship and excellence. Chapter Four focuses on the development of FASPAC—the six specific principles that should guide every member of the Papa John's team, just as they guided me when I made the first Papa John's pizza. And Chapters Six and Seven will introduce you to the two leadership paradigms that I have identified—the Head Coach and Kingship models. Spoiler alert: you don't want to be a King.

The rest of the chapters deal with other important business concepts and ideas, as well. You'll also hear about the times when Papa John's fell short—the times when we "fell asleep," as I put it. I can admit that there have been many times when Papa John's did not live out the principles that we preach. These times have been hard, not just for the company but for me personally. Papa John's is a part of me—it pains me when we aren't all that we can be or all that we should be. We are constantly reevaluating our practices in light of our principles to ensure that we are delivering on our promise to customers. This process is often painful. But sticking to our principles is never an easy task.

In any case, these lessons have been critical in helping me understand and clarify the ideas I discuss in this book. They have also helped me understand what separates Papa John's—and the companies like it—from the businesses that aren't acting in the best interests of society. Recognizing these differences has helped me develop tools to help principled business leaders identify and overcome the obstacles that are holding their companies back. Looking around America, it's sad to see just how many business leaders have forgotten their mission to make the world a better place.

To be clear, the business community is not my only intended audience. I also hope other would-be entrepreneurs read this book—the next generation on whose shoulders falls the burden of creating a better world. The education of future generations of entrepreneurs is critically important for continued progress and the long-term success of the American economy. We're always one generation away from forgetting the principles that make good businesses possible.

Most importantly, I hope that anyone with an interest in making the world a better place finds value in my story, my thoughts and the ideas that I've developed over the years. My family, my friends, my team members, my customers, my suppliers and many others have played an important role in turning Papa John's into what it is today. This "collaborative alliance," as I call it, has been crucial to our success. It is no less crucial for the success of any other company or, for that matter, any community or even any country.

No matter who reads this, I hope they take away this one message. Business requires principled people who are willing to work hard, take risks and innovate. The businesses that are run this way—the "good businesses"—take care of their people, create quality products and ultimately improve people's lives. Papa John's is where it is today because we did exactly that. We have made the world a better place, one pizza slice at a time.

Achieving this goal requires every ounce of our energy. To this day, I still focus on the small things, spending much of my time in the kitchen and the lab at Papa John's headquarters. I'm still passionate about constantly improving our pizzas. Our traditional, superior-quality Papa John's pizzas can always get better. Each small step we take in that direction is a step towards giving others—our customers, our team members, our friends and our families—something that makes their life just a little bit better. And once you do that, you're well on your way to making the world better, too.

That's what everyone should aspire to accomplish, no matter who they are or what they do. I wish the best life has to offer to anyone who follows this path—or better yet, to anyone who charts a new one. Godspeed!

1984

John converts a broom closet into a pizza kitchen.

1985

1st Papa John's opens in Jeffersonville, Indiana.

1986

Papa John's sells its 1st franchise (store #9).

1991

Papa John's 100th restaurant opening.

1997

Papa John's ranked #1 in Restaurants and Institutions Choice in Chains survey.

1998

Papa John's tops $1 billion in system-wide restaurant sales.

1998

First International store opened in Mexico City.

1999

Papa John's 2,000th restaurant opening

2012

Go Left Leadership Development Training launches.

2013

International store 1,000 opens.

2015

Digital Sales exceed 50% of all restaurant sales for first time ever.

2015

Launch of Papa Cares, Papa John's onsite health clinic.

1993

Papa John's files IPO.

1994

Papa John's 500th restaurant opening.

1994

Papa John's ranked #1 of best-run small companies by Business Week.

1995

Papa John's ranked 10th by Forbes in list of the nation's 200 best small companies.

2001

Papa John's becomes 1st pizza chain to offer online ordering at all traditional restaurants.

2008

Papa John's tops $1 billion in cumulative e-commerce sales.

2010

Papa John's tops $2 billion in cumulative e-commerce sales.

2010

Papa John's becomes the Official Pizza Sponsor of the NFL and the Super Bowl.

2016

Papa John's becomes the offical pizza of MLB.

2016

Papa John's eliminates artificial flavors, synthetic colors, and high fructose corn syrup from its menu.

2016

Ranked #1 in the American Customer Satisfaction Index for 15 of last 17 years.

2016

Papa John's 5,000th restaurant opening.

CHAPTER ONE

MICK'S LOUNGE

Someone much wiser than me once said that we stand on the shoulders of giants. I couldn't agree more. I was fortunate enough to stand on the shoulders of two giants—my father, Robert Louis Schnatter, and my "Papaw," my grandfather on my Mom's side, Louis Erman Ackerson.

You'd be hard-pressed to find two men who were more different than my Dad and my Papaw. That's why they were both so important to my development—they complemented each other and taught me different lessons. On the one hand, they were both incredibly entrepreneurial. On the other hand, one was successful in much of what he did, while the other failed time and time again.

That dubious honor falls to my father. He went to school to become a lawyer, graduating from the University of Louisville Law School in 1958. His career started brightly. He became the youngest elected city judge in the history of Indiana at the age of 26. After he finished his term on the bench, he ran for prosecuting attorney for two four-year terms, winning both times. He then dabbled in politics, including running for lieutenant governor, sheriff and a few other minor positions.

In between his various political pursuits—which were more like stunts than anything else—he practiced law. He excelled as a lawyer, specializing in criminal law. It still amazes me just how good he was at practicing law. He could pick up a case file on the way to the courtroom, read it for the first time and still clean his opponents' clocks. Sometimes he'd learn everything he needed while walking across Court Avenue from his office to the courthouse—a process that took about eight minutes. There weren't many people who could keep up with him, in the courtroom or in life.

Yet for all his promise, he was unable to turn his strong start and natural intelligence into long-term success. His lifelong goal was to be a successful entrepreneur. But he simply couldn't run a business.

It wasn't for lack of trying. Over the years, he was involved in numerous business ventures in or around our hometown of Jeffersonville, Indiana. All of them failed. Bob's Carpet Company—defunct. Central Solar Heating Company—defunct. Hunter's Lounge and Bar and Grill—defunct. Star Wars Wine Company—defunct. Southern Indiana Cable Vision—defunct. Barbara's Rustic Frog Inn—defunct. The only one of his businesses that ever made it was Mick's Lounge, and it was nearly defunct when I joined him as a business partner in 1983. But more on that later.

It's a testament to my Dad's never-give-up attitude that he kept trying new things. That's the sign of a real entrepreneur—they have a thousand ideas and they never stop trying to turn each of them into a reality. More than that, a real entrepreneur never gives up. Almost every innovation and advance in human history has been the result of trial and, yes, error. Before you figure out what works, you have to figure out what doesn't.

Bob Schnatter as the youngest city judge in Indiana's history, age 26

1960

One thing's for sure: my father discovered a lot of things that didn't work. He always made money throughout the years, but he was never good at managing it. That was not a desirable trait for someone who wanted to be a successful businessman. Things got so bad in the mid-1970s and early 1980s that my Dad wasn't paying our electricity and water bills for weeks or even months at a time. My Mom had to pick up a job clerking at the county clerk's office. He was also 12 months behind on the house payment at that point, so my Mom sold a piece of property on the river that my Papaw had given her several years earlier. The $12,000 she got from the sale got us caught up on the mortgage payments.

But like clockwork, my father would find himself in tough financial situations again and again. For instance, in 1984, he sold 36 percent of Mick's Lounge to one of our co-workers for $20,000. Only a few weeks later, he came back to that same co-worker and asked to borrow $2,000 so he could go to the 1984 Democratic National Convention. How he'd lost, misplaced, or spent the $20,000 in just two weeks will always be a mystery to me. It shows just how badly my Dad managed the money he made.

Our whole family—my mother, my father, myself, my brother Chuck and my sister Anne—was affected by his poor financial decisions. It was humiliating, especially for my Mom. She was and is a strong woman who demanded respect and did everything with integrity. Yet my father constantly disrespected her with his foolish life choices.

It didn't help that he sometimes gambled. He spent most days at his law office or at one of his various entrepreneurial experiments. He'd usually come home in the late afternoon for a quick nap, then head out on the town for a few drinks and a game or two of cards. He also loved the horse races. Before I turned 12, I learned by watching my Dad that "you can win a race, but you can't win at the races." I would later hear another saying that also summed this up—"To be a millionaire in the horse business, you need to start off as a billionaire."

Pictured from left – Papaw, Sara Ackerson, Mom, Dad,
Marie Schnatter, John C. Schnatter

Mom and Dad on their Wedding Day

To be fair, sometimes my Dad won big. One evening in 1977, he came home with a 1972 Chevy Impala. He won it playing cards. That car was a constant reminder of his nightly routine—literally. When he got back around 10 or 11 at night, he'd drive the car up the driveway, then swing a tight left turn to get it into the garage. But he sometimes cut it a little short and hit the brick corner on the side of the garage. My brother and I shared a bedroom immediately overhead. We heard the hit and felt the house shake. We slept in a bunk bed—Chuck on top and me on bottom—and the noise would wake us both up. We'd stick our heads off the side of the bed, look at each other and say, "Dad's home."

This was fun for us. We were just kids, after all. The same couldn't be said for my Mom, who had to work during the days and take care of the family alone most nights.

This had a profound effect on me as a kid. It showed me the type of man I didn't want to be. I wanted to provide for my family and be there when they needed me. I loved my father very much—he was, after all, one of the two most important people in my life—but even before I turned 12, I knew I wanted to succeed where my Dad hadn't. I wanted to make sure I never had a problem providing for my family and loved ones. I wanted to be a successful entrepreneur.

1969

My sister Anne, me (center), and my brother (buck

My mother played a key role in shaping my perspective on life. If I had to sum up Beth Ackerson in one word, it would be steadfast. She was the rock that stayed constant in the hurricane that was our family. Being married to my father, she had to learn to be self-sufficient. She knew that her three children would have to rely on her for support and care. She also knew that she had to teach us to be responsible, since her husband wasn't doing a good job. I learned from an early age that my Mom expected—no, *demanded*—the best from her kids. One time I came home from school with a report card that had five A's and one B. My Mom's reaction was classic: "What's up with the B? We don't make B's in this household."

To this day, I'm immensely grateful that my Mom pushed us so hard to succeed. I said earlier that I was fortunate to stand on the shoulders of two giants. In many ways, my Mom was even more of a giant than my Dad or my Papaw. I could stand on their shoulders—I couldn't climb high enough to get to hers.

Like most boys, I desperately wanted to have my mother's approval. She ingrained in me from a young age that I had to provide for my loved ones in order to have her respect. She made it very clear to me early on that if I wasn't successful and couldn't pay the bills, I was no good in her eyes. That would make me worthless—no, it would make me less than worthless. Letting my mother down was absolutely terrifying to me.

But that didn't mean that I wasn't willing to take any risks at all. For all his faults, my Dad greatly influenced me when it came to trying new things and getting my hands dirty. That was one of his biggest contributions to my personality and my approach to life and to business. Robert L. Schnatter had literally no fear of failure—that's why he started so many new ventures. His entrepreneurial failures were still entrepreneurial, even though they didn't pan out. He taught me from an early age that it's far better to try and fail than to never try at all. If you fall, you can still get up. You never have the chance to fall if you don't take a leap of faith in the first place. Every entrepreneur intuitively understands this. My Dad hardwired this essential concept into my head as a kid. It would take me decades to fully realize this. Looking back, I see now that my Dad modeled entrepreneurship on a daily basis. That deeply and profoundly influenced me as a young boy watching his father.

My Mom, my sister Anne, and me

Beyond the importance of risk-taking, my Dad taught me many other lessons. He was big-hearted. In between his various business ventures, he somehow found time to be an integral part of the Jeffersonville community. He took pride in giving back to those around him, even if he sometimes didn't provide for his own family.

One of his many side gigs was coaching my Little League team. I will never forget the time he bought baseball equipment for the kids in a nearby low-income community called Claysburg, where a large portion of the kids were African-American. It was the early '70s and racial tensions were still high across the country, yet my Dad always made a point to treat everyone equally. He recognized that everyone—no matter who they are, where they come from, or what they do—deserves to be treated with dignity and respect. I'll never forget the smiles on the kids' faces as my Dad handed them the baseball bats, balls and gloves. These kids eventually became my friends at Parkview Middle School and Jeffersonville High School. Yet that was only one of the countless things he did to bring people together and put smiles on their faces.

His love for his community—and his commitment to its success and well-being—deeply affected me. Dad was a firm believer that you should give people a hand up, but not a handout. (He never took any handouts either, despite his many failures.) In fact, he thought it was absolutely necessary to help those around him in any way he could. He told me many times that it is "obligatory to give back to your community because the community has given so much to you." This stuck with me. He helped me realize that everyone should strive to build mutually beneficial relationships within their communities.

This lesson is true at all times and in all places, including in the business world. How you treat your team members determines how they'll treat you, as well as how we all serve our customers. I would later learn that the customer's experience will never be better than the team member's experience. A successful relationship, whether at home or in the workplace, can't exist without respect and trust. Cultivating these traits is, as my Dad always said, "obligatory." There's no better way to put it.

1972

My Dad (back right) coaching Little League team
ages 10-12. I'm in the back row,
fourth from the right

1976

My Dad (back left) coaching my senior league team, I'm in the back row, second from the right

In short, Dad meant the world to me. He was instrumental in my early life. He showed me much that I wanted to emulate and much that I wanted to avoid.

Yet in many ways, my maternal grandfather Louis Erman Ackerson—my "Papaw"—was even more important to my development. He encouraged my entrepreneurial spirit, taught me the importance of good character and always pushed me to be the best that I could be.

More than anything else, he was a good man. If my Dad meant the world to me, my Papaw meant the universe.

When you met Papaw, you couldn't help but think that he was something special. He was over six feet tall and seemed to be carved out of marble. He was cool, he was funny, he made others feel comfortable around him. He lived most of his life in Louisville, Kentucky, which was immediately across the Ohio River from Jeffersonville. I spent my earliest years traveling down Interstate 65 across the bridge between the two cities at least once or twice a week, sometimes more often. In a very real sense, the river was the dividing line between the two biggest influences on my life. The Jeffersonville side was defined by my father, with his financial struggles, the resulting chaos in our family life and his constant entrepreneurial experiments throughout the town. The Louisville side of the river was something else entirely. Papaw's life was defined by consistency, prudence and diligence. His life, in a lot of ways, contradicted that of the life of my father.

Like my Dad, Papaw was an immensely talented lawyer, albeit in a different field. He practiced corporate law rather than criminal law. He graduated from the Jefferson School of Law—now part of the University of Louisville—in 1931 and founded his own law firm shortly thereafter. He built his reputation as a trustworthy lawyer who would fight for his clients and try to do right by them. Most of his clients stuck with him for years, including the partners at Kingfish Restaurants, local yacht club Louisville Boat Works, prominent banker Sammy Kline, Louisville real estate mogul Al J. Schneider and many more. When I was growing up, the firm was named Ackerson, Ackerson, Blandford and Kaiser. (The second Ackerson was for my uncle.) Later it became Ackerson, Ackerson and Blandford. The firm is still around to this day, although the name has changed several more times in the intervening years.

My Papaw was just as entrepreneurial as my father. Yet where my father was fearless, even foolish at times, my grandfather believed in taking calculated risks that had a high chance of bearing fruit. Failure was not an option—you only took a risk if the odds were on your side. Papaw certainly practiced what he preached. He invested in two other successful businesses on the side. Modern Concrete sold exactly what it sounds like it sold—concrete, bricks and mortar. Liquid Transport provided chemical distribution throughout the region. Just like Papaw's law firm, both of these companies are still around and are still successful today, although they now have different owners. I even built my house using Modern Concrete's bricks.

I believe Papaw's success was a reflection of the values he held dear. Like all of us, he wasn't perfect, but he always tried to play it straight, play by the rules, run a clean business and leave all his cards on the table—all while having fun and bringing joy to those around him. He once told me, "If you're a good person, you'll win; if you're a bad guy, you'll lose. You can't beat the system." He expected us to lead good wholesome lives, just like he did. That, more than anything, explains why I admired my grandfather as much as I did and why he had such an enormous influence on my life. He was an upstanding—and outstanding—human being.

I've spent the rest of my life trying to be half the man that my Papaw was. He was a good man who inspired those around him to also be good. He tried to make the world a better place however he could. And everyone around town knew it. That's exactly the sort of reputation, gained through good deeds, that everyone should try to cultivate. Papaw definitely did. And he influenced me and many others through his example.

So it shouldn't be a surprise that Papaw was more of a mentor to me than my own Dad. My Dad constantly traveled during his time as a lawyer and a politician. When he was gone, my Mom needed help taking care of me and my two younger siblings, who were at that point not even teens. Papaw stepped in to help. I saw him on a weekly basis for most of my formative years, mainly because my brother and I worked for him on the weekends. On the weekends when we didn't see him, Papaw would still swing by our house on Sunday mornings to bring us bakery goods. We continued this routine well into my teenage years.

I learned countless lessons about life, business and many other things from Papaw. For example, he taught me the virtue of saving. He still had the first nickel he ever made and he had a solid financial reputation around town and with local banks. I remember going with him to the hardware store and wondering why he never carried cash. I would ask Papaw, "How come you never have any money?" He responded, "I don't need any money. My credit is good." His word was his bond and everybody knew that.

At that point I didn't yet know I wanted to run my own business. But I did know my Papaw's honesty, trustworthiness, accountability, fairness and reputation were traits I needed to have. I admired Papaw for how he practiced his principles as a businessman. That may be why I ended up pursuing business later in life. I always wanted to follow in his footsteps.

Crucially, that's not because he made money or lived a comfortable life. Watching Papaw interact with his co-workers, customers and community showed me that entrepreneurs play a powerful role in making people's lives better. Papaw was instrumental in teaching me that businessmen have a moral duty to take care of those around them. I have tried to follow his example since before I founded Papa John's. For over 30 years, I have strived every day to improve the lives of my team members, franchisees, suppliers, customers and community. This gets to the heart of how our free economy works: you help yourself by first helping others. Papaw modeled this mindset as much or more than anyone I've ever met.

Papaw also taught me the importance of hard work, which I learned while doing odd jobs on his two-acre property. My brother and I spent most weekends helping him out with odd jobs on his property. He had no intention of letting us skate by when we were there. If we finished one task, he'd give us another one, and he always made us work hard and fast and to get the job done, until we were exhausted.

He also encouraged us to be mechanically inclined. I would often ride around Papaw's property on his tractor. It occasionally broke down. When it did, Papaw would simply tell me to "fix it," no matter what the problem was. I wasn't even eight years old when he said this for the first time. Then he just walked away and left me to my own devices. This was daunting at first, but it was an opportunity for me to learn with my hands. Every time, I tore the tractor apart to try and figure out what was wrong and how we could make it right. I'd get into the motor, the carburetor, the gear system—everything. I was trying to do what Papaw had asked—I was trying to find and fix the problem.

Sometimes I did, sometimes I didn't. But the outcome didn't matter to Papaw. What he really wanted me to do was to figure out how things worked. He encouraged me to be curious—to find opportunities and demand answers and get to the bottom of things. He wanted us to know how things were put together and how they were engineered, which left me with a profound curiosity about how things worked, and why. Once Papaw planted this seed in my head, I was no longer content with only figuring out how the tractor worked. I had to do the same thing with every other piece of equipment on the property. I got my hands on as many pieces of machinery as I could. I worked on them on top of the giant workbench in Papaw's basement. I could even get the tractor down there because Papaw had built a ramp from the backyard. The basement quickly became my home away from home—I must have spent hundreds of hours down there. Papaw would come down every now and then to see how things were going. I always told him, "I'm figuring it out." He was constantly encouraging my curiosity.

This is one of the greatest gifts he ever gave me. It profoundly affected how I approached the rest of my life. I still have to get to the bottom of everything, not just machinery. How a business works. How the world works. How life works. I remember once getting dragged to the principal's office in high school because I asked too many questions in Mr. Kennedy's chemistry class. There, Mr. Kennedy told the principal that I was disrupting his class. The principal replied, "Does he ask good questions?" Mr. Kennedy responded, "He asked real good questions." The principal responded, "Well, answer his questions." That was a direct result of Papaw teaching me to tinker with everything from such a young age.

That lesson was invaluable. It undoubtedly affected my own approach to both business and life, whether it was working on Papaw's tractor or improving the pizza at the very first Papa John's. In fact, I still tinker with Papa John's to this very day. I still spend much of my time in the kitchen and the lab at our headquarters, experimenting with our recipes and seeing how we can improve them.

But Papaw didn't just want us to get our hands dirty. Equally important in his mind was cleaning up your messes. If you're going to take something apart, you also have to put it back together. Sure enough, Papaw always demanded that we put the tractor back together again and put all the tools back in the box or on the wall. Then, at the end of the day, he would tell us to get cleaned up. We would take a shower, put on some nice clothes, and then Papaw would take us down to a nice restaurant for a burger or a steak.

He wanted to reward us for a job well done. He believed it was not enough just to work well and work hard; you also had to be able to go home and live a good life, however you defined it. I now model this in my own life, which is why I do everything I can to reward my team members for a job well done. I believe we should work our asses off during the day, leave everything better than we found it and then go home to lead a comfortable life with our friends and family. That's what Papaw did every day of his life, and he was one of the happiest people I've ever met. I want every member of the Papa John's team to be that happy.

Finally, Papaw was always my biggest believer. He never had any doubts I would succeed. Once a year from the age of 12 onwards, he would take me to the local Audubon Country Club to play a round of golf. He was member #1 because no one else came before "Ackerson" alphabetically, which I learned when I ordered Shirley Temples at the clubhouse bar. This was maybe the highlight of my entire year—it was like playing golf with God himself. From the moment we left the club, I couldn't wait to come back the next year. I spent the next 12 months thinking—no, dreaming—about it.

I vividly remember the very first round of golf we played there. We took a quick break on the 10th tee, a vantage point that allowed us to look out over most of the country club. Nestled between the rolling hills, we could see the clubhouse, the pool, the immaculately maintained landscape, everything. It was like being in a different world. As we stood there surveying this beautiful sight, I asked Papaw if he ever thought I'd be successful enough to become a member at a place like Audubon. He didn't even hesitate. "Yes," he told me. "You'll have the ability to buy this place and burn it down if that's what you want to do." I was only 12 years old when he said that. I had no idea what he meant. But in retrospect, I'm incredibly grateful that my Papaw thought I could achieve anything I wanted.

His belief never wavered throughout the years. When I started my own entrepreneurial adventure over a decade later, Papaw was always there to give me good counsel and reassure me that I could succeed and even thrive. I wouldn't be where I am today without Papaw's unceasing support and encouragement.

My Papaw
1955

All told, I was very lucky to learn so many lessons from the different personality attributes and lifestyles of my Dad and my Papaw. Their different approaches to risk-taking were especially influential. My father's fearlessness was his greatest asset. His inability to figure out what worked and what didn't work was his greatest weakness. He tried new things without figuring out why the last one didn't work. My Papaw's approach to risk-taking overcame this problem. Thanks to him, I learned that you have to be intelligent enough to recognize favorable outcomes. Trial and error is good only if you figure out how to avoid the same errors over and over. Tinkering goes hand in hand with apprenticeship—you try something new so that you can become better at your craft.

Even though my Dad and my Papaw had different ideas of what tinkering was supposed to do, they both believed that if you weren't tinkering, you weren't living. Another similarity is that both had a strong work ethic and a desire to overcome any obstacles they encountered in life. And they both had an attitude of "get up early, stay up late, get it done." In a reflection of just how important this is, I still tell my colleagues at Papa John's that they should approach each day with an attitude of, "wake up, be nice, kick ass and repeat." I wouldn't know these words without the influence of my Papaw and my Dad.

• • • • •

I tried to live by this philosophy even when I was just a teen. Thanks to my Papaw and my Dad, I was very conscious of the importance of hard work and diligence when I was hired for my first job at the age of 15. In the fall of 1977, I started washing dishes at Rocky's Sub Pub, a small, local and real Italian family-owned pizzeria in Jeffersonville. It was one of the few good restaurants in town—and the best possible place for me to learn what worked and what didn't in the pizza-making world.

Like many first jobs, mine wasn't fun when I started. I didn't want to wash dishes. (Interestingly, I've since changed my tune. I now enjoy washing dishes because it gives me a window into my past and helps me remember my humble beginnings.) But I'd learned from my Dad and my Papaw that I could rise through the ranks if I worked hard enough. The same day I started, I resolved to put my back into it, never complain, show initiative and climb the ladder of opportunity, even though I didn't even know where the next rung was.

I already knew what I wanted to do, however. From the moment I started at Rocky's, I had my eye set on pizza-making. After a few months of washing dishes, I was given the opportunity to make pizza dough and use the real, fresh-packed tomato sauce that was better than any pizza sauce I'd ever tasted.

This position was a good halfway point for me, but it was only halfway. I still wasn't making the pizza from start to finish. Unfortunately, I knew that going the rest of the distance would prove much more difficult. The Fondrisi family, the authentic Italians who owned Rocky's, believed that pizza-making was a great honor that required great skill and dedication. They were good Italians who took pride in their work and wanted to reserve it for the very best. That meant that

The original Rocky's Sub Pub

the Fondrisi brothers—Joe, John and Frank—had a monopoly on the job. They had certainly earned this privilege, given their insights into pizza-making that could only have been learned through their Italian heritage and years of trial and error.

A few examples of their expertise stand out in my mind. The Fondrisis modified the amount of yeast used in the dough depending on the weather. When it was cold outside, they used more; when it was warm, they used less. They changed this based on the seasons because the dough expanded more in the heat. They also taught me that fresh-packed pizza sauce was far superior to paste, a more common ingredient in the pizza industry. Sauce costs more, but it made a noticeable difference in taste—a difference customers were sure to appreciate. Rocky's bought its sauce from Stanislaus Food Products, the same vendor I would eventually use when I started Papa John's nearly a decade later. To this day, we continue to use Stanislaus' fresh-packed pizza sauce, a reflection of its high quality. It is a company I've always looked up to and respected.

Watching the Fondrisis work, I could tell that pizza-making was equal parts art and science, although from the outside it looked entirely like art.

And I knew I could break into this hallowed ground. I didn't want to take no for an answer—I still don't. So I kept improving and being intentional as I went about washing dishes. My big break came a few months later. One weekend, the Louisville *Courier-Journal* wrote an article about the restaurant scene across the river in Jeffersonville. Up to that point Rocky's had been struggling. That's also why John, Joe and Frank did all the work—they couldn't afford to hire anyone else. Yet when they opened up the paper that morning, they discovered that Rocky's Sub Pub had gotten a stellar review—the kind of review that can forever change a restaurant's future.

Frank, Joe, and John Fondrisi from Rocky's Sub Pub

We immediately felt the effects. That night, Rocky's was busier than it had ever been. The staff was overburdened and the kitchen needed relief. With no one else to turn to, Joe Fondrisi asked me to try my hand at making pizzas. My big chance had finally arrived.

This was an immense honor—and it was also terrifying. I'd only ever watched the Fondrisis make pizzas. I didn't really know what I was supposed to do. But once I stepped into that kitchen, I took to it like a duck to water—or maybe like tomato sauce to dough. I never went back to dishwashing from that point forward.

Me with my beloved 1971 Z28 Camaro

1978

Thus began my lifelong love affair with the pizza pie—an obsession that has not diminished since, even in the 54-year-old I am today. At the time, I hadn't yet figured out that I wanted to start my own pizzeria. But I was beginning to think about running my own business someday. Although I didn't know it at the time, I was starting to find the pieces for the puzzle that was my life. Now I had to start putting them together to make the puzzle complete.

In the meantime, I worked hard enough at Rocky's Sub Pub to buy my very first car, a gold 1971 Chevrolet Camaro Z28 for $1,600. This car would later be an integral part in the creation of Papa John's, as well as its future success.

• • • • •

A few years after I started at Rocky's, I graduated from high school and attended college in upstate Indiana at Ball State University. I briefly worked at Wendy's Old Fashioned Hamburgers before I left Jeffersonville. The grease alone was reason enough for me to avoid the burger-flipping business for the rest of my life. I coined a phrase based on my experience: "If you flip hamburgers, you'll kiss the floor of a pizzeria." I didn't go to college knowing that I wanted to someday open my own business, even though I'd always tossed that idea around in my head. Instead, I started as a criminal justice major. I wanted to follow in my family's footsteps—both sides. My Papaw, my Dad and my maternal uncles, Jon and Bob Ackerson, all graduated from the University of Louisville Law School. So would my brother Chuck and my daughter Kristine in the years to come.

However, I didn't enjoy the law nearly as much as I thought I would. I eventually switched to business after I saw a friend's textbook. I read over his shoulder while he was studying and was fascinated with the material. I've always believed I should go with my gut instinct, so I switched majors without a second thought.

I had to find a job to help me cover the cost of classes, as well as room and board. My freshman year, I began working nights at a local pizzeria named Greek's, which was owned by a man named Chris Karamesines. The mixture of education and experience—learning from Chris at Greek's and before that from the Fondrisi family at Rocky's—helped me begin to form ideas about what I thought a pizzeria should look like.

Both places taught me the importance of treating your team members like family. But the lessons didn't stop there. At Rocky's I learned about the fundamentals of making authentic Italian food, which would serve me well when I started Papa John's. The fresh-packed pizza sauce alone was a crucial part of my education. Greek's added more ammo to my arsenal. Chris Karamesines was passionate about using quality ingredients, which is why we mixed the sauce ourselves using whole-pared tomatoes. I liked the sweet taste of Greek's sauce so much that I later tried to replicate it at Papa John's. When we first started getting Stanislaus' fresh-packed sauce, I added in some sugar, basil and oregano at the store to make it taste more like Greek's sauce.

Years later, Stanislaus' owner and I cooked up a recipe he could make at the cannery. This meant I no longer had to recreate the sauce we used at Greek's in the back of Papa John's. It was now coming to me on a daily basis from one of the finest tomato sauce producers in the world.

Chris also taught me a lot about how to deal with volume and how to maximize productivity, whether in the kitchen, the dining room, the delivery process, or anywhere else in the business. Chris was a professional at running a high-quality pizzeria. Greek's did as much business in one night as Rocky's did in an entire week. The lessons I learned at both restaurants were critical to my entrepreneurial development.

Greek's Pizzeria at Ball State University

And I was developing fast. Even though I was only 20 years old and a sophomore in college, the allure of entrepreneurship was already so strong that I even considered dropping out of college to start a Greek's franchise in Bloomington, Indiana. Fortunately, my Mom and my Papaw convinced me to finish what I had started—another important lesson that has stuck with me to this day.

This didn't stop me from continuing to plan for my future, however. My time at Rocky's and Greek's, and my flirtation with starting a franchise, caused me to think about the nature of the small business that I dreamed about running someday. Even in 1982, I asked myself a simple question: How would I separate myself from the competition?

I already had a few ideas. In the early '80s, well over 60 percent of the pizza-making market was through local, independent pizzerias. The only "big boys" in those days were Pizza Hut, Domino's and Little Caesars, and none of them were very big yet. Pizza Hut owned variety. Domino's owned speed. Little Caesars owned price. If I wanted to start a pizzeria that could grow beyond its local roots, I knew the only place left for me to make my mark was in taste and quality. For that, my pizzeria would have to look and feel like an independent small business. It needed to feel like a mom-'n'-pop, no matter how big it got. And this didn't just mean making better pizzas. It also meant taking care of our people and treating them like family.

1982

**Chris Karamesines,
The Greek**

This led me to a few other conclusions. If I ever got to the point where I ran multiple pizzerias, I wanted each store to be the same—in quality, customer service and experience. With my limited experience, I had already learned that most companies that franchise look at each store independently, as if they ran 5,000 stores that are different in dozens of ways. But I looked at each store individually replicated 5,000 times—like a mom-'n'-pop, independent pizzeria. I wanted every Papa John's to feel and look and smell and taste like the first Papa John's, which I hadn't yet built. I firmly believed, and I still do, that your quality is only as good as your consistency—"incongruity breeds mistrust." This statement has been borne out during the dark times in Papa John's history. But more on that later . . .

My strong desire to differentiate my company from its competitors would later prove crucial to Papa John's explosive growth and high customer satisfaction.

I didn't waste any time following up on my goals. From the comfort of my dorm room, I began designing menus, identifying the equipment I needed and even sketching the layout of the pizzeria I had already built in my mind. I also started writing down recipes. My time at both Rocky's and Greek's had convinced me that I could make a better pizza than anyone else if I used better and fresher ingredients. Just over a decade later, "Better Ingredients. Better Pizza." would become Papa John's motto—a motto that millions of people around the world now hear or see every day.

But first, I had to come up with a name for my entrepreneurial experiment. So I reached out to a student I knew on the fifth floor of LaFollette dorm who was a marketing major from Chicago, Illinois. I asked if he would come up with a name and logo for my non-existent business. In return, I promised him that if we ever went big, I'd give him a free pizza a week for the rest of his life. Days later, he came back with the name "Papa John's" written in blue text on a white and red background.

It was exactly what I wanted. The exact same design would later hang above the door of my very first stand-alone Papa John's. But that was still three years away. In the meantime, the logo, my recipes, my drawings, my designs, my menus and my deepest hopes for my future pizzeria had to go on the back burner. So I packed them into a large cardboard box and placed it in my bedroom closet back home—waiting for the right time. That box would stay there for several years, essentially undisturbed. It's hard for me to explain just how important this box was. It had Papa John's inside of it—a potential $4 billion company contained within a cardboard box hidden in my closet. I had no idea what I had hidden away under a pile of clothes in my bedroom closet. That box was revolutionary, but its time had not yet come.

Sadly, the guy who designed the logo never claimed his pizza prize. To this day, I've never heard from him. He surely knows that Papa John's did in fact go big—bigger than I or anyone else had ever imagined. If he's reading this, I hope he contacts me immediately. I owe him more than $16,000 worth of pizzas. I'll even throw in another $16,000 in pizzas at no extra charge.

● ● ● ● ●

Despite my grand ideas, my own entrepreneurial experiment didn't quite start like I expected.

After only three short years, I left college to move back home to Jeffersonville in the summer of 1983, only one class short of graduation. I began taking a night class to finish my degree. I was dead broke. I applied for dozens of jobs, but no one would hire me—a depressing turn of events that left me down in the dumps. After several months, my Dad approached me with the only offer I ever got—and therefore, the best offer I ever got. He wanted me to help him manage his failing tavern, Mick's Lounge. The bar was named after a partner who was too busy running around town to actually run the business that had his name over the front door. Now my Dad needed someone to help him out.

1982

Papa John's Original Logo

It wasn't an ideal situation—not by a long shot. But I had nowhere else to go, so I quickly accepted my Dad's offer. He offered me $200 a week to join him as his new manager.

Little did I know that I was walking into a complete disaster. Mick's Lounge was easily one of the worst bars I've ever had the misfortune of walking into. The beer wasn't cold. The food wasn't good. The standards were low. The whole place was dirty. The employees were ripping off my Dad and Mick regularly. It was definitely the filthiest, dirtiest, smelliest, roughest, toughest beer joint in town—and I loved it!!!

None of those things mattered to me when I walked through the front door for the first time. Mick's Lounge was my first entrepreneurial adventure—running, managing and owning a business. I had an "Aha!" moment where I immediately knew that entrepreneurship was my life's calling—a gift from God!

Unfortunately, the bar was out of money—and not by a little. I learned that once I started getting my paycheck. It bounced as soon as I tried to cash it. That remained the case for my first 20 paychecks. Why? Because my father and Mick had somehow racked up $64,000 in debt owed to various vendors and banks. The debt was so large that even my Dad didn't know the full extent of his predicament. With Mick out of the picture, my Dad asked me to come in to lessen the damage before Mick's Lounge went bankrupt. My job was to keep my father from being left totally broke.

I didn't know what I was getting into. I literally had no idea how to run a business. But it was like a light switch flipped on in my head from the moment I set foot in Mick's Lounge. Saving such a dirty and downtrodden bar may not have been an ideal job, yet I knew I could rise to the challenge. I was in my element—I felt like an entrepreneur. On my third day on the job, I remember telling my Dad that I was going to turn Mick's Lounge around. I said to him, "Dad, I can save this place." He told me it was impossible, that there was too much debt. He was wrong. I knew in my heart and in my head that Mick's Lounge was going to make it. Now I had to make sure that happened.

I certainly had my work cut out for me. If I was going to succeed, I had to think like an entrepreneur. I had to start practicing everything I'd learned from my Papaw and my Dad, even though Dad hadn't done a good job at Mick's Lounge.

We needed to get patrons through the front door and I was willing to try anything to make that happen. There was plenty of low-hanging fruit at first. I came in early and stayed late to clean the place up. We repainted the interior to make it more appealing. We spruced up the serving area. We built a can-crushing mechanism to make sure we were cashing in on recycling. We figured out we could put exactly six 55-gallon trash cans full of recyclables—crushed aluminum cans—in the back of a van owned by Bob Ehringer, an early member of the Mick's Lounge team who eventually became our business partner after buying part of my Dad's and my stakes in the bar. The six trash cans fit snugly in his van. They also made the van reek of beer. But it was worth

Mick's Lounge *1983*

it: combined with the can-crushing device, this gave us a highly effective and lucrative recycling operation, pulling in an additional $120 a week in profits. This may not seem like much, but for a bar on the verge of bankruptcy it was a windfall we would be stupid to pass up.

In addition, we instituted nightly specials, deals and competitions. That included selling three Little Kings beers for a dollar on Tuesday, holding euchre tournaments on Thursdays and pool tournaments on Sundays, and so on.

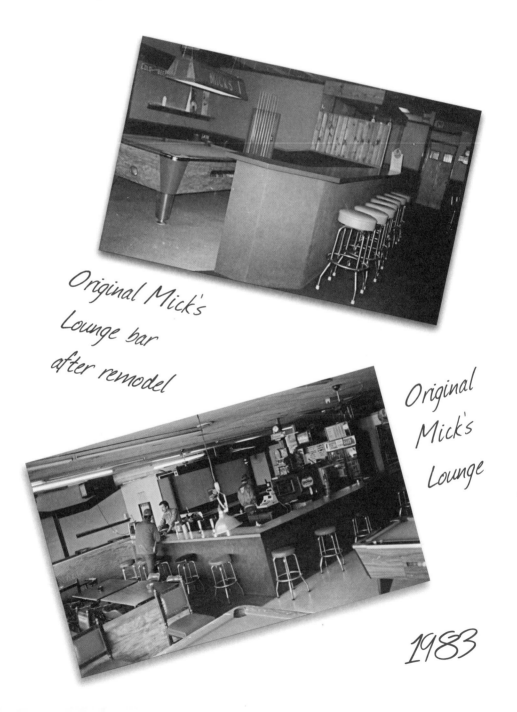

Original Mick's
Lounge bar
after remodel

Original
Mick's
Lounge

1983

As the saying goes, "opportunity arrives disguised as insolvable problems." We tinkered, like I'd learned from my Papaw. We used trial and error on more things than I can count. If something worked, we doubled down on it. If something didn't, we abandoned it without a second thought.

Bob Ehringer's van outside Mick's Lounge

55 Gallon garbage cans full of aluminum cans

1983

Sign for Tuesday beer deal

Euchre tournament tables on
Thursday nights

I also revamped the pricing system. When I started, beer cost 85 cents for premium and 65 cents for everything else. A game of pool cost 35 cents. None of this made sense to me—why ask customers to bring dimes and nickels when you could do everything in quarters? With this in mind, I cut the price of beer to 75 cents for premium and 50 cents for the rest, while upping the price of a game of pool to 50 cents. We established daily $1 lunch specials—a beer and a Mick Burger. My hunch was that customers would take the money they saved on beer—all of it in quarters—and spend it on the pool table. I had no intention of ever seeing a nickel or dime in Mick's Lounge again.

1983

Pool tables where we had our Sunday pool tournaments

It turned out that I was right. Within a month, revenues from the pool tables, pinball machines, poker machine and cigarette dispenser had jumped from $240 a week to $500. Mick's Lounge needed as much money as it could get in order to pay off the debt, so I promptly bought out the vendor who owned the pool tables and the arcade games. Until I bought them, they were all owned by Bill Cavanaugh, who had run Mick's Lounge before my Dad and Mick had bought it from him. (The bar was originally called Bill's Lounge II, because it was the second bar Bill owned. The Mick's Lounge sign kept the "II," even though there was no Mick's Lounge I.) Owning the pool tables and arcade games upped our weekly take to between $900 and $1,100 a week—a dramatic increase in a matter of months.

Our experiments with food deals were also reaping rewards. Now that Mick's Lounge was clean and friendly, the lunch crowd quickly increased. The $1 specials surely helped. In the span of a few months, we went from doing $40 a day in lunch sales to over $300. We were shocked.

One day, Charlie Moore, the owner of a nearby restaurant came over to talk to me about what we were doing. He was upset because Mick's Lounge had taken most of his lunchtime customers. I told him about our dollar deal with the Mick Burger and a beer. He wanted to see how much money we were actually making. Together, we crunched the numbers to figure out how much the ingredients in our lunch specials really cost—something I'd not done before. I never learned about "food costs" in college, even though it was a critical part of running a restaurant. Now I was learning this lesson in the school of hard knocks.

What an important lesson it was. Charlie Moore was a businessman and I was a gunslinger. I had a lot to learn. It turned out we weren't making any money at all. The total cost of the ingredients for a Mick Burger and a beer was $1.25. Despite our increase in lunch customers, we were losing a quarter with every sale. In terms of trial and error, this was definitely an error. As they say, "good judgment comes from having experience; experience comes from having bad judgment." But that's okay, we eventually fixed our pricing. We were bringing more people in the door than ever before. We were putting butts in the seats and slowly turning the bar around.

We may have been gradually moving towards the black, but it was already obvious I had a lot to learn about the daily ins and outs of running a business. One memory sticks out in my mind. I started at Mick's Lounge on Thursday, September 1, only a few days before Labor Day weekend in 1983. I remember it like it was yesterday. On the Tuesday after Labor Day, I made my first trip to the bank to deposit everything we'd made since I started five days earlier—between $4,000 and $5,000. In my youthful ignorance, I simply threw the money in a paper bag, brought it to the teller and dumped it on the desk for her to count. I didn't know I was supposed to sort the bills into denominations—standard business practices like that were foreign to me.

I kept this up for a few weeks. The teller was clearly getting frustrated with me. She regularly gave me some mean looks when I walked through the door—the kind of looks that say, "not this guy again." One day she finally snapped and told me I needed to count the money myself. It was my job, not the bank's job, she said. So I started counting and sorting the money myself before depositing it. That's another thing they don't teach you in college.

At least I didn't come to her with all the quarters we were making. After a few weeks and then a few months, Mick's Lounge was raking in a thousand dollars' worth of quarters on a weekly basis. I took those down to the bank's main branch every week, since it had a coin machine. I brought the quarters in two huge white bags that must have weighed about 30 pounds each. I always made sure to walk by the front of the bank so a cute teller working at the main desk could see me hauling two white bags full of thousands of quarters. As a 23-year-old guy without a steady girlfriend and working too many hours to get one, this was the best I could do.

Fortunately, some parts of running a business came more naturally to me. We were also hiring dedicated and talented team members. Ever since I started working at Rocky's Sub Pub, I understood the importance of identifying talent and taking care of the people who took care of me—whether as a manager or any other team member. "Loyalty is a two-way street." Today, "People Are Priority Always," or PAPA, is one of Papa John's most important principles. We were already practicing this in 1983, even though we didn't have a name for it yet.

I still remember the team members we hired. Roxanne came in as our main nighttime bartender. Sonny tended bar for the lunch crowd and the afternoon. Bob Ehringer came in to help rebuild the bar and pinch-hit with other jobs when necessary. He quickly became an invaluable part of the Mick's Lounge team. I've already described how he became my business partner after buying out part of my Dad's stake. Bob's wife Linda helped out, too.

But our best hire was Denise Robinson. Her husband was Glenn, a longtime customer and later one of our first delivery drivers. My Dad hired her to be our cook, but she had no experience whatsoever. "There's one problem: she can't cook," he said when he told me he'd hired her. I went ballistic. Then he told me we would pay her $2 an hour for three and a half hours a day. I looked at him and said, "You're crazy. You hired a cook that can't cook." We were so far behind on our bills and we owed money to everybody in town. We just didn't have $7 a day to spend on anyone, much less a cook who couldn't cook.

My Dad responded that you should "hire for attitude, train for aptitude." He was absolutely right. We still use this phrase with our team members even to this day. We drive the point home with another equally true saying: "if you think you can't, you're right, and if you think you can, you're right." Attitude would later become Papa John's core value #5 within our FASPAC framework, which I will discuss later.

I was learning this as I watched Denise become an integral part of our team. Like my Dad said, she had a phenomenal attitude and quickly developed the aptitude for her job. She's still with Papa John's to this day—a jack of all trades who's excelled on the administrative side of things. She was particularly good at bookkeeping, which never really interested me. I was always analytical and mathematically inclined, but I've always known that keeping track of records would have bored me to death. I would rather build, run and constantly improve the business itself. I have no doubt in my mind that Papa John's wouldn't be what it is today without Denise Robinson's hard work, dedication and loyalty over the past 30-plus years. She guards my back and I love her for it. Thank you, Denise.

Denise and her husband Glenn Robinson sitting at the Mick's Lounge bar

• • • • •

On the whole, Mick's Lounge was doing better than it had done in years. But we still weren't turning the business around fast enough to pay back our debts quickly enough. We were making enough money to pay our bills in real time, but not much more than that. The debt cast a dark shadow over everything we did. Nor did it help that we'd discovered even more debt after I started. One week we got a bill from the state of Indiana saying we owed $10,000 in back sales taxes. That was the first I'd heard about it, and now we had to add it to our massive tab. The bar was still in a big financial pickle.

We were getting desperate as a result, but I had no intention of throwing in the towel. So I put my most prized possession up for sale—my Camaro. In October of 1983, at the age of 21, I found a buyer willing to pay $2,800.

Selling that car was one of the hardest decisions in my life up to that point. Remember, I was a 21-year-old guy who probably put way too much stock in material things. I was devastated when I sold my Camaro—I actually teared up. I loved it. But I understood that I had to have skin in the game and make sacrifices in order to succeed. I had to make a personal sacrifice if I was going to pay down the bar's debts. This realization was painful, but it was a direct reflection of the values I'd learned working for Papaw when I was young. He taught me that if you get something for free you don't value it. Now, after selling my Camaro, I had all my skin in the game.

• • • • •

With the money in hand, the first debt I had to pay back was to Clark County Distributing. It was a beer distributor who supplied us with Michelob, Michelob Light, Bud Light and Budweiser—the King of Beers and by far our most popular beer. Mick's Lounge had somehow run up $16,000 in debt to the distributor before I was brought on board. Ira McKinley and his wife Ruth, who co-owned the distributor, were incredibly frustrated with us, understandably so.

I knew I had to show them I was good for it. Only a few days after selling the car, I paid them $2,000, all of it from the Camaro's sale. I hoped that by paying off such a large chunk of the debt at once, I would show Ira and Ruth I was sincere about paying them back.

They came to Mick's Lounge for lunch soon afterwards. I sat down with them to discuss how things were going. The conversation quickly turned south. Ira looked me in the eye and said, "I've never met anybody like you, John. You make me nervous." I told him, "I make everybody nervous." He responded by saying, "That's what scares me. I don't understand you." His next words nearly caused my jaw to drop to the floor: "I'm going to cut you off. I've got to cut my losses. I've had enough of the lies." To be fair, Ira had a point. He was downright furious with my Dad and Mick, who had strung him along for years, racking up debt, promising to pay him and then going back on their word. My $2,000 simply wasn't enough to make up for years of bad will and broken promises.

But that didn't change the fact that we needed the beer in order to survive. I was scared to death as I talked to Ira. I may have been a cocky 21-year-old, but that quickly evaporated when faced with a real crisis like the one I was facing now. The loss of beer—especially the King of Beers—would have been lethal to the bar. At this point, beer sales were roughly 90 percent of our revenue—without it, we'd go belly up in just weeks. As the saying goes, "you can't sell from an empty wagon." Without Budweiser at Mick's Lounge, that's all I had— an empty wagon.

Booth where I pled my case with Ruth, and Ira

1984

I knew I had to make my case and make it fast. At this point I was working close to 70 to 80 hours a week at Mick's Lounge, doing everything I could to turn it around. I got visibly upset as I told Ira just how hard I was working and how Mick's Lounge was already seeing significant improvements in revenues. I told him: "I gave you my guts, I just sold my 1971 Camaro Z28 that I loved." I pleaded with him, saying I was pouring my blood, sweat and tears into Mick's Lounge. I asked him why he didn't trust me when I was already doing what my Dad and Mick never did—paying him back. But he held firm, telling me he wasn't going to change his mind. Half in tears and scared out of my mind, I looked at his wife and said, "Ruth, I'm gonna pay you back. I promise. I'm good for it."

I meant what I said and I said what I meant. I was going to pay them back. I was good for it. I'd learned from my Papaw that a businessman always keeps his word.

To this day I'm not sure I ever convinced Ira that things really had changed. But I did convince Ruth. As I spoke to her, she looked back at me. Then she turned toward Ira and said, "Ira, give him the beer." The look between them probably lasted five seconds, but it seemed like an eternity to me. Ira then quietly said, "Okay." I had my beer. Mick's Lounge would live to see another day.

●　●　●　●　●

That episode taught me another important lesson: you have to fight every day to survive in the business world. "When you're up to your ass in alligators, try to remember the mission was draining the swamp." Our mission was to protect Dad's reputation, pay off the bills and prevent Mick's Lounge from going bankrupt. I resolved to start paying down our debts at a much faster rate so we avoided situations like the one with Ira and Ruth. However, I couldn't do this without money. I knew we could make the money back over time, but time was in shorter supply than money at that point. So I swallowed my pride and asked my mentor, Papaw, for a $15,000 loan.

Now Papaw had never liked Mick's Lounge, and he definitely didn't like me working there. When he did come in, he would always have the same thing—a cold beer and a bowl of bean soup. Yet even though he wanted me to be doing something else, he could tell I was using the lessons I'd learned from him to turn the bar around.

I said exactly that when I asked him for the loan. It was a difficult conversation. Humbling, too. At the end of it, he agreed to give me a line of credit. This was a further sign that Papaw believed in me. When I was 17, I was working at his property, doing odd jobs. This was when I was struggling with insecurity and questioning if I'd ever be good at anything. I asked Papaw, "Do you think I'll ever be successful?" He immediately said yes. He said, "Both of my sons are successful"— they were both prominent Louisville lawyers—"and you're three times smarter than both of them." He wanted me to do something big with my life, and was willing to help me do it.

Papaw's loan couldn't have come at a better time. It seemed like every week I was discovering new debts that I didn't know about— debts that even my Dad didn't know about. The credit helped us pay back the most pressing bills. But by this time, the bar itself was making more money than ever before. Our recent hires had completely transformed the food, service, atmosphere and everything else about Mick's Lounge. We were finally making a major dent in our debt.

It was only a matter of time before we paid it all off. Denise Robinson, who kept the books, came to me one day and said, "John, we're making serious progress here." She was right. By December of 1983, we'd paid back nearly half of our debts, taking them from $64,000 to about $32,000. Right after the start of the New Year, Clark County Bank loaned me another $32,000 to finish paying everything off. The only outstanding debt I had after that was around $10,000 I still owed from the $15,000 Papaw had loaned me. By the start of January, Mick's was making enough for me to repay him $1,000 every week.

I finished paying him back by the end of February in 1984. This gave me an immense sense of accomplishment. I was practicing everything my Papaw had taught me, and he was watching me succeed. But my joy was short-lived.

Only a few weeks later, he went into the hospital with a serious illness. Up to this point I was still meeting him for steak dinners on a weekly basis. I knew he was in poor health—so much so that most of his family didn't want to be around him anymore. I didn't care, though.

1935

I loved him so much, and he loved me. His physical limitations didn't matter to me—I wanted to spend every moment I could with him. Papaw was always teaching me something new and helping me become a better person. He had made me into the young man I was—into the man I was becoming. You don't just abandon someone like that.

But while I knew his health was bad, I didn't expect him to deteriorate as fast as he did in those last few weeks. I could hardly hold myself together as his health got worse and worse. In many ways, it was like watching my own father die—that's how much my Papaw meant to me. I couldn't bring myself to accept the fact that such an influential man in my life wouldn't be around anymore. No one had done more to teach me the values and the life lessons that eventually allowed me to build Papa John's. I wanted to help him—I wanted to save him—but there was nothing I could do.

I was there as he neared the end. I'll never forget the last words he ever said to me. I was standing by his bed and he gave me a look of love that only Papaw could give. Then he asked, "By the way, did you ever pay me back that fifteen thousand bucks?" I'd finished paying him back just a few weeks before, but we'd never closed the loop and confirmed that we were all square. He never had any doubts that I would; he just wanted to double-check. I smiled at him and jokingly replied, "Papaw, my credit is good"—the same words he told me when I was only 8 or 9 years old. That was the last time we spoke.

Papaw, Louis Erman Ackerson, passed away on March 26, 1984. He left behind a family that loved him dearly, including a devastated 22-year-old who always imagined his grandfather would be there to help him and teach him.

I still miss him. There's so much more I wish I'd said to him—so much more I wish I'd learned from him. Yet his legacy lives on in the company his grandson built. Along with my Dad, Papaw was one of the two men most responsible for teaching me the lessons and the values that have always defined Papa John's and enabled it to flourish like it has. My grandfather's guidance and influence on my life cannot be overstated. My Dad had always dreamed of success, but my Papaw actually taught me how to be a success. That means Papa John's even-

Papaw with his wife Sara Ackerson

tual success was Papaw's success. I only wish he'd lived long enough to see that name hang above the doors of our 5,000 stores. His smile would have been even bigger than mine on our opening night.

Hopefully he was already proud of what I'd accomplished. By the time Papaw passed away, the comeback was officially complete. It was March of 1984 and Mick's Lounge was in the black. Seven months earlier it had been all but guaranteed to go under—now we were making more money than ever before and growing by the day. My first foray into the business world was already a success. But it wasn't enough. I wasn't fulfilled, not by a long shot. I knew I had to find a new challenge. Papaw would have wanted me to keep pushing myself. He would have wanted me to find something new to tinker with—something that could transform my own life and the lives of those around me.

Now I had to answer that question. What would my next challenge be?

—— • ——

Papaw being Papaw

CHAPTER TWO

GO LEFT

"Go Left."

Papa John's wouldn't exist without these two simple words. "Go Left" is our guiding philosophy. Let me be clear: this has no political meaning whatsoever. The phrase itself is drawn from a life event I experienced when I was 23 years old—more on that later—and its meaning is entirely entrepreneurial. When we go left, we take the more difficult route. We do what needs to be done, no matter how hard it is, because the harder choice is usually the right one. We challenge the status quo and see things through to the end. We believe that if we take risks, we can succeed and excel and make the world a better place. Even if we fail, we can pride ourselves on trying our hardest. And when we make a mistake, we own it and we take the hit. Then, like my Dad and my Papaw always did, we figure out what we did wrong and try again. We never give up—we never stop going left.

I can't emphasize just how important this concept is. At Papa John's, we have developed an entire culture of entrepreneurship around Go Left. Our entire executive leadership team has gone through this train-ing. In 2016, we began rolling it out to team members at our headquarters, and then to the Papa John's team at our more than 5,000 stores around the world.

My ultimate goal is for every team member, no matter who they are or what they do at the company, to understand and embody the Go Left mindset. When they confront a problem or identify an opportunity for growth, I want them to ask themselves: "How can I Go Left in this situation?" Put another way, I want every single team member to act like what we call an "intrapreneur"—a person who acts like an entrepreneur in a large company. Incredible things will happen if we can foster this kind of workplace. We'll make even better pizzas. We'll go above and beyond the call of duty through improved customer service. We'll create more jobs and more opportunities for people who need them. We'll find new and exciting ways to help our communities and our neighborhoods. And our team members will find countless ways to grow and improve their own lives—as well as the world around them. That's what Go Left is all about.

At this point, you might be asking, "Where did Go Left come from in the first place?" To answer that question, we have to go back to before we ever made our first Papa John's pizza. We have to go back to 1984, immediately after my Papaw died.

• • • • •

My Papaw's death in March of 1984 left me utterly devastated. The most important person in my life had just passed away. I had hundreds of questions I wish I had asked him. Most importantly, I wanted to ask him what I was supposed to do next.

I had literally no idea. Ever since I was a kid, I always wanted to find something I was good at. Every kid thinks this at one point or another. We're all hardwired to seek success. Even before we can describe it, we know that we want to find that one thing, whatever it may be, that can give us happiness and fulfillment. My theory is that's why we're so curious and adventurous when we're young—we're looking for what we're supposed to do.

Like many people, I still hadn't found what I was looking for by the time I graduated college. Up to that point in my life I'd been a decent student, a decent athlete and hopefully a decent person. But I always felt like I had to work twice as hard as the other kids simply to be above average. I didn't want to work hard just to be in the middle of the pack—I wanted to find something where I could work hard *and* get ahead. I had a partial taste of what this was like when I washed dishes and made pizzas at Rocky's Sub Pub as a teenager and at Greek's when I was in college. Then again, I wasn't really sure what I was looking for at that point.

I thought I'd finally found it when I walked into Mick's Lounge for the first time. I liked running a business. I worked hard. I put in long hours. I saved the bar from going under in just over seven months, paying off $64,000 in debt by building a business that gave customers what they wanted. I thought I'd finally found something I was good at. I'd finally found my inner gift. I could run a business and be happier than I'd ever been—and that's saying something for a 22-year-old.

But I didn't *love* Mick's Lounge. When I meet with groups of young people today, whatever level of education, whether in elementary school or in a college classroom, I tell them all the same thing: find something you're good at and that fulfills you. Without both of these components, you'll always have a feeling like there's something else you should try. Fortunately, America's system of free enterprise creates countless opportunities for people to match their talents and skills to their interests. The possibilities are literally limitless. Our country's long history of innovation, entrepreneurship and upward mobility proves just what can happen when people are free to pursue their dreams. Anyone, regardless of where they are on the economic ladder, can climb that ladder by finding something where they excel and where they find a sense of purpose.

I hadn't found that balance yet. I was certainly good at running Mick's Lounge, but I didn't actually like the bar business at all. I didn't enjoy all the drinking, smoking, cussing and the nightly fights that came along with this line of work. It was a rough business that affected everyone who participated in it. Before he died, Dad and I observed that people would come to Mick's Lounge to get drunk at night, then they'd go to his law firm in the morning to get divorced. That was disappointing and disheartening, to say the least.

I didn't want that life—and I didn't want to be complicit in helping others live it, either. I had to find something else, something actually fulfilling.

It didn't matter that by this point Mick's Lounge was making a significant amount of money. That's the type of business I describe as "lose-win." Yes, I personally was winning, as were my team members. But I didn't feel like I was making a positive contribution to my community. The values that I held dear—the values that I learned from my Dad and my Papaw—were more important to me than just making money. Can anyone honestly say that Mick's Lounge was helping people and making the world a better place?

I knew it wasn't. And I knew I couldn't live out the many lessons I'd learned from Papaw so long as I worked at Mick's Lounge. I wanted a "good business"—one that helped people and improved the world around it.

Fortunately, I already had half of the equation figured out. I really excelled at running a business, so my next task was to find out what would fulfill me. I was slowly starting to figure this out the longer I worked at Mick's Lounge. I thought back to my time in college and two things stuck out in my mind: my time making pizzas at Greek's and all the hours I spent coming up with my first ideas about a pizzeria named Papa John's. Then I thought back even further, to my first job washing dishes at Rocky's Sub Pub at the age of 15. That's when the seed was first planted—and now it was finally sprouting. I loved making pizzas. It was both fun and fulfilling. I had loved it from the moment I stopped washing dishes and started making pizzas. And once I started, I was instantly hooked. Slapping the dough, spreading the sauce, placing the toppings, slipping it into the oven, serving it to happy customers—the whole process gave me a sense of purpose, a feeling of accomplishment and profound enjoyment.

The more I thought about it, the more I realized I had to start making pizzas. I loved making pizzas. I love it to this day. I always will.

This gave me an idea. Why don't I combine my love of pizza-making with my skill at running a business? My instinct told me this would be even more fulfilling—that the whole would be greater than the sum of its parts. I'd learned over the past seven months that getting a business to run smoothly gave me a sense of fulfillment. When Mick's Lounge was firing on all cylinders, I was, too. It just clicked. Wouldn't it click even more if I actually enjoyed the type of business I was running?

I knew I had to try. Now I just had to figure out how to get pizza-making into the Mick's Lounge mix.

I found my answer late one night in March of 1984, shortly after my Papaw passed away. I was 22 years old. I had just finished a night shift and the bar was completely empty. With a beer in hand, I glanced around Mick's Lounge, and my gaze settled on a broom closet at the back of the bar. Now, I'd walked into that broom closet every day for the past seven months to get the broom and the dustpan. But I never thought anything of it. Up until that moment, it was just a simple closet that served a simple purpose.

It came to me in a flash. This was where I could start selling pizzas. This was where Papa John's would officially be born.

To this day, I don't know why I thought this, or why it happened when it did. It was a broom closet, for goodness' sake. But I just knew it was right from the moment it entered my head. I immediately got up from my seat, walked over to the closet and started scoping it out to see just what was possible. Within minutes I had a good idea of what I was going to do. When I finally left Mick's Lounge, well into the wee hours of the morning, I scribbled a note on a lunchtime guest receipt and left it on the cash register for our lunchtime bartender, Bob Ehringer. It read: "Bob—I've gotta bigg'a damn'a idea'a." I was hinting to him that I had an Italian concept in mind. Hopefully he got the joke!

When I got home I immediately went to the clothes closet in my bedroom. It contained my greatest and my most secret treasure: the cardboard box I'd been hiding under a pile of clothes for the past two years. I'd only gotten it out once to show my friend, Jim Fry, over the summer of 1983. He and I had been friends since we were five years old. His mom was our Cub Scout den leader. (He's now a Papa John's franchisee in Oregon and has been a trusted friend for 50 years.) It had my recipes, my drawings, my designs, my menus and the never-before-used logo for Papa John's. Taken together, these items made up my dream for my future restaurant—a dream I'd forgotten once I started at Mick's Lounge. I was so excited for what I was about to do. Words still can't describe it.

Bob Ehringer and me sitting at the entrance to the broom closet

I was dredging up a dream I had more or less forgotten for over two years. Saving Mick's Lounge had taken every ounce of my energy; I simply hadn't had the time to entertain any other ideas. But now the bar was doing fine and I was ready for the next challenge. Papa John's was that challenge—I was ready to turn my dream, years in the making, into a reality.

I'm not sure if I slept at all that night. I went back to Mick's Lounge around 10:30 a.m. the next morning so I could prep the bar and the kitchen before customers started arriving at 11. My Dad, Denise and Bob were already there, outfitting the steam table in preparation for cooking. I didn't waste any time: I introduced them to "Papa John's." I brought the pizza box with me to work. As soon as I got there, I opened it and showed everyone its contents. I explained every little detail. I told them how much thought I'd put into opening my own pizzeria someday. Finally, I told them I thought we could really do something big if we made a better pizza using better ingredients.

It would be years before we made "Better Ingredients. Better Pizza." our slogan. But we were already getting close. Our first was actually "Homemade Pizza the Way You Like It," which we started using when we were in the broom closet. After that we switched to "Fine People Serving Great Pizza," shortly after we moved into the first official Papa John's in 1985. Our thought behind this phrase was that we were not only in the pizza business, but also in the people business. (This is still true.) But we replaced it with "Made from Scratch with the Finest Ingredients" only a few months later in December 1985. We simultaneously trademarked "Delivering the Perfect Pizza," which we used once or twice in 1986. Then we started using it exclusively in 1989. It was our slogan up until we finally came up with "Better Ingredients.Better Pizza." in the mid-1990s.

This back-and-forth may seem confusing, but all of these different slogans attempted to get at the same idea. All four showed our desire to convey Papa John's commitment to its mom-'n'-pop roots. That's why we emphasized "homemade" and "fine people" and "made from scratch." They also showed our early commitment to a good product—"homemade pizza" and "great pizza" and "the finest ingredients" were in many ways early versions of our current slogan. Of the four we tried out, our second one—"Made from Scratch with the Finest Ingredients"—came closest to what we wanted to convey. But it wasn't until 1996 that "Better Ingredients. Better Pizza." became Papa John's official slogan. That may have been more than a decade after Papa John's started, yet one thing is hopefully clear: the idea behind it was a crucial component of my dream from the very beginning, even before we had a name and a trademark for it. We kept updating our slogan to better capture what Papa John's was all about. By 1996 we finally had it right.

But that was still more than a decade away at this point. We didn't even have a slogan when I introduced my team to Papa John's for the first time. They had a million questions for me. They probably thought I was crazy—I was now suggesting a radical change in our business, and it had only occurred to me less than 12 hours earlier. But I had also built a big bank of trust with them over the past seven months. No one had thought we could save the bar when I started, yet that's exactly what we had done. They had confidence in me as a leader. They were willing to collaborate with me on this new project, even though they knew almost nothing about it. Within an hour after I walked into the bar that morning, everyone had bought into the Papa John's dream.

It didn't take them long. They only had to listen to my voice to figure out that I liked the idea of making pizzas. But once they saw what was in the pizza box, they figured out that I *loved* the idea. The excitement was palpable—you could feel it in the air. I was bouncing around Mick's Lounge like a kid. They wanted to feel that same level of excitement. Even though they'd only learned about Papa John's moments before, I could already tell that my dream was starting to become their dream.

As I would later learn, this is a crucial part of successful leadership. Your co-workers and colleagues have to buy in to what you're doing. This can't happen if a few key things aren't present in the business. You need clear communication. You need clear expectations. You need kindness and mutual respect at every level of the organization. And you need to be consistent in how you interact with people. When all of these things are present, you can join together in a collaborative alliance. You can't just be a visionary—you need to put the pieces in place so that others will see, believe in and follow that vision. A leader who can't bring people along is no leader at all.

Denise's husband Glenn slinging dough inside broom closet, with cigarette nearby

Dad was the first to sign on. He never really knew how to deal with me throughout his life, mainly because he knew he couldn't keep up with me. But he also knew he could trust me to win. He'd seen me save Mick's Lounge over the previous months. Well before that, he'd been counting on me to win ever since I was 8 or 9. When I was young, he would sometimes take me down to the local Eagle's Club to play pool. He would start missing the easiest shots after a few drinks. Once that began happening, he would look at me and say, "Don't miss." We won almost every time. Dad trusted me after that. That's why he didn't hesitate to become one of the first team members in the new Papa John's experiment. The others followed his lead shortly thereafter.

So we got to work, wasting no time. Our first conversation about my vision for Papa John's happened before the lunch rush, and we started to work shortly after the dinner rush that same night. We found a sledgehammer and started breaking down the broom closet's outer walls. I knew that I had to make it larger if I had any chance of fitting pizza-making equipment—especially the oven—inside. We worked for the rest of the day and well into the night, breaking down the walls and figuring out how we were going to rebuild it as a mini pizzeria.

As we worked together, I explained more to my team about what we were going to do at Papa John's. I figured we could sell $5 pizzas in the back of the bar and 50-cent beers in the front. If it turned out to be a moneymaker, we'd eventually shift everything away from the bar business to the pizza business. (This eventually happened when I sold Mick's Lounge three years later in 1987.) Even then, I had no doubts whatsoever that we could make it work. What I didn't know was that we could make it big—*really* big.

After the first day of work, we shifted to a nightly schedule. We still had to run Mick's Lounge during the day, after all. Over the next few weeks, we started rebuilding the walls further out, so that the closet went from a small rectangle to a larger rectangle with a narrow cubby-like area at one end. (It was shaped kind of like Oklahoma when we were done with it.) We worked late into the night—sometimes all night—and kept Mick's Lounge open for business as usual. Customers were still coming in for lunch, for dinner, for drinks, sometimes gawking at the ongoing construction project behind them. It must have looked strange. But I didn't care—I was on my way to finding fulfillment. Just building the damn thing made me happier than anything I'd ever done.

We made good progress. In early April, a few weeks after we started, I took a trip down to Food Equipment Supply on Main Street in Louisville, Kentucky. I went in search of pizza-making equipment—anything I could find, really. It was owned by a guy named Tony Manley. We had worked together before when I was remodeling Mick's Lounge shortly after I started there. We had a good working relationship, built on trust and mutual respect—the keys to any relationship, whether work-related or personal. That's why he loaned me $1,640

**First Baker's Pride oven
in the broom closet**

worth of used pizza equipment. I would have bought the equipment myself, but I was tapped out after recently borrowing $32,000 from Clark County State Bank and $15,000 from Papaw. Fortunately, Tony knew I was good for it.

We were now at the point where the broom closet was ready for us to start installing equipment. It was going to be a tight fit. Even with the recent expansion, the room was still dominated by the furnace that heated the rest of the bar. It was in the back, catty-corner to the broom closet's entrance. Next to the furnace and opposite the door, we put in the biggest piece of equipment: a small Baker's Pride pizza oven. It was also the most expensive item by far. I could have used a Blodgett's oven, a cheaper option that I first learned about when I worked at Rocky's. But I'd been introduced to Baker's Pride at Greek's. It was a strong, well-made, powerful oven that could handle volume. With two decks, it was large enough to cook eight fourteen-inch pizzas at a time—four on each deck. Even though I hadn't yet made my first Papa John's pizza, I was sure that we were going to be busy.

On the other side of the furnace, we put in a prep table where we could make the pizzas. At one end we installed a tabletop mixer to make dough. We attached a cheese grater to the front of the mixer—a simple way to improve productivity. We set up an industrial can opener for the various types of cans we used—our pizza sauce, olives and mushrooms all came in #10 cans. And on the other side of the room, we set up another prep table, where we could cut the cooked pizzas and box them for delivery.

The entire operation was set up so we had easy access to the back door of Mick's Lounge, which was right next to the entrance to the broom closet. From there, we could start delivering pizzas around Jeffersonville with ease. Furthermore, we could do it without interrupting the flow at Mick's Lounge itself. It turned out that starting in the broom closet forced us to be even more productive than normal. We only had a tiny area to work in—the lack of space made us acutely aware that we needed to make every square inch count.

It only took us a few nights to install everything. Then we started ordering the ingredients—the building blocks for the better pizza we were going to make. We ordered them from Lombardi Foods out of Chicago, the same vendor Rocky's had used when I worked there. They had high-quality products that were memorable for customers.

The best, to my mind, was the fresh-packed tomato sauce—not tomato paste, which most other pizzerias used. Lombardi bought its fresh-packed sauce from Stanislaus Food Products, based in Modesto, California, in Stanislaus County.

I'd tasted Stanislaus' fresh-packed sauce for the first time when I was a 15-year-old washing dishes at Rocky's. The difference was obvious. That's why the first Papa John's pizza was made with Stanislaus' fresh-packed tomato sauce. In fact, every pizza we make today is made with fresh-packed sauce—much of it comes from Stanislaus. It's simply the best. I've been using their "stuff," as Stanislaus owner Dino Cortopassi calls it, for over 31 years at Papa John's.

As for all the other ingredients, we stuck with Lombardi for a few years before moving to International Foods out of Indianapolis. I thought they had better quality products at a more competitive cost. To me, however, the cost was secondary to the quality. Businesses operate under one of two mindsets: efficiency or quality. Efficiency is undoubtedly important—we're always trying to be more efficient at Papa John's—but for us it is always secondary to quality. Even before we made our first pizza in the broom closet, I knew that quality was the name of our game. That's why we now own our own distribution system, so we can control and measure everything from the farm to the fork. It's the perfect mix of productivity, vertical integration and superior, high-quality results.

• • • • •

By April 11, roughly two weeks after we started rebuilding the broom closet, we were finally ready to start making pizzas. It was go time.

Unfortunately, we didn't have a good sense of what we were doing and things didn't start out quite like I'd planned. The first Papa John's pizza I ever made wasn't exactly a winner. I burned the crust, burned the cheese and put on way too many toppings. I was pretty perplexed at this less-than-stellar start. But the simple fact was that I'd lost my touch after so much time out of the game. It'd been two years since I'd last made a pizza and I'd clearly become rusty. It wasn't quite like riding a bicycle—that was much easier than making an excellent pizza. It would take me two to three months before we were proud of the pies we were churning out.

Thankfully, owning Mick's Lounge protected me from failure. The bar covered my overhead and expenses, giving me the freedom to experiment until I perfected the Papa John's pizza. I needed this buffer in order to get my bearings. Without it, we might never have succeeded.

There wasn't much of a "we" at first. I was making all the pizzas for the first few months. My reasoning was simple: I had to get a good grasp of what I wanted and how I would do things. It was up to me to create and deliver the better pizza, made with better ingredients, than any other pizza in Jeffersonville, Indiana. It was also up to me to figure out how to maximize productivity. I just needed some time to figure out how I would accomplish these goals. I was certain Papa John's would eventually deliver a quality product, even if it took me a few months to get going. As the saying goes, "chance favors the prepared mind." My first few months making pizzas in the broom closet was when I prepared myself for the challenges ahead.

Unsurprisingly, we didn't sell many pizzas in the first few weeks. In fact, most of what we made was shared between the staff and the customers at Mick's Lounge. They were our first "focus group"—testing what I made, taking it home and telling me if it was a winner or a dud.

One complaint we got early on was that we were "dump trucking"—putting on too many toppings, which made the toppings and the cheese slide right off the crust. I originally thought that customers would want a fully loaded pizza. One of our early suppliers in Louisville told me in no uncertain terms that I had to put fewer toppings on to prevent the pizzas from falling apart. What good was a pizza whose toppings fell off a few bites in? Interestingly, this same supplier would later publicly predict to the media that Papa John's wouldn't last. He was right about the first thing, but we sure proved him wrong about the second.

Each pizza got better and better over the next few months. Unfortunately, our initial business model certainly wasn't sustainable at all—mainly because we didn't actually have a business model. We needed customers—people who could tell the difference between a good pizza and a superior pizza, and wanted the superior one. One thing I completely overlooked was how to market my product to a wider audience.

I was making pizzas out of a broom closet at the back of the bar, for God's sake. I couldn't advertise on the front door because there wasn't a front door—and even if there had been one, I might not have realized what I was supposed to do with it. I was convinced at that point that I just needed the best pizza in order to win.

This was only partially true, as we quickly learned. The only way we could prove to customers that our pizza was superior was, well, if we actually had customers. We needed to get butts in the seats—or rather, orders on the phones.

We tried a number of tactics. We printed menus with the Papa John's logo and handed them out at Mick's Lounge. We ordered door hangers to hand out around town. We gave out dollar-off coupons so that our $5.99 pizzas sold for $4.99. We told our family and friends to tell their family and friends. We tried everything—that's what entrepreneurship requires.

One gamble was to run an ad in the Clark County *Evening News*. It advertised a deal for Monday Night football: a pizza and a six-pack of beer for $10. I thought this was a surefire way to boost business. It wasn't. It turned out that most guys who want a six-pack used it as an excuse to leave the house for a few minutes or even a few hours. They would much rather come to Mick's Lounge, knock a few back and then take the six-pack and the pizza home. We might have had better luck if we offered to deliver the pizza and nothing else. Regardless, I learned my lesson when we didn't make any money on the promotion. But that's the nature of entrepreneurship—you keep trying new things until you find the ones that work. If you fail small and often, you can quickly get a good sense of what works.

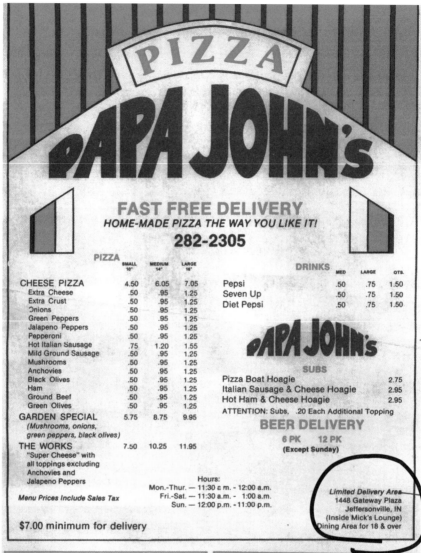

PIZZA PAPA JOHN'S

FAST FREE DELIVERY
HOME-MADE PIZZA THE WAY YOU LIKE IT!

282-2305

PIZZA

	SMALL 10"	MEDIUM 14"	LARGE 16"
CHEESE PIZZA	4.50	6.05	7.05
Extra Cheese	.50	.95	1.25
Extra Crust	.50	.95	1.25
Onions	.50	.95	1.25
Green Peppers	.50	.95	1.25
Jalapeno Peppers	.50	.95	1.25
Pepperoni	.50	.95	1.25
Hot Italian Sausage	.75	1.20	1.55
Mild Ground Sausage	.50	.95	1.25
Mushrooms	.50	.95	1.25
Anchovies	.50	.95	1.25
Black Olives	.50	.95	1.25
Ham	.50	.95	1.25
Ground Beef	.50	.95	1.25
Green Olives	.50	.95	1.25
GARDEN SPECIAL	5.75	8.75	9.95
(Mushrooms, onions, green peppers, black olives)			
THE WORKS	7.50	10.25	11.95
"Super Cheese" with all toppings excluding Anchovies and Jalapeno Peppers			

Menu Prices Include Sales Tax

$7.00 minimum for delivery

DRINKS

	MED	LARGE	QTS.
Pepsi	.50	.75	1.50
Seven Up	.50	.75	1.50
Diet Pepsi	.50	.75	1.50

PAPA JOHN'S

SUBS

Pizza Boat Hoagie	2.75
Italian Sausage & Cheese Hoagie	2.95
Hot Ham & Cheese Hoagie	2.95

ATTENTION: Subs, .20 Each Additional Topping

BEER DELIVERY

6 PK   12 PK
(Except Sunday)

Hours:
Mon.-Thur. — 11:30 a.m. - 12:00 a.m.
Fri.-Sat. — 11:30 a.m. - 1:00 a.m.
Sun. — 12:00 p.m. - 11:00 p.m.

Limited Delivery Area
1448 Gateway Plaza
Jeffersonville, IN
(Inside Mick's Lounge)
Dining Area for 18 & over

$3 OFF LARGE Summer Fever at $2 OFF MEDIUM	$3 OFF LARGE Summer Fever at $2 OFF MEDIUM
PAPA JOHN'S	**PAPA JOHN'S**
Means Big Savings	Means Big Savings
"MADE FROM SCRATCH WITH THE FINEST INGREDIENTS!"	"MADE FROM SCRATCH WITH THE FINEST INGREDIENTS!"
WITH FAST FREE DELIVERY	WITH FAST FREE DELIVERY
Minimum of 3-Toppings	Minimum of 3-Toppings
Good thru Oct. 12, 1984	Good thru Oct. 12, 1984

The first Papa John's menu

1984

Flyer identified Papa John's in the back of Mick's Lounge

And that's exactly what we did. After a few of our initial ideas flopped, we came to an important realization. We had to find the people who liked to eat pizzas and wanted them delivered. The question was, where were these people?

Well, you have to "hunt where the ducks are," so I started by looking at other pizzerias. Specifically, I was interested in the ones that specialized in delivery rather than dine-in. The obvious example was Domino's, which had started in Michigan 24 years earlier and expanded into Jeffersonville several years before. Every night after I'd wrapped things up at Mick's Lounge—between 1 and 3 a.m. most nights—I would head down to the closest Domino's. My target? The dumpster. It contained dozens, sometimes hundreds, of deli slips that had customers' names and addresses and orders. I would crawl in the dumpster to find this hidden treasure.

I now had a long list of potential customers, all from the dumpster database. I sent each of them a personal letter. It simply read: "To the pizza lover who this concerns. Papa John's makes better pizzas. We'll give you half off on your first order. Give us a try." It finished with our first phone number, (812) 282-2305, and my personal signature—John H. Schnatter.

This may not have been glamorous, but it was incredibly effective. Domino's eventually caught on—how, exactly, I'll never know. A few years later they started dousing the deli slips in water, making them unreadable to anyone. But by that point, Papa John's was well on its way to success. We didn't need to dumpster-dive for customers anymore.

The combination of these various tactics worked. Within a month of my first pizza, we were doing between $600 and $700 a week in sales. By May, we were up to $1,000 a week. By July, we were averaging between $1,500 and $2,000 a week—the breakeven point. I had no idea how long it would take us to reach this point when I had started three months earlier, but I was shocked that it took so little time. Word was getting around town. More and more people wanted a taste of Papa John's pizza.

Almost all of our business was delivery at this point. The few who came to pick up pizzas in person, or even to sit down and eat it there, typically didn't come back. They would walk into Mick's Lounge confused. Where was Papa John's? They certainly weren't expecting a broom closet in the back of a bar. Needless to say, it wasn't a family-friendly environment, even though that's what I ultimately wanted to create. I already knew we needed a stand-alone store if Papa John's was ever going to have that mom-'n'-pop feel that I wanted.

Our most popular pie was pepperoni, which accounted for one out of every five pizzas we sold. The next most popular were cheese, "the works," and sausage—they were each roughly 6 or 7 percent of our orders. Interestingly, these percentages have hardly changed in the past 30 years.

By July, I was devoting almost all of my time to the broom closet—business was that busy. I was up from 11 a.m. until about 3 a.m. every day of the week except Sundays, when I left before midnight. I would nap in the broom closet during the day, when pizza orders were few and far between. I slept on the prep table with a pizza bag as a pillow. We forwarded the phone to the main bar—(812) 283-8096—during these hours. Denise was bartending during the day. When an order came in, she would write it down, come back to the broom closet and wake me up. Then I would make the pizza, deliver it, come back and repeat.

Nighttime was a different story. We were up to between 10 and 15 orders an hour from the dinner hour onwards. I finally had to bring others in to help me. The first was Bob. Glenn pitched in, too. And so did my only brother, Chuck.

Chuck came to work for Papa John's in the summer of 1984. Before he came aboard, I gave him two options. His first option was to work for $10 an hour—a very good wage in the mid-1980s. His second option was to work for $3.55 an hour—minimum wage—in exchange for 10 percent of the company. I also wanted him to manage the broom closet for a few months. I wanted him to do this so I could enjoy my summer. I'd been working between 60 and 80 hours a week for the past nine months. I had enough time to go on a few dates, but not nearly enough to start a steady relationship with someone. I wanted to live a little bit—I was still a 22-year-old.

But Chuck didn't have any interest in my proposal. He said, "No thanks. I'll just take the ten bucks an hour. I want to enjoy my own summer." So I kept running the broom closet by myself for the next few months. He would later get a small percentage of the company when we went public in 1993, but it wasn't nearly as much as he would have gotten if he'd wanted to work harder in 1984. Chuck is still kicking himself to this day—he made a $250 million mistake.

Chuck was an invaluable member of the team. His legal insight was especially helpful—he could do some of the paperwork, compliance and office-related work, none of which was my strong suit. He started law school the following year. This was actually a great thing for Papa John's.

I made him another deal right before he went to law school. I'd pay his tuition if he did our legal work for free. That's exactly what he did for the next few years. He went to class, studied and worked during the day. Then, at night, he did most of our legal work. (Papaw's old firm, Ackerson, Blandford and Kaiser, also did some of our more complicated legal work in the first few years.) Chuck was already well on his way to becoming a good lawyer. In addition to helping out at Papa John's, he was an intern at the local law firm Greenebaum, Doll and McDonald, one of the top law firms in Kentucky. He went to work there full-time shortly after he graduated from law school. We actually made them our official law firm around 1987. Their firm was one of the leading experts in the country on franchising, which was very useful for us at that time.

Bob Ehringer and me making pizzas in the first Papa John's restaurant

1985

ARTICLE VIII
Incorporator(s)

The name(s) and post office address(es) of the incorporator(s) of the Corporation is (are):

Name	Number and Street or Building	City	State	Zip Code
John H. Schnatter	2505 Utica Pike, Jeffersonville, IN.			47130
Robert A. Ehringer	705 Graham St., Jeffersonville, IN.			47130

ARTICLE IX
Provisions for Regulation of Business and Conduct of Affairs of Corporation

("Powers" of the Corporation, its directors or shareholders)
(Attach additional pages, if necessary)

The Board of Directors, by majority vote, shall conduct the affiars of the Corporation

THIS DOCUMENT MUST BE SIGNED BY ALL INCORPORATORS.

I (We) hereby verify subject to penalties of perjury that the facts contained herein are true. (Notarization not necessary)

_____
(Written Signature)

John H. Schnatter
(Printed Signature)

_____
(Written Signature)

Robert A. Ehringer
(Printed Signature)

_____
(Written Signature)

_____
(Printed Signature)

This instrument was prepared by Daniel R. Marra
(Name)   , Attorney at

Law,   412 E. Court Avenue,   Jeffersonville,   Indiana   47130
(Number and Street or Building)   (City)   (State)   (Zipcode)

Articles of Incorporation

Chuck was and is a steadfast lawyer. One of his most important contributions was in regards to Papa John's actual name. When we incorporated, I wanted to name it just that—Papa John's. Chuck had a better idea—Papa John's International. His reasoning was that changing a company's name later on in the game would cost us $50,000. We had no intention of forking over that amount of money, then or ever.

We were years away from opening our first Papa John's internationally—that didn't happen until 1998 in Mexico. But we knew it was only a matter of time before we moved out of the broom closet and into the record books. We just had to work hard and then the endless expansion would come. We may have been young and excitable, but we were also determined to turn our wildest dreams into reality.

So we incorporated the business as Papa John's International. Chuck was right: the name hasn't changed since.

• • • • •

1965
Brother Chuck and Me

Chuck was there to see some of our first successes. I remember one Tuesday night in July when we sold over $200 worth of pizzas. We couldn't believe our success—we thought we were rich. Chuck and I were jumping up and down like little kids. We were operating out of a broom closet, of all places, and yet people were still buying our pizza and loving it. It seemed to us like Papa John's was already on track to become a phenomenon.

For my part, I was more fulfilled than at any point in my life. Every moment making pizzas in the broom closet was a moment well spent. Each pizza started with the dough—making, kneading, slapping, tossing it. Next came the sauce. This was my favorite part. I found great joy in spreading the sauce evenly. It was an art that required precision. So did the next step: scattering the cheese. The key here was "edge-locking" the melted cheese to the crust. Getting this right ensures that the cheese and toppings don't fall off when you start eating a slice.

My Brother Chuck and Me later in life 1996

The final step before putting it in the oven, of course, was adding the toppings. When we started, we already had most of the variety that we offer at Papa John's stores today—all the basic toppings were there. Yet we didn't have nearly the same quality. We were still learning how the better ingredients could turn into the better pizza. It would take us some time before we found the best ingredients out there, although we already had Stanislaus' unbeatable fresh-packed sauce.

But it wasn't just the pizza-making that captivated me so much. Sure, I enjoyed the work in the broom closet. But I enjoyed the rhythm of running a business so much more. I was in my element when everything was running at a high level, when the trains were all on time. It was as if Papa John's was a finely-tuned watch. Friday nights were especially intoxicating for me—that's when we were busiest and had to get everything right. When everything clicked, something in my mind also clicked. Similarly, when the business wasn't firing on all cylinders, neither was I. I still spend time each week ensuring that Papa John's is on top of its game. No matter how successful we get, there are always ways for us to take things to the next level.

The business wasn't going to take off, however, until we got our product to a better place. Every day, we sought to improve the quality of our pizzas. We did, little by little. Nor was quality our only area for growth. We also needed to make the pizzas and get them in people's hands much faster. It initially took us roughly five minutes to make each pizza, six minutes to cook it, a few seconds to box it and 15 minutes to deliver it. I always pushed myself to do better. Each week I got faster and faster, eventually shaving off a minute or two from the whole process. To this day, we're always looking for opportunities to increase speed and maximize productivity without sacrificing one iota of quality. Every second saved is a second sooner the customer gets his or her order. We must never forget that the customer's satisfaction is what keeps us in business.

By the late spring of 1984, only a few months later, we were clearing more than $2,000 a week—40-50 pizzas a day, on average. We were getting so many orders during peak hours that I was forced to divide my attention between answering the phone and actually making the pizzas. I hated that damn phone. The ringing would interrupt me in the middle of my art. This would inevitably affect quality, which was unacceptable to me. Bob, Glen and Chuck had to start helping me more at this point so I could focus on what mattered most: the pizza. The Papa John's team was beginning to form, and we were all dedicated to making it a success.

We were going gangbusters by the fall. By November weekly pizza sales were closing in on $3,000—an incredible feat given that we'd only been making pizzas for half a year. At the start of 1985, we were having record weeks of $3,500 or more. Pizza was now nearly half of the bar's overall revenue. Beer, wine and food sales were holding steady at around $7,000 a week. The pool tables were bringing in about $1,000 a week.

All told, the combination of Mick's Lounge and the broom closet pizzas amounted to nearly $600,000 in annual revenue, with projected profits of over $100,000 per year. By this point I was on my way to achieving some of the financial goals I'd set for myself a few years before. Like almost everyone in this world, I definitely wanted to be successful. But I also needed realistic goals in the short term. I settled on one such goal in my early 20s: I wanted to make $50,000 a year and have $50,000 in the bank. I thought if I had this much money, I could finally get a date. I'd always looked at money through the lens of "I'm broke," so I foolishly thought that women were only interested in guys who could take them to fancy restaurants and let them shop. I had much to learn—my wife Annette would tell you I still do—but my intentions were good. I wanted to provide for my future family.

The broom closet was doing so well that I could now set my sights higher. I no longer had to struggle to make a decent living. Now I could concern myself with making it big.

There I was, a 23-year-old running a business that made over $100,000 a year through 50-cent beers, 50-cent games of pool and $5 pizzas. I'd built up a bit of a reputation around town by that point. Jeffersonville, Indiana, was used to Boy Scouts—people who did business as usual. I was a gunslinger. I was willing to try things that others weren't. To be clear, I never believed in breaking the rules. Good business requires acting lawfully, and good business has always been what Papa John's is about and why we're so successful. What I mean is that most others were content to do things the way they'd always done them, whereas I was willing to innovate. My sleepy hometown wasn't too keen on my style, but then again, you can't take style to the bank.

And the bank was where I was headed next. My 8 months of making pizzas had only confirmed to me that I didn't want to be in the bar business anymore. I only wanted to be in the pizza business now. So in February of 1985, I marched my way down to Clark County State Bank, which had previously loaned me the $32,000 to get Mick's Lounge back in the black. This time I asked for an even bigger loan—$40,000.

The bank approved the loan without much of a fuss. With the money in hand, I went to work building the first Papa John's. And I already knew exactly where I was going to build it: right next to Mick's Lounge.

Mick's Lounge technically extended to the corner of the strip mall where it was located, Gateway Plaza. But the bar only used about three-quarters of the total space. The rest of it—an area roughly 1,100 square feet in size—had been used as storage for as long as I'd been at Mick's. Before that, it had actually been one of the first Kentucky Fried Chickens in the area. That was before KFC's heyday. As business had grown, the wildly successful restaurant had moved closer to highway 62. Then, as now, highways were a great opportunity to expand your customer base.

Lucky for us, KFC left behind a room perfectly suited for a pizzeria. It even had tile floor—a luxury in those days. In the mid-1980s, a tile floor was a sign that your restaurant was doing pretty well. It cost a substantial sum of money, and for good reason: tile never wore out. The few places that had them were successful chain restaurants or long-established independent stores. Papa John's was neither of those things—at least, not yet. But we had a room that was perfect for what we wanted to do. I thought to myself, why not transform it back into a place where good people served good food?

A real tile floor, which was a luxury to me, as opposed to vinyl ...

1985

It was like rebuilding the broom closet, but on a much larger scale. We had a significant amount of work to do. Of course, we were confident we'd get the loan before I even went to the bank, so we'd been working on the storage area for at least a few weeks. Back in those days, we didn't have the money for plumbers, framers, electricians and so forth. If we were going to do this, we had to do it ourselves. That meant building Papa John's between shifts at Mick's Lounge, between pizza deliveries from the broom closet and between the time when the sun set at night and when it rose the next day. I slept in the bar a few days a week, so I could get more work done. Luckily, we had a little loft area built near the entryway to the broom closet. It was actually right above the table where I pleaded with Ira McKinley and his wife Ruth not to cut off our supply of beer. That tiny little area became my part-time home off and on for the next few months.

Before...
1983

The first order of business was getting the pizza-making operation into its new home. After cleaning out the storage area, we moved the oven and the prep tables into the back of the storage space, where it would remain for years. We built a corridor—I called it the "umbilical cord"—that connected the soon-to-be Papa John's to the broom closet. The next thing we did was knock down part of the wall between Mick's and the storage area. In its place we built an eight-foot opening to connect the two rooms. This is how we got heavy equipment, tools, lumber and everything else in between the bar and the storage area. We even temporarily put two pool tables in the storage area so we could maximize revenues at Mick's Lounge while we were building Papa John's.

...and after
1985

1985

1985

The Passageway
to Papa John's

And of course, we started to build the pizzeria itself. My uncle and Bob were good with their hands—they could build and fix almost anything. They were also skilled at layout and design. Today, we use computer programs to create models of our stores. In 1985, we had to make those models in real life. Bob and my uncle did just that. They made miniature paper scale models of the tables, chairs and counters, which we arranged in a scale model of the room. Once they had everything set up, I gave them my input—I wanted to make sure everything was perfectly aligned with my vision. I wanted to maximize productivity while giving our customers the best experience possible. Once we figured out how we wanted the layout to look, we went to the hardware store to buy the materials. Then we came back and built the restaurants ourselves. We tinkered with store layouts for at least the first 100 Papa John's.

Entrance to the corridor between the first Papa John's and the broom closet

Construction of the first Papa John's

1985

1985

We made great progress over the next few weeks. We also decided to renovate Mick's Lounge simultaneously—why not? I've always believed that if something can be improved, you should improve it. Don't waste any time. In fact, the longer you wait, the less likely it is that you will reap the full rewards. Entrepreneurs who play the waiting game aren't entrepreneurs for long. You have to get your facts and then make your decision. Dithering can lead to disaster.

In everything we did at Mick's Lounge, we sought to maximize productivity and improve the customer's experience. Our biggest change was to the original bar where drinks were served. Originally, it had a hideous island that sat awkwardly right in the middle of the floor, forcing bartenders to go around it to get to customers on the other side. It was easily the most awkward part of the entire Mick's Lounge operation. So we tore out the entire bar area and rebuilt it without the island. We built a much smaller one that could serve the same number of customers while cutting the number of bartenders down from two to one. This improved customer service, facilitated more interaction between patrons and dramatically improved productivity. It also freed up additional space. We consolidated all the pool tables in one area, rather than scattering them across nearly every corner of Mick's Lounge.

First Papa John's ready for business!

1985

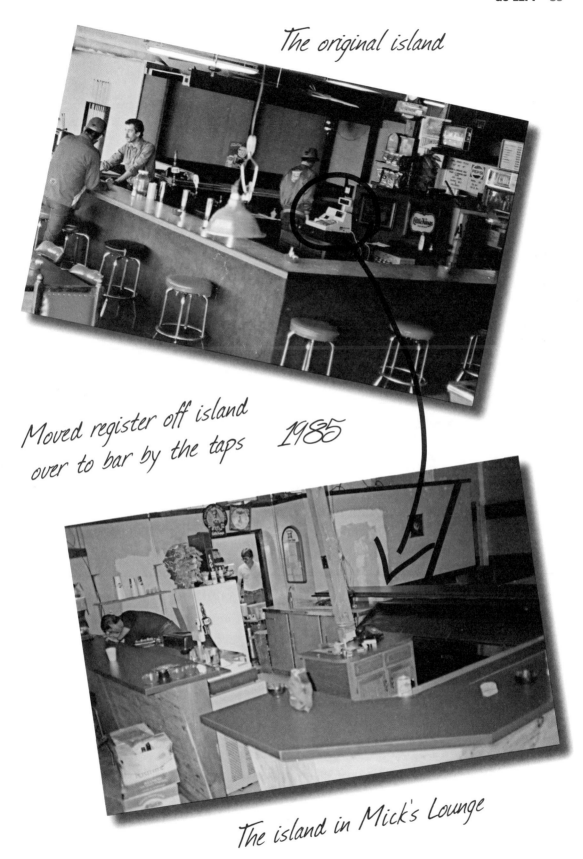

The original island

Moved register off island
over to bar by the taps   1985

The island in Mick's Lounge

Mick's Lounge plate lunches advertised in the window

We also made improvements in the kitchen. We installed a walk-in refrigerator. We bought new cooking equipment for Papa John's that allowed us to expand our menu. At Mick's, we served plate lunches including meatloaf, country fried steak, pot roast, mashed potatoes and gravy, homemade soups and, of course, our famous Mick Burgers. Everything new that we tried was designed to expand our options and keep our patrons happy. We never forgot that the customer comes first. It's a simple truth of the business world that customer loyalty is won—and lost—one customer at a time.

A few smart renovations stick out in my mind more than others. The bathroom, for instance. Whenever we only had one bartender on duty, they had to take the cash register till with them every time they used the bathroom. This was the only way to prevent theft. If we left the till in the cash register, someone could simply take the entire register and bolt with it. This isn't a hypothetical—it actually happened once in 1984.

But it turned out the bathroom wasn't that safe, either. Some of our customers discovered they could move some of the ceiling tiles, creating a little cubby just big enough for someone to fit in. Occasionally, a drunk customer would find their way up there before the night ended. Some mornings we came to work and found that some customer had spent the whole night. That's actually how the cash register got stolen. Someone stashed themselves in the cubby just before the bar closed. Once we all left, they dropped down and stole as much stuff as they could take. Not only did they take the cash register, they also took a bunch of beer and food and let themselves out the back door. They probably made off with $1,000 in cash and goods. Obviously, we couldn't let that happen again. We fixed this glaring problem with the renovation by placing three-and-a-quarter inch press boards over the walls and ceiling, screwed in as if they were bars in a prison cell. To this day, the bathroom in Mick's Lounge looks like it could be in a county jail.

Maybe this helps explain why I wanted to get out of the bar business so bad. A family-friendly pizzeria wouldn't have to deal with any of these shenanigans.

We constantly dealt with money shortages as we built Papa John's and remodeled Mick's Lounge. Sure, the bar was making plenty of money, but we turned around and spent every cent of profit on construction. Our banker, Jim Wheatley, was constantly calling me to say we'd overdrawn our account. He threatened to charge us $15 a day when we did this. Luckily, he only charged us a few times a week rather than every day. This actually worked out better for us. A loan would have cost more in interest than the overdraw fees did on a weekly basis. So we kept overdrawing the account until Papa John's was built.

By the middle of March, we were only a few weeks away from finishing all the renovations. The bar looked better than ever. Papa John's was almost ready for its grand opening. It still surprises me that we'd only been at it for maybe a month and a half. Then again, everyone involved was committed to making the Papa John's dream a reality. We were almost there. Little did I know my Dad was getting ready to die.

Remodeling Mick's lounge

1985

• • • • •

This is where the "Go Left" story truly starts.

I learned what Go Left means in late March, 1985. The first Papa John's was less than three weeks from opening its doors. My Dad never lived to see it. On March 18, a Monday, Robert Louis Schnatter went to the hospital with an illness. He didn't think it was anything serious; he just wasn't feeling well. But he got steadily worse over the next three days. By Friday, it was clear that something was terribly wrong. He wouldn't live much longer. He was on his deathbed.

This came as a complete and total shock to everyone who knew him, especially me. A 23-year-old doesn't expect his 51-year-old parent to pass away—that thought had never even entered my mind. This meant that the two most important men in my world would soon no longer be with me. They had taught me almost everything I knew. Now one was gone and another would soon follow. When I truly realized this for the first time, I thought to myself, "I guess I have to go it alone."

I've already described how my work ethic and outlook on life were the result of both my Dad's and my Papaw's influence. Nearly two decades later, I started searching for my old Z28 Camaro because it was my most important connection to these two men. I drove it to my Papaw's house to work for him on weekends. I drove it to my Dad's law firm to get lunch with him a few times a week. With both of them gone, the Camaro was the most tangible thing that linked me to the people who shaped me into the man I was today. We ultimately found the car—but that's a story for another time.

My Dad had been my friend, my coach and my business partner. Ever since I came to help out at Mick's Lounge a year and a half earlier, the two of us had formed an excellent team. He called me *ace;* I called him *champ.* He was the front-of-the-house guy, bringing people in, making them feel at home and helping them have a good time. I was the introvert in the back. It was my job to get the operations and the products right. It was Dad's job to get people in the door and make them feel at home. He would get in around 8:30 in the morning to start prepping the steam table and preparing food. I'd take his place when I got in at 11 so he could head out towards the courthouse to find new customers. While my Dad made the rounds, both inside and outside of the bar, I was coming up with new ideas. I was making sure that the beer was really cold, the burgers and fries were really good and hot and the pizza was really the best in town. He was making sure people were there to enjoy everything. Our different roles and styles worked, making Mick's Lounge more than the sum of its parts.

We had also built a great team together. Dad had been responsible for bringing in most of our best people, including Denise, Glenn and Roxanne. He inspired me to work hard so that our team could taste success.

But my Dad had given me another reason to work hard. He'd always had financial troubles with this or that, but the few years I'd worked with him at Mick's Lounge were especially bad. He started out in tremendous debt—so much that he didn't even know about all of it. He and my Mom were also going through some pretty serious problems. They ended up divorcing in 1984 after 23 years of marriage.

It's an understatement to say that my Dad was in a pretty rough spot. For me, saving Mick's Lounge and then building Papa John's was a chance to make everything good. It was a chance to get him back on his feet, to give him something new to be a part of. It wasn't just my dream—it could be his, too.

These thoughts were flying through my mind as I stood next to my Dad on his deathbed. It was Friday, March 22nd. Next to me was my sister Anne, who was midway through college, and my brother Chuck, who was halfway through law school. We were in the middle of the intensive care unit. Our emotions were out of control. At one point my Dad's twin brother, Richard Schnatter, asked me point blank: "When are you going to pull the plug on that son of a bitch?" I couldn't believe he was asking me this—it was insulting and painful and maddening all at once. I immediately shot back, "I never give up on anyone and I'm sure as hell not giving up on my old man." My uncle looked me in the eye and said, "You're the leader now."

I sure as hell didn't want to be the leader, especially right then. My Dad was dying before my eyes. But I also knew I had to step up and do right by the family. I remember asking myself several times, "What does a leader do in a situation like this?" I didn't know the right answer—I was really scared—but I was pretty sure that a good leader got the input of the people he or she trusts most. Collaboration was key. I turned to my brother and sister, who were sitting in the corner of the ICU. It wasn't just my Dad dying in the other room—it was their Dad, too. We were a team. So my siblings and I promised each other that we'd do everything we could do to keep our Dad alive. We realized we were in this together. We were the only hope he had of making it. And we made a vow to do the right thing no matter how much it cost or how hard it was. We weren't going to let Dad die by pulling the plug.

But we didn't know how much longer we had with him. We had to make preparations for the end, no matter how hard it was. I told Chuck and Anne, "Go in there and tell Dad you love him and no matter what you'll always be with him." We each took turns telling him that. By this point it was in the late evening on March the 22nd. I was the last to go into the room. It was horrifying for me. My Dad was convulsing on the hospital bed by this point. At first I didn't know what to say or do—I was frightened and upset watching my Dad suffer like that. But I knew I had to be strong. I walked up next to his hospital bed. I told him I loved him and I would always be with him. He looked me in

1984   *People sitting at the Mick's Lounge bar, I'm tending bar and running pizzas*

the eye for a good five seconds. It was a look I'll never forget. It said, "I'm in trouble and I don't know how to get out of it." It was absolutely terrifying. After a few more hours, I left the hospital to head home for the night, assuming Dad would still be there when I came back the next morning.

Only a few hours later at 3 a.m. on Saturday, March 23, 1985, I got the call. The voice on the other end said, "Come to the hospital now." I immediately knew my business partner, my friend, my coach, my Dad was in trouble. As I walked into the hospital about twenty minutes later, medical staff wheeled a double-decker gurney by me. I couldn't tell there was a body on the lower deck because a sheet was draped over the whole thing. I immediately stopped one of the doctors to ask, "Where's my Dad?" He told me, "He's dead. He just went by you." Robert L. Schnatter was dead at the age of 51, and I hadn't even been there when he died.

We held the funeral the following Tuesday. Hundreds of people came—a testament to the effect my Dad had on his community. He may not have been successful in his business ventures, but he was loved and respected and viewed as a good man—something that's even more important than success. It was a fitting tribute for him, one that I will never forget.

As this happened, I built around myself a protective mental shell to help me get through this difficult time. I felt numb. I didn't know how else to deal with my Dad's death, so I retreated inward. The most important person in a young boy's life is his father—and I had just lost mine. It had been eight days between my Dad going into the hospital and his funeral—eight days of emotional trauma and confusion and chaos.

It's impossible to explain just how devastating it was to lose both my Dad and my Papaw—the two most important men in my life—in the span of only a year. This taught me a lesson that I never wanted to learn. You can't expect your most important relationships to last forever. One person always ends up burying the other. But that's the deal. Learning to live and love on life's terms is something I learned at 23 years old burying my Papaw and my Dad.

Even so, amazing things can still come out of terrible sadness. That happened after Papaw died—that's when I broke down the wall to the broom closet. Another transformational thing occurred as my Dad's life was ending.

Standing in the ICU the night before he passed away, I realized something. As I reflected on the lessons Dad taught me, I realized that if I could get through this, I could get through anything. It was like my father had given me a parting gift—the gift of confidence. It was inspirational. My Dad's last act was to convince me to finish what I started. As we buried him a few days later, I knew that it was now up to me to take charge and be the leader. In my moment of tremendous pain, I suddenly found a tremendous sense of purpose. Dad had never feared failure—it would be an insult to his memory if I started fearing it now.

I woke up the next morning with a feeling I didn't expect. I had every reason to be depressed and downtrodden after everything that had just happened. Instead, I felt relieved and *determined*. I wanted to go *do* something that would make my Dad proud. So I booked it over to Mick's Lounge without delay. We had saved it from bankruptcy just over a year before. As I walked in, in front of me was a group of about ten of our regulars sitting at the bar drinking beer even though it was only 10 in the morning. To the left was a doorway in a brick wall. Beyond that doorway stood the half-completed pizzeria that we'd spent the past two months building. The room was full of dust, tools and trash. My future was in that room.

I took a few steps into Mick's Lounge. The bar was on my right and the doorway to Papa John's was on my left. I looked right, at everyone sitting at the bar. They turned around and looked back at me, staring. They hadn't seen me in five days—I'd been at the hospital and the funeral home watching Dad die, followed by a few days grieving with my family. They were waiting to see what I would do. Then I looked left again, at the doorway to Papa John's.

I looked back and forth a few more times. I could have gone to the bar and drowned my sorrows. That would have been the easy choice, given what had happened over the past week. My Dad—one of the two most important men in my life—was dead. All I had to do was sit down, grab a beer and spend a few days wallowing in misery. But that wouldn't have been the right thing to do. I wanted to honor my father's memory, just like I had tried to honor Papaw's memory the year before when I knocked down a wall in the broom closet. If they had both still been alive, they would have wanted me to finish the job and turn my dream into a reality. They would have wanted me to build a pizzeria that served great pizza and that made people happy.

I knew it would be hard. But I also knew I had to do it. I had to turn my dream into a reality. I had to build Papa John's. I had to go left.

So I went left. I picked up a hammer and some nails. I started putting tongue and groove paneling on the walls. I built that dining room. I built that first Papa John's. And then we built a pizza empire. The rest is history.

— • —

Putting up tongue and groove paneling

CHAPTER THREE

THE FIRST PAPA JOHN'S

The first Papa John's officially opened about two and a half weeks after my Dad passed and just over a year after my Papaw died. The date was April 11, 1985. Coincidentally, this was the one-year anniversary of when we started making pizzas in the broom closet.

Such a rapid transformation—from broom closet to a stand-alone store in less than 12 months—was only possible because of the two men who raised me. My Dad and my Papaw equipped me with the tools and the skill set that enabled me to start my own entrepreneurial adventure. They gave me most of the ammunition I needed to go into battle. Yet I always expected them to be alongside me. Now they were both gone, leaving me to start my adventure on my own.

But I was up for the challenge. I was definitely scared, but I was also confident. My Dad and my Papaw trained me to be ready for anything, even as they were passing from this Earth—remember that my Go Left moment happened right after my Dad died. I knew I couldn't feel sorry for myself. I had to find my strength in the midst of adversity. The best thing I could do to honor their memories was to take what they taught me and turn Papa John's into a success—one day, one pizza, one customer at a time.

That officially started with our opening day. When we completed the store's finishing touches on the morning of April 11, I looked around to survey what we'd built.

We'd come an incredibly long way in such a short amount of time. Only three months before, I would have been standing in a dank and dusty storage room, dreaming about what we were going to do. The month before that, we didn't even have plans for the space.

If someone had said we would be standing in a brand-new pizzeria only three months later, I wouldn't have believed them. Yet that's exactly where we were now, and we'd built it ourselves. I had this overpowering sense that I had finally found what I was supposed to do. I was only 23 years old, yet my whole life up to this point had been an education in how to start and run my own business, whether it was fixing tractors in my Papaw's basement or turning Mick's Lounge around alongside my Dad. I will always be an apprentice in business—learning, experimenting, improving. Opening the first Papa John's was the biggest calculated risk of my young life.

1985

Front of first Papa John's

Pizzas baking in the 2nd oven in the 1st Papa John's store

Crankin' it out in the 1st Papa John's

1985

My Mom
and sister on
opening night

Family and friends
at grand opening

Denise and Glenn
with other friends
at first Christmas
after grand opening

We kicked off the grand opening with some festivities. The night before, we invited our friends and family over for a test run. Beyond those of us who worked there, between 15 and 20 people stopped by that evening. My Mom came, along with my brother Chuck and my sister Anne, and so did a few friends from around Jeffersonville. By this point we had roughly 16 employees shared between Mick's Lounge and Papa John's. Even those who'd only worked with us for a short time were like family to me. You only had to look around the brand-new pizzeria that night to see it. Everyone was happy. The team was grinning from ear to ear. We were proud of what we'd already done and what we were getting ready to do. We finally had the "good business" that could make a positive difference in our community. Dad and Papaw would have been proud.

And the pizzas we made that night were the best we'd made up to that point. It was a good sign for our official opening the next day.

We only went up from there. Our first day saw us sell between 40 and 50 pizzas—double what we would have served on a comparable day in the broom closet. Within seven days, we were selling 800 pizzas a week—more than double what we had been doing in the broom closet. Papa John's was off to the races.

A huge part of our initial success can be chalked up to something incredibly simple: having an actual building branded with "Papa John's". It turns out this goes a long way towards getting butts in the seats. Even before we opened, people would stop by every few days to ask what we were building. We must have had dozens of people knock on the front door in the weeks leading up to our grand opening. Interest only grew when we installed a 27-inch-by-79-inch awning and a four-by-eight-foot sign over the front door. We also put three signs on the side of the building—all of which featured the Papa John's logo or name—and I personally crafted two handmade stained glass windows for the front. It also featured our first slogan, "Homemade Pizza the Way You Like It." People finally had a name for the construction project they'd seen over the past two months. Hundreds of potential customers now drove by every day and saw what we'd built. Many would stop by to try out the new pizzeria in town.

I can't overstate just how transformative this was—and how I didn't see it coming. I may have turned Mick's Lounge around over the past year and a half, but I had no experience with actually *starting* a small business, much less making it a success. I clearly had a lot to learn. To this day I have a lot to learn—like I said, I will always be an apprentice in the world of business. In any case, simply having a front door with a sign over it was the single most effective marketing tactic we had used up to that point. It was also the most basic. In business, like in life, you have to "get yourself in a position to get lucky." Getting a front door allowed us to get lucky.

It was clear from the start that Papa John's wasn't going to crash and burn. In fact, we were already flying higher than we initially expected. Like most pizzerias, our busiest days were Friday, Saturday and Sunday. The weekend crowd is crucial to any restaurant's success—the pizza business is no exception. Mondays were, and still are, our least busy days, even with Monday Night Football. Nothing comes close to the weekend scene. By the end of our first month, we had nearly tripled our sales compared to when we were in the broom closet. Our entrepreneurial experiment was already bringing in almost $9,000 a week in sales. We were bringing more in than Mick's Lounge, which by that point had been open for four years.

I thought this was normal for a pizzeria. How could I have known any better? I was at the bottom of the totem pole when I worked at Rocky's and Greek's, so I never had a chance to look at their books. Even if I had been able to do so, I wouldn't have understood what I was seeing. Now I ran my own pizzeria. I wanted to know how I stacked up against the competition. One day in early June, I went down to the local Domino's off of Grant's Plaza—the same Domino's where I had

1985

Hand-crafted stained glass that my uncle and I made. Even when we were half-broke, we took pride in our work fished deli slips with customer information out of their dumpster. I asked the manager what their weekly sales were. To my surprise, he said they averaged around $6,000 per week. We were already selling 50 percent more pizzas than the leading pizza chain that had been around for 25 years.

This was proof that we were on to something with Papa John's. Even before I started making pizzas in the broom closet, I developed a fundamental belief that "you can't make good wine from bad grapes." Put another way, I believed that people could tell the difference between a mediocre product and a superior one, that quality would always win. Everything we'd done up to that point, from the suppliers we chose to the equipment we purchased, was geared towards making a quality pizza. I knew that if we ever lost our focus, we'd have a mountain to climb to win back our customers' trust.

Papa John's store #1 with my pickup truck

1985

And here was the proof that we were on the right track. The first Papa John's store was less than two months old and we were already beating our biggest local competitor. I honestly thought I was the luckiest guy in the whole world. I'd been dead broke less than a year and a half earlier. No one would hire me. I thought I was unemployable. Now I was employing others—and more importantly, taking care of them. I had finally found something I was both good at and found fulfilling. My dream as a kid had finally come true. I hope that everyone, no matter who they are or what they do, experiences this feeling in their own lives.

I can only hope that my Dad and my Papaw were looking down on me, smiling. Here I was, only weeks after opening the first Papa John's, yet already we were going down the right path—and fast. I was living the life my Dad always wanted to have and the life my Papaw taught me to have. To me, it seemed like they were living vicariously through my success.

I left Domino's with a bounce in my step and a smile on my face. It didn't matter that I was only 23 years old—I thought I could conquer the world. I thought to myself: "If we could beat 'em in Jeffersonville, Indiana, why couldn't we beat 'em in the whole world?" I had to take Papa John's to as many people as I could, one store at a time. What were we waiting for?

● ● ● ● ●

First we had to make sure we could continue running the first Papa John's at a high level. Fortunately, we didn't encounter any major hurdles in the first few months. Sales continued to increase throughout 1985, with nearly every week seeing an improvement over the previous one. With business getting better and better, my thoughts naturally turned to expansion. If Papa John's was going to conquer the world, we probably needed to build a second store.

I always knew I wanted to have multiple stores ever since I came up with the Papa John's concept in college. Actually, I wanted to have hundreds or even thousands of stores spread across America and the world. Massive expansion was always part of the Papa John's plan.

Now we had to figure out where we wanted to go next, and when we wanted to do it. We were only on the first step of a very tall staircase.

I already had a vision: I wanted Papa John's to have the best pizza in Southern Indiana. So that's where we focused in the first few years. We weighed the options and visited a few nearby towns as we searched for a good location. We settled on Clarksville, immediately to the northwest of Jeffersonville. This was the natural place to go. It was only four or five miles from the Jeffersonville store. I knew we needed to be tight-knit in order to stay on top of our game. We also needed each new store to be contiguous with an existing one. If the delivery areas touched without overlapping, we could maximize our geographic footprint as well as the number of customers we could reach. It also created a better system for supervisors, who could devote more time to ensuring productivity and quality at the stores they oversaw. Proximity breeds better performance across the board.

We have always tried to ensure that our expansion follows this simple formula. If we expanded too far too fast, I feared we would start to lose the quality that was central to Papa John's identity. We needed to be disciplined and have our fundamentals down pat before we did anything else. Interestingly, some of Papa John's franchisees don't understand this concept. This is especially true overseas. They'll try to open up stores that are 20 miles apart or more. Unsurprisingly, many of these stores end up closing.

Eventually they catch on that the winning path is to build contiguous stores—what we modeled from the very start. Growing in concentric circles, rather than random potshots, is one of the keys to Papa John's continued success. Building extensions off of a single foundation is always better than trying to build multiple foundations in different locations. Your marketing, distribution, leadership, brand recognition, quality, productivity and customer satisfaction all benefit from this approach. I can't stress that enough—and it's because I stressed it so much that Papa John's was able to expand so fast without sacrificing our traditional, superior-quality pizzas.

We would start to prove this with the Clarksville Papa John's. But first we had to build the actual pizzeria. It wasn't quite as much work as the first Papa John's, but we still had our work cut out for us.

Clarksville
store under
construction

1985

The store itself was on Highway 131, roughly a mile from I-65, the main highway heading into Jeffersonville and Kentucky after that. We leased the front of the building because we couldn't afford to buy the whole thing ourselves. (We would do that later.) Just like the first store, we pretty much had to build the interior. We once again made scale-model mock-ups so we knew where everything would go. Once we figured that out, we got to work turning our crude figures into a full-scale pizzeria. Several months of hard work and construction late at night and on weekends did the trick.

The finished product looked almost nothing like the first Papa John's. Our business model was already changing by this point. We built the Jeffersonville store under the assumption that we'd be doing roughly the same amount of business through dine-in and delivery and carryout. That's why the first Papa John's had a full dining room, including fancy silverware and china, cold mugs of beer and an extensive menu with things like fried zucchini and fried mozzarella sticks—my personal favorite. Although we did just fine from a monetary standpoint, it was already becoming clear that the dine-in experience wasn't what our customers wanted most from Papa John's pizza.

Clarksville store ready for business 1985

In the mid-to-late 1980s, the pizza business was moving more and more towards delivery and carryout, rather than in-house dining. We still had a decent number of customers who came in to sit down and eat a pizza in the Jeffersonville store. But it became obvious that most of our customers wanted to have fresh, hot pizzas come to them—not the other way around. In fact, we repeatedly heard from our early customers that they wanted a superior pizza delivered straight to their door, for a great value. That's what they asked for, so that's what we gave them. This decision was crucial to Papa John's initial success—we weren't afraid to abandon our initial business model in favor of a better one. Every entrepreneur has to be humble enough to know when they're wrong. You have to listen to your customer rather than yourself. To this day, we do everything we can to listen to our customers so we can give them something that meets—and exceeds—their expectations. That's how you develop loyal customers. And we love our loyal customers.

This is a valuable lesson for any would-be entrepreneur. I'd even say it's one of the most important lessons of all. It turns out the phrase "the customer is always right" has a much deeper meaning than the one that most people think. We're in the business of creating something that customers enjoy—something that makes their lives better. That requires recognizing what the customers want and making sure we're giving it to them. If we do that, everybody wins. The customer gets what they want and the entrepreneur gets their business. But if we don't do that, we have no right to be in business at all.

Dino Cortopassi, one of the owners of Stanislaus Food Products, the company behind Papa John's fresh-packed tomato sauce, once told me a fictional story that sums this up. It starts at the annual convention of "Snappy," a dog food manufacturer. The company CEO stands up in front of a few hundred of the company's employees. He starts to rile the crowd up, as if it was a concert or a big game. He yells out, "Who's the best?" The crowd roars back, "Snappy, Snappy, Snappy!" Then he asks, "Who's got the best quality?" The crowd roars back again: "Snappy, Snappy, Snappy!" Then the CEO gets serious: "Then why are our sales down 20 percent?" A deathly silence falls over the room for a few seconds, until a new employee at the back of the auditorium gets up and says, "Because the dogs won't eat it." Put another way, the company wasn't selling what the customer wanted, so the customer was disappearing. If the dogs didn't like the dog food, then Snappy wasn't long for this world.

This joke stuck with me. When Papa John's rolls out a new product, I ask my managers to answer a simple question: "Is this what our customers want?" If it's not selling well, then we pull it without a second glance. We're in the business of making customers happy, which means selling them what they want.

Admittedly, selling what customers want isn't the only thing you need to succeed. It's only the first of three things. You need to be best in your class. You need to have a passion for what you do. And you need to have a business model that works. All of these are equally crucial. Papa John's had the first two parts in spades. The broom closet's success—followed by the first full store's success—definitively proved that we were the best pizzeria in the Jeffersonville area. Our passion was also obvious. You only had to look at us as we made the pizzas to see that we loved what we did. Our passion was also reflected in our rapid expansion. We wanted to bring Papa John's pizza to everyone we could.

Now we needed a simple and effective business model to match our ambition. Our first store was doing fine, monetarily, but we could tell we would do even better if we abandoned dine-in and doubled down on delivery and carryout. After a lot of thought and number crunching, we came up with a simple formula that would guide Papa John's starting with store #2. We would spend $100,000 building every store. Once it got up and running, we expected it to do $10,000 a week in sales while spending $1,000 a month in rent. Our overall goal was for each store to earn 10 percent in profits.

That was our business model: $100,000, $10,000, $1,000 and 10 percent. Yes, it was simple, but it was also effective. Every successful chain restaurant has its own unique business model, some catchier than others. McDonalds calls theirs "QSC," which later turned into "QSCV." This stands for Quality, Service, Cleanliness and Value, and each individual store is measured according to each of these factors. It works for them; our system works for us.

We tested out our new model with the Clarksville restaurant, which had its grand opening on October 31, 1985. This was just a few weeks before I turned 24 years old. We also did a small advertising blitz, including ads in the local newspaper, door hangers in the delivery area and, of course, personally signed letters to the customers whose addresses we found in the dumpster of the local Domino's. Things started off slowly, with the store doing maybe $2,000 to $3,000 a week in sales. But just like the broom closet, it picked up with every week. Sales doubled after a few months as word got out about the new pizzeria in town. To help keep costs down, we set up a paging system that allowed us to send team members home when we weren't busy and then bring them back when things picked up. Our early stores definitely wouldn't have been profitable without this system. We were operating on a shoestring budget and didn't have any expendable cash. It would be that way for many years, pretty much up until we went public in 1993.

Then again, that's the cost of taking a risk and opening up a small business. Every team member—no matter how senior or junior they are—needs to believe in the business' mission and make sacrifices for it to succeed. I tried to instill this in literally every single person we hired. Papa John's is my life's work; I still make sacrifices to make sure it succeeds. I want everyone around me to have the same mentality. When they don't—especially people at the top—then the company runs into trouble. We would learn this the hard way later on. But I also have hundreds of stories of team members who did make sacrifices for Papa John's. I've already mentioned some. I'll mention many more in the pages ahead. Papa John's is blessed to have so many great people on the team.

The new business model showed promise in terms of profitability and customer satisfaction. This gave us the confidence to continue using it as we expanded. We were already building our third Papa John's even when we opened our second. I didn't want to waste any time. After Clarksville, we went to the next town over: New Albany. We may have been changing our business model, but we had no intention of changing the geographic strategy that allowed us to cover 100% of customers in a given area.

Just like before, we identified a building that was close to the Clarksville store—three and a half miles away, to be exact. It was on Grant Line Road, one of the most heavily trafficked arteries in New Albany. We fixed the place up, installed the right equipment and hired some new people. Our third store was ready to go by late November, 1985, less than a month after the second store opened. It followed the same path as Clarksville—a decent financial start followed by sustained improvement. Our business model was proving to be a winner. From that point on, we focused on delivery and carryout because that's where the customer interest was. The only store that still has a dine-in area is the Jeffersonville store. It's actually moved locations three times since we first opened it in the broom closet in 1984. The first move, as I already mentioned, was next door when we built the first stand-alone Papa John's. A few years after that we moved it to another location just up the street, and in the following years we moved it across the street near Highway 62. Despite all this change, it still has a sit-down area to this day. It's an important part of our history that we should never forget.

1985

New Albany store under construction

The New Albany store kept improving over the following months. We definitely weren't firing on all cylinders yet, but we were getting close. The main store was making enough money to finance continued expansion. The new stores, meanwhile, were getting close to turning a profit. Fortunately, the Jeffersonville store was a cash cow. It was making enough money to both cover the initial losses at new stores and finance continued expansion.

But we still had a lot of room to improve, even in Jeffersonville. We were doing everything we could at this point to boost Papa John's name recognition. We didn't have the money for major advertising campaigns at this point, relying instead on door hangers and word-of-mouth. In the summer of 1986, we built a little kiosk that we could cart around town. We set it up in downtown Jeffersonville on Spring Street during special events, hoping to get our name in front of families who were out enjoying the town's festivities. Funnily enough, we didn't have the money to decorate the thing. We had to take the red awning and the Papa John's sign off the main store and attach it to the top of the kiosk—that's how little money we had.

New Albany store ready for business   1985

Papa John's kiosk with the awning off the front door and sign from side of the building of the main store. Didn't have the money for 2 signs and 2 awnings so we made do

1985 & 1986

The kiosk didn't make much money, either. Then again, it wasn't supposed to. It was just a good way to get the Papa John's name in front of people's eyes. We were a scrappy little company willing to do everything we could to boost our brand.

But we also knew that little marketing maneuvers like door hangers and the kiosk weren't the ticket to long-term success. For that, we needed to keep building stores. Our initial strategy was to own the Southern Indiana area, which we had nearly achieved in roughly a year. This only whetted our appetite to expand our horizons. We had to test our mettle somewhere else. Directly to the south was the big fish: Louisville. The biggest city in Kentucky was less than a mile away from Jeffersonville, across the Ohio River. But that one mile might as well have been 100 miles. Louisville was a different world, economically and socially. It was booming. Southern Indiana was sleepy by comparison. Our goal was to tap into this much larger market. It would be a big test of whether Papa John's was ready for the big time.

So we took the leap of faith. In the fall of 1986, right before I turned 25 years old, we started to build store #4 on Lower Brownsboro Road. It was close to where I-71 and I-64 merge in the downtown Louisville area. It opened on December 1, 1986. We were hoping this would give us a massive influx of customers and make Papa John's an instant success in a huge metro area. Instead, we got our asses handed to us. The store struggled for well over a year. We hoped it would cut into the customer base of a nearby Domino's, which was doing gangbusters. We later learned they were doing so well because they had established good relationships with the hotel industry in downtown Louisville. They had a stranglehold on this market that would take years to break. In the meantime, we were the new kid on the block and we didn't have the name recognition necessary to dethrone Domino's.

Lower Brownsboro Road store ready for business

Even though this was a disappointment, the store's struggles didn't make it a failure. In fact, I'd say it was a big success. I'd learned from my Dad that failure helps you figure out what doesn't work. That gives you a better chance of eventually finding something that does work. With this lesson in mind, we realized we had to focus on what worked before we could make huge inroads into the Louisville market.

So we doubled down on the Southern Indiana strategy. This may seem counterintuitive to many readers. Most people's natural inclination is to follow the saying, "the squeaky wheel gets the grease." The Brownsboro Road store was definitely the squeaky wheel. My thought, however, was that we should keep greasing the other three wheels that weren't squeaking—the stores in Jeffersonville, Clarksville and New Albany. They were the ones making money. Therefore, they were the only ones that could finance continued growth. Why would we devote scarce resources to something that wasn't giving us a return on investment?

In retrospect, I wish we hadn't gone to Louisville first. Lexington would have been the better choice. On the one hand, it would have put a serious strain on our infant distribution network—Lexington is over 70 miles away from Louisville. However, it had a built-in audience for a brand-new pizzeria: The University of Kentucky. Tens of thousands of college students would have made a Papa John's location a success. In fact, we proved this when we built our first store in Lexington, our 18th overall, on November 16, 1988. It was our first outside the Louisville metro area. It was also one of our biggest successes. The Lexington area has always been one of the most profitable areas for our company. Wildcat country is Papa John's country.

But it's not just about location. A lot of our success in Lexington can be chalked up to Mike Smith, a store operator who started his Papa John's career in the city. Today he is our vice president of operations, where he continues to make Papa John's a better company. He has developed more profitable store operators than anyone else in the history of the company. He's one of our great leaders. Papa John's is better off because of him.

In any case, we were still three years away from moving into Lexington. In the meantime, we had to keep getting better with what we already had. We had plenty of places to improve.

For starters, we needed to build a "commissary"—a central location where we could make and distribute everything our stores needed. This would help us manage and measure the quality of all our ingredients; it's easier to hold everything to one standard when it's all coming from the same place. We recognized this from the moment we opened up the second store in Clarksville. For the first year or so, we set up an *ad hoc* commissary in the corridor at the first Papa John's. If you recall, we had originally built this to serve as an "umbilical cord" between the broom closet and the pizzeria while the latter was under construction. Once it opened, however, we didn't have much use for it. The first commissary gave it a new purpose.

We loaded it up with everything we needed. We put in a World War I-era dough mixer, a used Hobart T-80 with three gears that had a capacity of 80 quarts. (A new Hobart 80-quart mixer would have cost us $10,000—about $9,740 out of my price range.) The room also had one prep table where we hand-cut and hand-rounded each dough ball, a scale for weighing them, another prep table where we cut and prepared the veggies and more. There was very little machinery or automation at this point. In fact, we folded every pizza box by hand, stacking them as high as we could go. We established a daily schedule for the commissary. We'd make ingredients all morning long. After the lunch rush ended, between 1 and 5 p.m., we'd pack up our new delivery truck—a used dually we bought from a local Budget Rent-A-Car—to get the next day's ingredients out to the stores.

We were still working hard—usually 10 to 12 hours a day, six-and-a-half days a week. Sunday night was my only time off. By this point I was shifting towards doing more supervising and long-term strategic planning. I worked in the commissary a lot when it first opened because I wanted to make sure everything was made with an eye for quality. Once I was sure of that, I devoted my days to identifying new places for stores and helping existing ones stay true to the Papa John's vision. My goal was to guarantee quality without micromanaging. I did everything I could to get a store to a self-sustaining, profitable place. Once I could tell a store was on the right path, I'd do everything I could to stay out of the way. If I walk into a store and it's firing on all cylinders, the best thing I can do is pat the manager on the back and then get the hell out of there. You have a major problem when tinkering turns into micromanaging.

1984

The corridor between Mick's Lounge and the first Papa John's stacked
with pizza boxes and aluminum cans in 55 gallon trashcan
(The umbilical cord)

But there was still plenty of tinkering to be done at the commissary. The small set-up in the corridor got the job done for the first year, but we knew it wouldn't work in the long run. It didn't even make sense in the short run. We clearly needed a bigger space by the time we built the third store in New Albany. We needed something much bigger to make sure every store was supplied with everything they needed. If we didn't do this fast, we risked jeopardizing our promise to make our pizzas with better and fresh ingredients. That was something we weren't willing to do.

Me and Bob putting the Papa John's logo on the 1st distribution truck

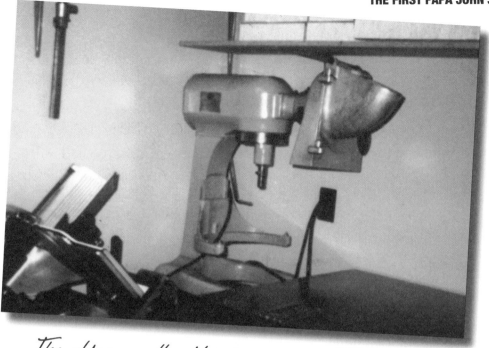

The older, smaller Hobart mixer, we had to make 30 batches a day, which was a pain in the ass...

Now we just needed to find the best place. It didn't take much looking—the Clarksville store occupied part of a building which had only a few other tenants. We didn't have the money to buy the building outright, so we asked the owners—Bob Waiz, a prominent realtor, and Sam Volt, a prominent tax attorney—for help financing it. I thought their cooperation was a sign of the community's growing belief that Papa John's was something special—men of that high caliber typically didn't sign on to something unless they thought it was worth their time. That was probably partially true, but I later found out that we overpaid them for the building. "Live and learn," as the saying goes.

We chose this location for the simple reason that it was in a central location between all our stores. We figured a commissary here would increase productivity and therefore make us better at getting the best product to customers in the quickest way. We didn't need the whole building when we first opened the Clarksville Papa John's, so we rented out part of the first floor to an optometrist and the top floor to a local karate school. We then began using the whole building when we built the commissary, as well as the first official Papa John's office space. Each floor was 26 feet by 123 feet—about 3,000 square feet total. It got the job done. But it definitely wasn't the perfect setup. For instance, the building didn't have a loading dock, so we had to bring everything in by hand through a side door. This was exhausting and time-consuming. I knew that wouldn't work for us long term, but in 1986 we didn't have any other options. We had to make do and suck it up.

We also had to upgrade our equipment. We were doing serious volume at this point—roughly 4,000 pizzas a week across all four Papa John's. Unfortunately, some of our machines were absolutely ancient. The World War I-era T-80 mixer is the best example. It was so old that it would break every few months. The main culprit was the drive shaft, a deceptively complicated piece of equipment that repeatedly snapped. When this happened, it was a total disaster that could slow us down for hours at a time—an emergency for a pizzeria that promised your pizza would be ready in 20 minutes or less. The only thing that kept us going in these situations was my uncle Bill, a machinist at the Naval Ordnance Station in Louisville, who was talented enough to make drive shafts himself. He would make them at his own day job, hide them in his pants and then bring them to me.

Our constant struggles remind me of a Winston Churchill quote: "Sometimes doing your best is not good enough. Sometimes you must do what is required."

We couldn't keep this up, especially since our volume was constantly growing, putting even more stress on this ancient machine. I needed a new mixer and fast. So I called up Chris Karamesines, the Greek who ran Greek's, where I made pizzas in college. I've always viewed Chris as one of my mentors—he taught me as much about making pizzas as anybody. He was also quite a character. He had a voice you could never forget. When I told him my predicament, he yelled at me through the phone: "JOHN! JOHN! I thought I taught you better than that! John, John, don't use a T-80! You need an M-80!" I didn't know what that was. He kept going: "You got a World War I machine, John! John, you got the wrong machine! The M-80 is a much bigger and stronger model. You don't even have to take it out of first gear. I can't believe you're that stupid!"

After messing with me a little more, he gave me the number of a farmer in Greenville, Indiana who had the M-80 mixer that I needed so badly just sitting in his barn. Apparently it was from a Greek's franchise that had shut down in the past year. Chris' parting wisdom was that I shouldn't pay more than $250 for the machine.

I wanted to solve this problem quickly, so I got in my pickup truck and drove up to get the M-80 mixer. My girlfriend (and future wife) Annette joined me. Sure enough, the heavy-duty piece of machinery was sitting in the back of the farmer's barn. After some haggling, the farmer agreed to sell the mixer to me for $220. After I handed over the cash, he thanked me and started walking away. I ran after him, saying, "Hey, how am I supposed to get this thing in the back of my pickup truck?" He responded: "That's your problem, pal."

1986

The pickup truck we used to pick up the M-80 mixer from a barn in Greenville Indiana

I was angry, mostly at myself. But there was nothing I could do about it. So I asked him, "Well, how'd you get the mixer in the barn in the first place?" He told me he used a tow truck, which had a small crane on the back. I didn't have any choice, so I called the nearest tow truck to come hoist the mixer into the back of my pickup. That cost me another $40, pushing me over budget on this one project. I was pretty pissed off.

Once the mixer was in my truck, I faced another big problem: getting it back to the commissary in Clarksville. The mixer itself was a top-heavy monstrosity that weighed 1,200 pounds. My truck, an '84 Toyota, weighed 2,800 pounds. The mixer looked so top-heavy sitting in the truck bed, I was afraid the truck would roll over on the hour-and-a-half drive back to Clarksville. Even worse, it was starting to snow. There we were, driving down I-65, slipping and sliding all over the snow-covered roads while carrying a massive piece of machinery in the bed of my pickup truck. At one point, Annette asked me, "Is this safe?" I wanted to impress her, so I didn't even hesitate to say, "Oh yeah, we're fine." I was hoping she couldn't tell I was terrified on the inside.

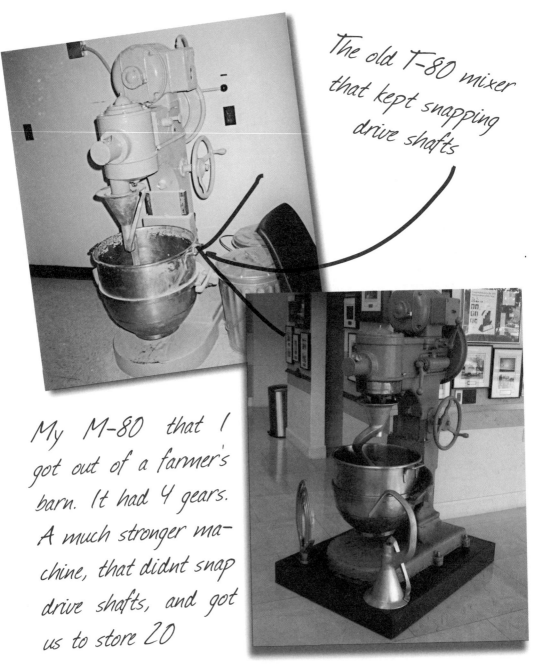

The old T-80 mixer that kept snapping drive shafts

My M-80 that I got out of a farmer's barn. It had 4 gears. A much stronger machine, that didnt snap drive shafts, and got us to store 20

Fortunately, we got back to Clarksville without any problems. But then we had to get the mixer into the building. We set up a winch attached to the Papa John's sign and used it to hoist the mixer out of my truck. After that, we set up some dowel rods in the parking lot and rolled the mixer onto the sidewalk, which was flush with the parking lot. Then we rolled the machine into the actual building. Anyone who saw this from the street probably thought we were stealing something or were part of a slapstick comedy routine. But that's what things were like at that point. We didn't have any spare cash to spend on projects like this. Our focus wasn't on frills—it was on delivering a better pizza to as many people as we could. When it came to projects like this, we just had to put our backs into it and stay devoted to the original Papa John's vision. It would have been easy to cut corners here and there, but I wasn't willing to let that happen. You can't make a traditional, superior-quality Papa John's pizza by cutting corners.

By late 1986, the Clarksville commissary was up and running. It immediately benefitted the business. Just like we expected, it helped us improve our productivity, which helped us double down on quality. As Ray Kroc, founder of McDonald's, once said, "Your quality is only as good as your consistency." We learned through trial and error that your customers stop trusting you when you give them something different every time. They wanted a quality Papa John's pizza, nothing else. Now that every pizza at every store was being made with ingredients produced in a central location, we could ensure consistency across the board. There's no excuse for a Papa John's pizza to be of lower quality than the best Papa John's pizza. That was true in 1986, and it's still true today.

With the commissary complete, we could now refocus on expanding. The Clarksville commissary could handle up to 20 stores, and we were well on our way to reaching that many locations. Business kept improving by the week. By early 1987, we had even gotten the Brownsboro Road location to a good place. It was finally making profits in line with our business model. That gave us confidence that we could continue expanding in the Louisville market. To accomplish that, we bought three Dino's Pizzeria franchises that were going out of business. This roughly doubled the size of the company in a matter of weeks.

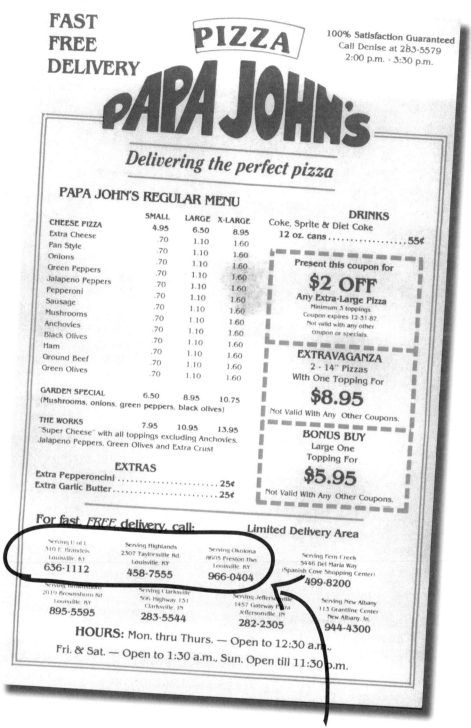

FAST FREE DELIVERY

PIZZA

PAPA JOHN'S

Delivering the perfect pizza

100% Satisfaction Guaranteed
Call Denise at 283-5579
2:00 p.m. - 3:30 p.m.

PAPA JOHN'S REGULAR MENU

CHEESE PIZZA	SMALL	LARGE	X-LARGE
Extra Cheese	4.95	6.50	8.95
Pan Style	.70	1.10	1.60
Onions	.70	1.10	1.60
Green Peppers	.70	1.10	1.60
Jalapeno Peppers	.70	1.10	1.60
Pepperoni	.70	1.10	1.60
Sausage	.70	1.10	1.60
Mushrooms	.70	1.10	1.60
Anchovies	.70	1.10	1.60
Black Olives	.70	1.10	1.60
Ham	.70	1.10	1.60
Ground Beef	.70	1.10	1.60
Green Olives	.70	1.10	1.60

GARDEN SPECIAL   6.50   8.95   10.75
(Mushrooms, onions, green peppers, black olives)

THE WORKS   7.95   10.95   13.95
"Super Cheese" with all toppings excluding Anchovies,
Jalapeno Peppers, Green Olives and Extra Crust

EXTRAS
Extra Pepperoncini .... 25¢
Extra Garlic Butter .... 25¢

DRINKS
Coke, Sprite & Diet Coke
12 oz. cans .... 55¢

Present this coupon for
$2 OFF
Any Extra-Large Pizza
Minimum 3 toppings.
Coupon expires 12-31-87.
Not valid with any other
coupon or specials.

EXTRAVAGANZA
2 - 14" Pizzas
With One Topping For
$8.95
Not Valid With Any Other Coupons.

BONUS BUY
Large One
Topping For
$5.95
Not Valid With Any Other Coupons.

For fast, FREE delivery, call: Limited Delivery Area

Serving U of L
310 E. Brandeis
Louisville, KY
636-1112

Serving Highlands
2307 Taylorsville Rd.
Louisville, KY
458-7555

Serving Okolona
8605 Preston Hwy.
Louisville, KY
966-0404

Serving Fern Creek
5446 Del Maria Way
(Spanish Cove Shopping Center)
499-8200

Serving Brownsboro
2019 Brownsboro Rd
Louisville, KY
895-5595

Serving Clarksville
506 Highway 131
Clarksville, IN
283-5544

Serving Jeffersonville
1457 Gateway Plaza
Jeffersonville, IN
282-2305

Serving New Albany
113 Grantline Center
New Albany, In
944-4300

HOURS: Mon. thru Thurs. — Open to 12:30 a.m.
Fri. & Sat. — Open to 1:30 a.m., Sun. Open till 11:30 p.m.

Old menu showing Dino's (no relation to Dino Cortopassi of Stanislaus Food Products) locations converted to Papa John's   *1987*

That year also saw the first Papa John's franchise. Remember: I knew I wanted to franchise my future pizzeria ever since I worked at Greek's in college. I didn't even have the Papa John's name when I figured that out. We were able to move forward with this much sooner than I expected thanks to our quick growth. By this point, my brother Chuck was working at Greenebaum, Doll and McDonald, a prominent Louisville firm and one of the leading franchise experts in the country. Our old firm—Ackerson, the one founded by my Papaw—had served us phenomenally well. But Chuck was so integral to the business' legal work that we had to follow him to his new firm. It also helped that Greenebaum had the specific business experience we needed for our growing company. It was the right fit at the right time. As I've said before, you have to get yourself in a position to get lucky. Greenebaum helped us get into that position, no doubt about it.

With Chuck's help at Greenebaum, we got the franchising paper-work finalized and filed the UFOC—the Uniform Franchise Offering Circular—in June of 1987, when I was only 25 years old. Our first fran-chisees were Scott and Roger Roalofs. They went to the same church as my uncle John Ackerson, my mother's brother. He introduced me to them and we instantly hit it off. Scott had experience managing a local Domino's, so he knew the ins and outs of the pizza business. And he could tell right off the bat that Papa John's had a superior product.

They opened their first store in Fern Creek, Kentucky, a small neighborhood in southeast Louisville. The Fern Creek store started off slowly at first, which made Scott and Roger very nervous. But like the Lower Brownsboro Road store, it only got better with time. To-day it's one of Papa John's best-performing stores. They subsequently built another Papa John's in the Louisville metro area, with similarly good results. Scott and Roger were not only our first and some of our most successful franchisees, but also our most faithful. They've never wavered, not once. They've seen the company's ups and downs, our highs and our lows, but they've always supported me and stuck with Papa John's for over 27 years. They're great people from a great family, and they run a great operation.

That's the kind of relationship I've tried to cultivate with all our franchisees, whether it's my childhood friend Jim Fry, my best friend Tim O'Hern or some of the franchisees I mention later in this book. I want to make sure I'm working with honorable people who understand Papa John's and share our vision. If you're not 100% committed to "Better Ingredients. Better Pizza." Papa John's is not for you. We make a promise to our customers and our team members, and we expect to deliver on that promise. Loyalty is a two-way street—the pizza business is no exception. We always try to do well by people, no matter which side of the counter they're on. In fact, we're in the people business more than we're in the pizza business—something I have tried to emphasize for over 30 years.

Most of our early franchisees were people who I knew personally. Some were family friends—or even family. For example, my wife, Annette, started her own franchise in 1988. We met the Wednesday before the Kentucky Derby in 1986. We've now been together for over 30 years. She's been by my side—or two steps ahead of me—for almost all of Papa John's most important moments.

I'm a truly lucky man. She is an incredible woman who is better than I am in every way. It turns out that running Papa John's is no exception.

Here's the proof. While we were dating, and even after we got married in 1987, Annette would often ride with me in my pickup truck when I visited the various Papa John's stores. I thought she just enjoyed hanging out with me. Nope. She was learning how to run her own business. In 1988 she became a minority owner of a Papa John's store on Bardstown Road in Louisville. It wasn't doing great when she started—it was only doing $1,200 a week in sales. Within a few months she had it up to $2,000, then $3,000, and then eventually $12,000 in weekly sales. Annette was on fire. She was running her business better than I was running mine.

Annette was doing so well that she started to make her co-owners jealous. They were some guys I'd known for a couple years. They were also chauvinist pigs who thought they could run a business better than any woman ever could. Annette was proving them wrong. So how did they react? They fired her.

That's right, a Papa John's store fired Papa John's wife. I can't tell you how angry that made me. Not only was she better than them at running the store, but the store was basically hers in her heart. Her mom had sewn the drapes on the windows. Her dad and I laid the floor and built the counters. And she built it into a juggernaut in the early

Papa John's system. When she told me what had happened, I stormed over to the store. I walked in and told them, "This is my wife's store and she wants it back. You're out and she's in." One of them responded as if he was a mob boss: "If you get rid of us, you'll never do another deal in Louisville." I wasn't going to back down. I knew my wife wanted the store, so I told them I'd buy them out of the business. I didn't have the money, but that didn't matter. I went and borrowed money from basically everyone I knew. Sure enough, I was able to buy them out, and good riddance.

Besides, she's a better business owner than I am. Today, her store does over $30,000 a week in sales—50 percent higher annual sales than the corporate average and double the franchise average. A big chunk of her success can be chalked up to Stephen Klan, who helps run her store and has been with her since the very beginning. They have what I call a "collaborative" alliance—a mutually beneficial relationship that is a win-win for everyone involved. But it goes without saying that I'm a little more partial to Annette than I am to Stephen. She is still involved with the business on a daily basis. She never stops amazing me with her insight, dedication and sheer will to succeed. Maybe that's what drew me to her in the first place.

● ● ● ● ●

Looking back on our early years, it shocks me just how fast we expanded. At the time, I didn't really realize how impressive our growth was. In 1984 we were selling pizzas out of a broom closet at the back of a bar. By 1985 we had a stand-alone store. By the end of 1986, we'd expanded to three stores in Southern Indiana and one in Louisville, Kentucky. By the middle of 1987, we had seven Papa John's locations spread across the Louisville metro area. We were expanding faster every year.

We were also working harder than ever before. Most of our locations weren't profitable for the first three to six months. As for the stores that were making money, those profits definitely weren't finding their way to our pockets. Our goal was to take care of our team members and keep our stores clean and in good working condition. Then we reinvested almost everything we made right back in the business.

I was relentless about this. I saw that Papa John's was improving as we got more experience. The constant expansion forced us to find new ways to improve the business, whether in the stores themselves, the commissaries, our marketing, or anything else we did. We found a new conveyer-belt oven that cooked pizzas faster while using less money. We replaced the Papa John's signs on the front of our stores with green awnings, which were much more visible and had an instant impact on the number of people walking through our doors. We discovered a Wendel mixer that made more and better dough. We made so many improvements I can't remember them all. All of the improvements cost money—sometimes a lot—but it was well worth the investment. We staked our name on making a quality product, which is why we've done things the hard way ever since Papa John's started.

Our hard work was undoubtedly paying off. The bigger we got, the better we got—something that can't be said about a lot of businesses. And the better we got, the bigger we got. It seemed to me that Papa John's was on the right path. Unfortunately, not everyone agreed.

The ownership of Mick's Lounge and Papa John's had changed a fair bit over the previous two years. Before the pizzeria ever existed, my Dad and I split the business—I owned 51 percent and he had 49 percent. One of our first team members, Bob Ehringer, subsequently bought a big chunk of my Dad's stake—34 percent—and 2 percent of my stake for $20,000. We killed two birds with one stone by doing this: I got someone to help me run the bar, and my Dad got some money to pay off some of his many debts. Little did I know that giving up that 2 percent would come back to haunt me later.

This arrangement was still intact when we started building the broom closet. Then, when Dad passed away in March 1985, his brother Bill asked if he could have his deceased brother's remaining 15 percent of the company. I never should have given it to him. Those shares should have stayed in the immediate family, with me getting 5 percent, my brother Chuck getting 5 percent and my sister Anne getting the last 5 percent. Maybe I made this foolish decision because of everything that was happening at the time. I wasn't thinking straight—my Dad was dying, for goodness' sake. But I couldn't go back on my word, so we went through with the deal. That's the breakdown we had when we incorporated Papa John's: I had 49 percent, Bob Ehringer had 36 percent and my uncle had 15 percent.

This arrangement worked for the first few years. Bob was one of our hardest workers. He started at Mick's Lounge in 1983 as a bartender. He quickly grew in importance and was one of the first to sign on to my vision for Papa John's. In fact, he was the first person I told that I wanted to build a pizzeria in the broom closet. He was also the first person other than me to make Papa John's pizzas. My uncle, meanwhile, started helping out right before my Dad died, when we started building the first stand alone Papa John's. As a supervisor and machinist at the Naval Ordnance Station, he helped us with each store's layout. When we held our grand opening on April 11, 1985, both Bob and my uncle could rightly take pride in what we had created together.

The relationship stayed relatively strong from 1985 until 1987. But then things started to turn south. At that point, none of us were really benefitting financially from Papa John's. That was by explicit design: almost all of our profits were immediately going back into the business to fuel continued growth. This was always part of our plan, and everyone had known about it from the start. We were talking about it even when we were building the broom closet, before we ever sold our first pizza. We knew it wasn't about making ourselves rich. It was about making Papa John's a success—first in Southern Indiana, then in the Louisville metro area, then throughout the country, and finally across the world. Before we could benefit ourselves, we would have to make sure we benefitted millions of others by bringing a better pizza made with better ingredients into their communities and neighborhoods. That's what Papa John's was all about. We had to keep our focus.

My uncle, unfortunately, didn't understand that. He was in his 60s and just wanted to make money. He saw the money we were making at the stores but didn't understand why he wasn't seeing it in his bank account. Nor did he understand why we were still working so hard. He thought if you were an owner you could just sit back and rake in the dough. This helped explain why he wanted to stop building new stores immediately. In his mind, we had plenty of stores that were doing fine. He wanted us to skate from that point forward. Worst of all, he began bringing Bob over to his side, slowly but surely. The two of them spent a lot of their time driving between stores to do maintenance. My uncle used this time to fill Bob's head with all kinds of nonsense and false promises.

It was never much of a surprise that my uncle would start belly-aching like this. It was a surprise to me that he was able to bring Bob over to his side eventually. In one sense, I get where he was coming from. Bob and I had spent the past three years working more or less nonstop. We were working full-time at Mick's Lounge and then at Papa John's. We were both exhausted and wanted to see the fruits of our labor. But I didn't understand my uncle's point of view. Whereas Bob and I worked hard, he only helped out sometimes on the weekends. As time went on, he helped less and less. By the time he started making noise, he was hardly doing any work. He just wanted the money. He thought the best way to do that was to just stop building. Once he brought Bob over to his side, their argument became that we had more than enough stores. So why not stop building and start putting the profits into our own pockets?

But I would have none of that. They wanted to stop building; I wanted to build more and more. I knew in my heart and in my mind that Papa John's ultimate success depended on us continuously growing. It wasn't enough for Papa John's to serve the best pizza in Louisville—we had to serve the best pizza in the world. I had a vision. Now I had to stick to it.

Unfortunately, my uncle's unhappiness kept growing. So did Bob's, to a lesser extent. Since 1985, the three of us had met every Sunday morning to discuss the company's current state and our plans for the future. These meetings became unbearably tense in early 1987. My uncle knew exactly what he wanted: more of the company's profits going into his pockets. By this point we had between 15 and 20 stores, most of which were making a decent amount of money. But he didn't understand the difference between profit and cash flow. All of our cash was spoken for before we even made it. It was going to finance new stores and to make up for losses at the stores that had just started or were struggling. He didn't get that—he just saw the dollars and cents and thought he deserved some of 'em. One night, he and I really got into it, yelling at each other about the direction of the company. We canceled our weekly meetings after that.

Meanwhile, my uncle's work ethic started deteriorating dramatically. He was no longer willing to put any skin in the game. As the owners of the company, it was our duty to work just as hard as everyone else—no, to work *harder* than everyone else. If we truly believed in what we were doing, we had to model it for everyone else. A leader's job is to inspire their co-workers. My uncle was no longer doing that. He wasn't happy and he wasn't afraid to let others know. The rest of our team members started to notice, and standards started to slip. This was potentially devastating for a business as young as Papa John's. Actually, it's potentially devastating for a business of any size. The attitude at the top—whether it's in the boardroom of a major company or the back closet of a mom-'n'-pop—affects the attitude everywhere else. A bad attitude in leadership is like a cancer that can spread throughout the entire organization.

It looked to me like everything we'd built together was starting to fall apart—like Papa John's was in mortal danger. Worst of all, there was little I could do about it. I'd spent my whole life identifying problems and then fixing them. But there was no path for me to fix this problem. With only 49 percent of the company under my control, I was basically a bystander. I wanted to keep building stores. My two co-owners wouldn't let me.

It was then that I realized I needed full control of the company. Papa John's was my life's work, but I couldn't do everything necessary for it to succeed. As the saying goes, my stock certificates were too thin for wallpaper and too thick for toilet paper. Since Papa John's was a private company at that point, my shares were essentially worthless until I cleared the 50 percent mark. But I had no idea how I was going to get there.

Then an opportunity just fell into my lap. While all of these troubles were going on, Bob bought himself a nice speedboat. He really enjoyed it and spent most of his free time tinkering with it and taking it out on the river. He called me up one day in early 1988 to ask me for $20,000. He needed the cash to pay for a new muffler that would help make the boat go faster by five miles an hour. Clearly, I wasn't going to do that without getting something in return. I told him I'd give him the money if he gave me 2 percent of his shares in the company. He agreed.

This gave me 51 percent of the company. I still can't believe it—majority control of Papa John's ultimately came down to a muffler on a speedboat, of all things. If that muffler had never existed, then neither would the Papa John's empire. Stranger things have happened, but not by much.

Now this by itself didn't solve my problems—my uncle was still relentlessly bugging me to divert more of our profits away from building the business and into his pocket. But there was nothing he could do to force me to do things his way. I finally had the leverage I needed—the *freedom* I needed—to keep Papa John's on its upward trajectory. The company was safe again.

By this point the relationship between my uncle and me had completely deteriorated. Bob and I were still on relatively good terms. He actually didn't know whose side to take anymore. But it was crystal clear that the three of us could no longer function as a team. In fact, we hadn't really been a team for the previous few months, given how fractious our relationships had become.

Now, I'd already faced plenty of difficult situations, even though I was only 25. My Dad and my Papaw—the two most important people in the world to me—had both passed away within a year of each other. We built Papa John's in the midst of this, through a combination of hard work, determination and always "going left." We had to forge ahead in order to get ahead. The situation with Bob and my uncle was a different kind of difficult. For the first time, it felt like Papa John's was going backwards. It was heartbreaking to watch this happen to my life's work—my life's dream.

But we were finally on the right path once I gained control of the company. Unfortunately, Bob and my uncle were still unhappy. We kept up this uneasy relationship for another two years—I didn't see any way out of it. Then, in the fall of 1988, we finally figured out an amicable way for us to part ways. I would buy them both out of their stakes in the company. The appraiser we hired valued the company at around $400,000—a huge increase from the $1,600 with which we started Papa John's only a few years earlier. Given that the company was growing, we agreed to up the valuation to $700,000. They got 49 percent of this total and agreed to be paid over time, as neither I nor Papa John's had the cash to pay them immediately. This gave them more cash flow than they had been receiving, and it also stopped them from being a constant thorn in my side. It was a win-win for everyone. Most importantly, it was a win for Papa John's.

We signed the paperwork on October 6th, 1988, about a month and a half before my 27th birthday. It was a sad day, considering the history we had together. Bob had been an invaluable part of the first

Papa John's team. My uncle had also helped out in important ways—I'll never forget how he helped get us new drive shafts when the old ones snapped on the T-80 mixer. But neither of them were the great leaders that Papa John's needed. A leader is someone who takes his team where they want to go. A great leader is someone who takes his team where they *need* to go. In order to do that, they have to believe in the company's vision with their heart and know in their mind how to make that vision a reality. After that, they have to inspire their team members and spur others to be the best they can be.

Bob and Bill couldn't do that. How could they inspire others when they didn't believe that Papa John's best days were ahead of it? When people sell their stake in something, whether it's one share or a million shares, they're basically saying they think the value is going to go down. The person buying thinks the opposite—they think the company's value is going to get higher. I have always believed in Papa John's. Bob and my uncle no longer did.

And they could not have been more wrong. Once they were out of the picture, I could do everything I wanted to make my vision of Papa John's a reality. Not coincidentally, Papa John's really started to take off shortly after this episode came to a conclusion. That's the real shame of what happened with Bob and Bill. They got in a hurry. They wanted quick money. And they blew their opportunity to be a part of something really special. They would have literally made millions if they only had patience. Such is the price of emphasizing short-term gains over long-term success. No matter how smart it seems, it always comes back to bite you in the end.

• • • • •

Papa John's really hit its stride once this whole episode was behind us. We had grown pretty fast in the late 1980s. We opened no fewer than 10 stores in 1988, doubling the company's size. We had more than 20 stores at the end of that year, only four years after Papa John's started in the broom closet. Best of all, most of them were making decent money, which allowed us to finance continued expansion. That year also saw us open our first stores outside of Southern Indiana and Louisville, on the University of Kentucky campus in Lexington. By the end of 1989, we were closing in on 40 Papa John's stores spread between the two metro areas. Little did I know we would start expanding even faster in the early 1990s. Papa John's was in the best possible position to get lucky. I never knew I'd be in this position as a 27-year-old.

We were growing so fast our existing infrastructure couldn't keep up. The year 1989 saw us move out of the Clarksville commissary in the back of the Clarksville store. The lack of a loading dock was a real problem, given the volume we were doing. We'd been using it for about two years by this point. But once we hit the 20-store mark, it became clear we needed a much bigger facility to keep every Papa John's stocked with fresh ingredients.

I did everything I could to keep the commissary in the Southern Indiana area. Once I realized we had to find a new location for a bigger commissary, I went to the mayor of Jeffersonville. He had actually been the coach of my senior league baseball team in middle school, and his son and I had played together on the high school team that went to the state championships. He and I had a solid relationship. I told him, "I'm gonna build a big company and I need more warehouse space. Is there anything you can do to help me?" I thought for sure he would figure out a way to help us to move to the Clarksville Industrial Park, only a few miles away from the existing commissary. Instead, he suggested I look at Louisville instead.

I wanted to stay in Indiana. It was my home. It was where I started Papa John's. But Jeffersonville, Indiana wasn't going to work, so we settled on the next best thing: Jeffersontown, Kentucky, on the outskirts of Louisville and only about 10 miles away. In 1989 we moved into a new location on Data Drive. We were growing so fast by this point that we needed to build a larger commissary in late 1990—and even that one was too small by 1999. That's when we built a commissary attached to the Papa John's world headquarters in Jeffersontown, off of Papa John's Boulevard. It serves roughly 600 stores in Kentucky, Indiana, Ohio and Tennessee. Since it's attached to our headquarters, I often walk through it to see if there are any places for us to improve productivity or introduce new techniques. There always are. There always will be. And we'll always find 'em.

First real commissary in Clarksville, IN

Data Drive, Commissary #2, Jeffersontown, KY (where they tried to hide the dough in Chapter 4)

The front of Data Drive Commissary #2

The Bluegrass Drive commissary #3,
Jeffersontown, KY

Papa John's Headquarters, with commissary #4
hooked on the back, Jeffersontown, KY

In a sign of our commitment to always improve, we're always introducing new technology, techniques and best practices to make both the commissary and our stores more productive and the pizza more delicious. We even build things ourselves if we can't find what we want in the market. A good example is the "leveler" we use in the stores before we put the fresh-packed pizza sauce on the dough. I invented this device myself to make sure that a consistent amount of fresh-packed pizza sauce is spread on the dough. The person making the pizza fills up the sauce ladle to overflow, then runs it under the leveler to get the perfect amount. It also saves the pizza-maker time and improves productivity, which means the customer gets their traditional, superior-quality Papa John's pizza that much faster. Every second counts in the pizza delivery business.

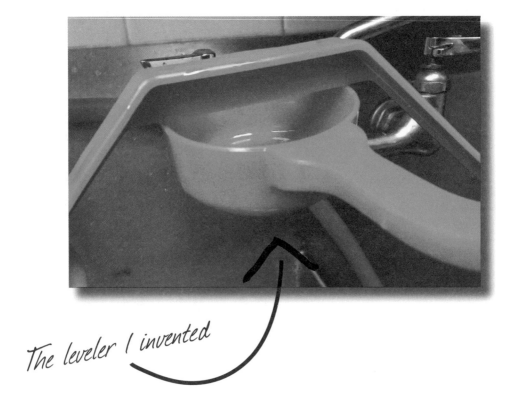

The leveler I invented

We also did—and still do—our fair share of innovation at the commissary. Take the example of our dough preparation. We initially struggled to make smooth dough balls. This was a big problem: the rougher the dough ball, the worse the pizza. We have always rounded each dough ball twice, even back when I was making pizzas in the broom closet. Early on we did both in quick succession—one right after the other. The second rounding, however, was when the dough balls would get rough. I could feel it. I could see it. And I didn't know how to fix it.

Then I stumbled across the solution by accident. Once day, while putting dough balls through the rounding machine, I was interrupted by a phone call that lasted about four minutes. When I hung up, I discovered the dough ball had rested, and that when I put it through, the end result was smoother than ever. It turned out we needed to let the dough ball rest for four minutes in between rounding sessions. This simple change allowed the dough ball to come out smooth on the second round. Today we round each dough ball twice. In between each rounding, we let the dough rest for four minutes in a massive apparatus we built ourselves. It has a conveyer belt that allows us to produce 11,000 of these perfectly smooth dough balls an hour. Once it's done resting, we put it through a "Round-O-Matic" for the final step. This results in the near-perfect dough balls from which every Papa John's pizza is made. We're also trying to find a way to make perfectly round and flawless dough balls, something no pizza company has ever done.

The dough "resting machine" in the Papa John's commissary

At this point in the company's history I was obsessed with improving the commissary system. At the time, Domino's, Pizza Hut and Little Caesar's were the only three chains with a truly national presence. They knew what they were doing. My goal was to figure out what they were doing, then do it better. If Papa John's had any hope of doing that, we had to double down on vertical integration—the combination of different stages of production under one roof. I also saw the need to implement full-scale automation, especially in the dough-making process. Sure enough, we started implementing a lot of revolutionary techniques and groundbreaking technologies in our commissary. We were trying so many new things that the Jeffersontown commissary was like a science lab.

We were really getting the hang of the pizza business by this point. Our first few years—especially the initial struggles at the Lower Brownsboro Road store in Louisville—taught me a lot about where to build my stores. "Location, location, location" really does matter, especially in the restaurant business. We figured out that in order for a Papa John's to be successful, it needed to be located on the side of the road where people are driving home after a long day's work. All they have to do is turn right—40 percent more effective than turning left. There also needs to be easy ingress and egress for cars, along with parking right next to the store. It also helps if the store is right off a highway or major road, where plenty of people can see it. If we found a place that met our criteria but was just outside of our business model's price range, we felt it was worth paying a little more money at the front end to make more money at the back end.

We also started investing in marketing and advertising in a whole new way. Up until late 1988, we had mainly dabbled in this area ourselves. We put out a newspaper ad here, did a small-scale promotion there, and so on. We needed to up our game if we were going to compete with the big boys outside of Kentucky. So in 1988, we hired Gibson, McKnight and Miller, a local advertising firm based in Louisville. They came up with our first television ad, which featured a little character named "Papa John's" who showed up in the pizza box. In retrospect, the ad is hilariously awful. Fortunately, some of their other ideas proved excellent. They were the ones who reminded us that we trademarked "Delivering the Perfect Pizza" a few years earlier—we made that our slogan, thanks to their recommendation. They were also responsible for the first major change in the Papa John's logo. The first logo was red, white and blue. Gibson, McKnight and Miller urged us to swap out blue for green to give the logo a more Italian feel. The logo has changed a few more times since then, but the colors from 1989 are the colors you see today. On the next page I'll show the evolution of our logo through the years.

Screenshot of the 1st television ad

1988

Papa John's logo with green text

1989

1984

1989

1994

PERFECT LOGO

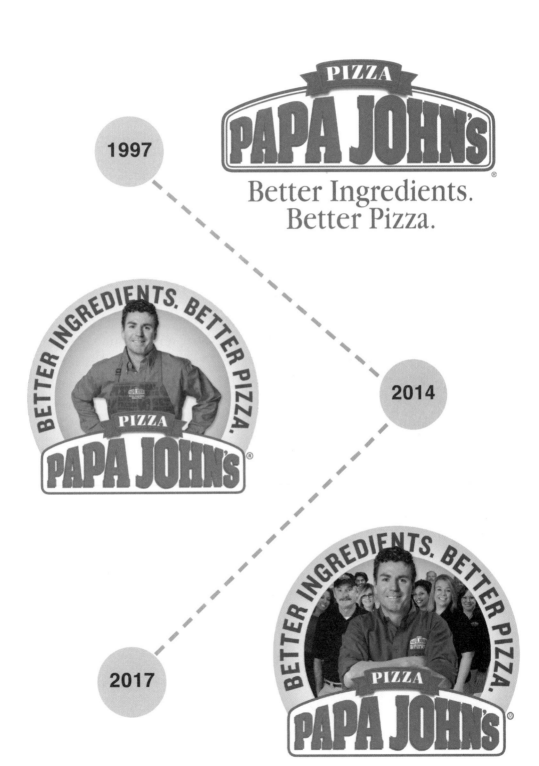

In 1989 we upgraded to Freibert Advertising, run by Bob Freibert. He is great to work with and is excellent at marketing. His first contribution was a television ad featuring popular country-music singer Earl Thomas Conley. Bob was our marketing guy when he had our first major marketing victory. *Louisville Magazine* hosted an annual awards dinner where they honored the "Best of Louisville" across a number of categories. We often bought a table at the dinner, although we never expected anything would come of it. So there we were at the 1989 awards ceremony when the "Best Pizza in Louisville" category came up. To our shock, the announcer opened up the envelope and yelled out "Papa John's." We freaked out.

This was a huge deal—no, it was bigger than huge. It put us on the map like never before. This award was coveted by independent pizzerias in the Louisville area, of which there were many that made an exceptional pizza. It was unheard of for a chain to win the award. In fact, I think Papa John's may have been the first. This was an enormous validation of our business model. Even before I opened Papa John's, I wanted it to have the attitude, mindset and superior product that characterize most independent pizzerias. Now we were being recognized for it in a major, public way. The next day, with the award in hand, I walked into Bob Freibert's office. I showed him the framed certificate and told him, "We've got the goods!"

BEST OF LOUISVILLE
A ★ W ★ A ★ R ★ D

BEST OF LOUISVILLE

PRESENTED TO

Papa John's
Pizza to Your Door

Louisville
MAGAZINE

Best of Louisville award, this put us on the map like never before

1989

This put us on the map in a whole new way, especially once the hardcopy version of *Louisville Magazine* went out. Everyone in town read it. We leveraged this as much as we could. With Bob's help, we used it to solidify our dominance in the Louisville area. We saw a remarkable improvement in our finances in a matter of days. Some stores saw permanent revenue jumps of 15 to 20 percent over the next few weeks. In 1990, we were still burning through money fast, all in the name of continued expansion in and around Kentucky and Southern Indiana. At one point, I went to the bank and got a million-dollar line of credit—a remarkable feat when you consider that five years earlier, we could hardly get a $32,000 loan. I burned through that pretty quick. Fortunately, that's when we got the award. The resulting revenue boost was nothing short of a godsend.

Almost overnight after winning the award, Papa John's had new opportunities to break into new markets—not just in Kentucky but in neighboring states. The closest major metro areas were Nashville, Indianapolis and Cincinnati. We swiftly started building stores in all three cities. Then we started building more stores in the smaller cities in between—backfilling, as we call it in the business. By the end of 1990 we had 46 stores.

We reached another major milestone on June 10, 1991, when I was 29 years old. That's when we opened up Papa John's Store #100. It was in Clarksville, Tennessee, a town about 30 miles outside of Nashville. Since the third or fourth Papa John's store, I'd always thought that store #100 would be the turning point for us financially. I knew we'd always have to work hard, but I thought we'd get to a point where we didn't have to take out hundred-thousand or even million-dollar loans from the bank. I thought we'd finally be making more money than I could spend on expansion. It turns out I was wrong.

We definitely weren't at that point yet. For the rest of 1991 and early 1992, we kept moving forward like we always had—taking our profits and plowing 'em right back into new stores. By this point we were moving into new cities and markets, using the same concentric-circle strategy we use when selecting where to build individual stores. We were building—or planning to build—a Papa John's presence in Cincinnati, Dayton, Cleveland, Indianapolis, Nashville, Memphis, St. Louis, Atlanta, Charlotte and more.

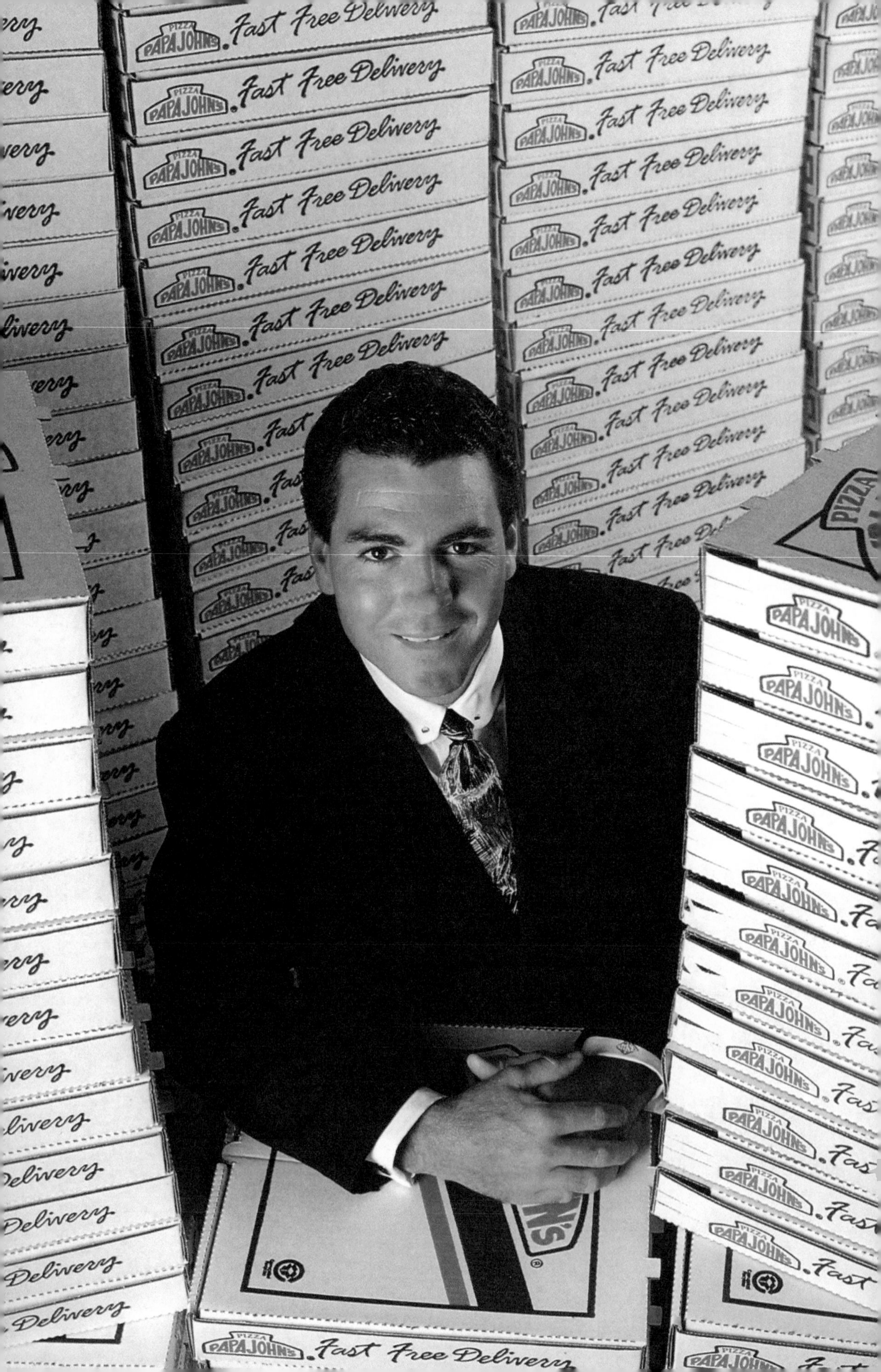
PIZZA
PAPA JOHN'S
Fast Free Delivery

Our breakneck expansion meant we were still scrounging for money. By 1991, I needed a fresh infusion of capital in order to keep expanding at our current rate. I went back to National City Bank, which had given me a one-million-dollar line of credit only a year earlier. Surprisingly, they turned me down. I had to get that credit in order to keep Papa John's expanding. Fortunately, local Louisville restaurateur Rick Sherman, the CEO of the national hamburger chain Rally's and a former executive with Church's Chicken, stepped in to help me out.

Rick and I first met in February, 1991. We were introduced by a franchisee for both of our companies. Rick wanted to know how he could get involved with Papa John's, which was a huge vote of confidence in the company, given how much experience Rick had. After spending just a few days with him touring some of our stores, it was clear to me that Rick and I could have a great working relationship.

Rick was instrumental in getting us the capital we needed. But it came at a price. He'd get me three million dollars from the bank if I gave him one-and-a-half percent of the company. I agreed. He immediately went down to a different bank with the same balance sheet, the same income statement, the same everything that I had used a few weeks before. The bank gave him the line of credit on the spot. It also dropped the interest rate to below-market levels and eliminated the personal guarantee requirements. Even though another bank had just turned down the same deal, with the exact same financial statement, the new bank knew it would be foolish to turn it down when Rick Sherman was behind it. If someone with his experience believed in that kid John Schnatter—I wasn't even 30 yet—then that was all the bank needed to know. Just like that, Rick got a piece of Papa John's.

He also started helping out on the business side. He joined our board of directors and became the latest in our growing list of franchisees. Early on, he recommended we set up a national purchasing program so Papa John's could buy direct from suppliers, instead of through brokers. This system saved us 2 percent on food and paper costs almost immediately. He's a great negotiator. He brought a lot of value to Papa John's in a short amount of time.

Papa John's 1993 Annual Report

Most importantly, Rick was the first person to bring up the idea of going public. He planted the idea in my head right after we became business partners. I didn't think much of it at first. I didn't think we needed it. In September of 1992, we opened up Papa John's Store #200. Fittingly, it was in Louisville—our heartland and our homeland. We were doubling in size every year now. Now it slowly dawned on me that we could expand even faster if we turned to Wall Street for help. An initial public offering on Wall Street would dramatically expand our financing options, giving us the ability to grow even further and faster.

I especially had my eye set on making inroads in the Deep South and Florida, especially Orlando. We had already opened the first Florida Papa John's in February 1993 in Orlando. I was pretty sure that pizza delivery and carryout would be a phenomenal success down there, with Disney World and the many other attractions nearby. I thought that Papa John's, with its superior product, could go gangbusters down there.

I slowly came to realize that going public was the best way to achieve these goals. More than that, it was the best way to do what I set out do when we started selling pizzas out of the broom closet. I always wanted Papa John's to not just make it, but to make it big. We incorporated the company as Papa John's International because we knew we would someday want to take it beyond America. I thought the sky was the limit, but compared to the big pizza chains of the day, we were still flying pretty close to the ground. I never had any doubt that Papa John's pizza was the best pizza in America—now I just needed to bring it to as many people as I could.

So I agreed to take Papa John's public. With the help of Rick Sherman and my brother Chuck, we started laying the groundwork for an initial public offering. Rick put us in touch with investment bankers and potential investors, since he had strong relationships with people across the country. Chuck once again provided the legal help—he was still working at Greenebaum, Doll and McDonald at this point. It was a very intensive process that required significant due diligence and more paperwork than I could have imagined. After several months of nonstop preparation, the big day was set for June 8, 1993. There would be 232 Papa John's spread across the Midwest and the South when the bell rang on Wall Street at 9:30 a.m. that morning.

The build-up to this day wasn't the best experience. For my part, I was very disappointed in the two investment banks that arranged everything—they will remain nameless. They failed to maximize the value the initial shareholders would receive in the IPO, thereby costing us millions of dollars. Worst of all, I saw that coming from a mile away. We initially structured the company so that I owned 61 percent, Chuck Schnatter and company president Dan Holland owned 4.3 percent and Rick Sherman owned 2.3 percent. The banks wanted to price the stock at $12 a share. I had spent the previous few weeks on a cross-country roadshow, talking to potential investors in preparation for the big day. I saw excitement everywhere I went.

Given what I was seeing around the country, it was as clear as day that Papa John's was going to be successful from the moment the opening bell rang on Wall Street. So I told the investment banks we needed to price the stock closer to $20 rather than undervalue it. They would only go as high as $13, which infuriated me. I wanted more. They refused and then gave me an ultimatum: *Do it our way or you'll be ruined.* I didn't have much of a choice. They held all the cards. I was only 31 and had never done this before. What was I supposed to do?

I was ultimately proven right in the end. The stock opened at $13 and closed at $17.50 on the first day. Then it kept rising. Within a matter of weeks, we were at $20 a share. Wall Street loved us from the get-go— we had a cookie-cutter business model that made a quality product and could be replicated anywhere in America. Papa John's was profitable in almost every market where we had a presence. (Atlanta was the only exception at that point, mainly because of its size.) Investors could see that we had tremendous growth potential. They rewarded us the day we went public. In less than a day Papa John's International became worth $344 million. I couldn't believe it—I still can't. Ten years earlier, I had been broke and hadn't had a job. Even the day before, I didn't have enough money to take my wife on a vacation. That changed overnight. We could hardly believe this was really happening.

The first Papa John's stock certificate

This was an incredible day for everyone involved in Papa John's success. Less than ten years before, I'd started my first post-college job working at a near-bankrupt bar. Through hard work and determination, we built a team that built a pizzeria in a broom closet and then a company that expanded to more than two hundred stores in less than a decade. This is a profound testament to what's possible when you set your mind to something and build a collaborative alliance with those around you.

More importantly, it's about *what* you set your mind to do. That's what I was focusing on that night. It doesn't matter if the company is worth $3 million, $30 million, $300 million, or $3 billion—all milestones we've crossed. The company's value will never change how we operate, how we think and how we implement. What really mattered—and what still matters most—is whether we are practicing the values that my Dad and my Papaw taught me years ago.

Those values have always been the same. They always will be the same. Take risks. Tinker. Treat everyone with respect. Encourage entrepreneurship within the company so that we're always improving.

And remember that we are still apprentices who have a lot to learn and can always do better. If we practice all of these things on a daily basis, we'll be much more successful at fulfilling our promise to use better ingredients to make a better pizza. We'll also create value and opportunities for our franchisees, our suppliers, our shareholders, our team members and our customers—what I call a win-win-win-win-win situation. It's what makes the world a better place.

That's what was on my mind the day we went public. We'd come a long way since we opened up the first Papa John's, surrounded by friends and family. But we were still a long way away from achieving the vision that inspired me to knock down a wall in a broom closet and start making pizzas in it. We were still a small company in the grand scheme of things. I still wanted to do something bigger.

I had no intention of losing my focus, and I still don't. When it comes to building a business, *focus* is the most important word in the Merriam-Webster Dictionary. But the most important word *overall* is *people*—and people are what we're focused on at Papa John's.

I have a story that helps illustrate what I mean about the importance of focus. People often ask me, "What's the difference between Papa John's today and when you were making pizzas out of a broom closet?" Interestingly enough, I once posed a similar question to a friend of mine who was a very successful farmer in Modesto, California for 65 years. I asked him, "What's the difference between today and 65 years ago?" His answer was simple: "Well, I've always been a farmer at heart, but today the only difference is I get new equipment."

That resonated with me. It made me realize I've always been a pizza maker at heart, from the broom closet in 1984 to going public in 1993 to today. The only difference is I now get new equipment.

CHAPTER FOUR

—— • ——

CORE VALUES

To ignore the past is to cut short your future. That's why I've told you so much about my Dad and my Papaw. They are Papa John's past, so understanding who they were and what they taught me is crucial to our future. But the foundation of Papa John's was actually built long before either of them were even born.

Let me take you back to 1867. July 19 of that year is actually one of the most important dates in Papa John's history. That's the day my 23-year-old great-grandfather arrived in the United States of America aboard a fully-rigged iron sailing ship named the Reichstag. His name was Martin G. Schnatterer, and he brought with him the DNA that would later become Papa John. I had arrived in America.

My great-grandfather is the source of the entrepreneurial instinct that runs in my family. He came from the German state of Baden, where he was a talented young craftsman who specialized in wood joining and table-making. Yet despite his talent, his future didn't look bright—at all.

America in 2016 is on the path to becoming what Germany was in 1867. It was profoundly *not* a land of opportunity. If you believed the wrong thing, the government attacked you. If you became successful, the government took your money. And if you dared go against the whims and will of society's rulers, the government beheaded you. In other words, the government was the greatest enemy of industrious, hard-working Germans like my great-grandfather. It stood in their way and prevented them from pursuing their dreams and making the world a better place. A prosperous society that benefits everyone can't exist without free markets, free exchange, freedom of speech, freedom of religion, freedom of association and so many other freedoms. None of these could be found in the country where Martin G. Schnatterer was born.

My great-grandfather wasn't willing to live in that kind of society. So he fled it. He left behind everything, including his family, his friends, his community and his country.

Think about that for a moment. Things were so bad in Germany that he left everything he knew and sailed into the great unknown when he was just 23 years old. He came to America on a three-month voyage with only the clothes on his back. He was a trendsetter, too—Ellis Island was still 25 years away from opening its doors. But like millions of others, my great-grandfather came to America in search of a better life. He didn't know where to find it. But he believed that America was the place to look for it. He believed that through hard work and perseverance he would be able to find new opportunities and build a new life—a life that was better than anything he'd ever imagined.

Ultimately, he came to America so that his children and grandchildren could have a chance to live the American Dream and so that his great-grandson could have a chance to become Papa John.

They say a picture is worth a thousand words, which is why I have included a picture of Martin G. Schnatterer. He's wearing a borrowed three-piece suit that doesn't fit him, but it doesn't matter. You just have to look at his face to see how determined he was. A fire burned in his heart, and nothing could put it out. He was the type of guy you just didn't mess with. He was going to find a better life in America, no matter what got in his way.

My Papaw and my Dad were my mentors, but Martin G. Schnatterer is my hero.

That was—and is—the promise of America. Our system of private enterprise is the most revolutionary economic system in human history. It empowers people to match their talents and their skills with their interests. It allows them to pursue what makes them happy. It allows them to speak their minds, tinker and explore new and better ways of doing things. In a country like ours, anyone with a great idea can turn it into a reality.

And that explains why America has been the envy of the world for most of its history. The possibilities are literally limitless when people are free to pursue their passions. Until recently, our system of government fostered a society where most people benefited themselves by benefitting others. Entrepreneurs created products and services that enriched and enhanced the world around them. This simple yet radical concept explains why our country has done more than any other to make people's lives better. Unfortunately, this system of free enterprise is increasingly under assault by a government that grows bigger with every passing day. Yet America's unrivaled prosperity didn't happen because of politicians or bureaucrats—men like the Founding Fathers and Martin G. Schnatterer were actually *fleeing* nations where the government called the shots. Instead, it happened because of hardworking people like my great-grandfather and millions of others like him, men and women who just wanted an opportunity to pursue their dreams.

There's never been anything else like it. And it called to my great-grandfather from halfway across the world.

He answered that call, which eventually took him to Jeffersonville, Indiana. Like his descendants, my great-grandfather was an entrepreneur at heart. He was a doer, not just a talker. He started off as a cabinetmaker for the Jeffersonville, Madison and Indianapolis Railroad. He eventually opened up a business that specialized in fine china, framing and glassmaking. Amazingly, he set up shop less than two miles from the first Papa John's. His store was located at 109 Spring St., just steps from the Ohio River and within sight of downtown Louisville, Kentucky. If you stood there today, you'd still see a lot of what you would have seen in the mid-to-late nineteenth century. The area is rich with history.

Martin G. Schnatterer in a borrowed suit (left)

The Reichstag (above), passenger manifest (below)

MARTIN SCHNATTERER,
CHINA GLASS
AND
Queensware, Picture Frames,
BRACKETS, ETC.
109 SPRING STREET,
JEFFERSONVILLE, IND.

1892

Along the way, my great-grandfather started a family, having seven kids overall. Much of his family—myself included—has stayed in the area to the present day. Martin G. Schnatterer instilled in his children the values that caused him to leave his country and come to America. He taught them about the importance of hard work, treating your customers and co-workers with respect and constantly trying to improve the world around you through innovation and entrepreneurship.

Don't take my word for it. On October 18, 1902, the *Jeffersonville Evening News* printed his obituary, which sums up everything that made Martin G. Schnatterer a great and influential man. He was one of the "substantial members" of his local community. He "accumulated considerable property by a life of industry and frugality." I believe the most important line in his obituary is this: "For more than two years he had been in failing health, but he refused to cease his employment until a few weeks ago, when his strength would no longer permit him to continue at his bench." That's why Martin G. Schnatterer is my hero. I hope to be half the man he was.

And that is why I include my great-grandfather's story. Martin G. Schnatterer believed in and modeled a specific set of principles. Those principles then guided his daily practices. Those same principles are what guide our practices at Papa John's today. Before we can understand where we are going, we first have to figure out where we came from.

China Glass advertisement in City Directory (above)

JEFFERSONVILLE EVENING NEWS
18 Oct 1902

SPARK OF LIFE

Takes Its Flight From Body Of Martin Schnatterer.

Death came to the relief of Martin Schnatterer, who lived at 338 Spring street, Friday afternoon at 4:30 o'clock. He had been ill for a long time of Bright's disease and his demise had been anticipated for the past two weeks. For more than two years he had been in failing health, but he refused to cease his employment until a few weeks ago, when his strength would no longer permit him to continue at his bench.

Mr. Schnatterer for several years had been engaged in the China and queensware business in the house where he died, the family residing in the living apartments, but he continued at his trade, that of a cabinet maker, his wife looking after the details of the store during the day.

The birthplace of Mr. Schnatterer was in the Black Forest, Germany, December 22, 1842, and would soon have been 60 years of age. At the age of 21 he came to the United States, and immediately thereafter to Jeffersonville, where for 19 years he was a cabinet maker for the J, M. & I. road. After that he opened a china store, but he wanted to be actively employed, and went to the shops of the car works, and followed his trade till a few months ago.

Mr. Schnatterer was one of the substantial members of St. Anthony's Catholic church, and of the C. K. of A. He accumulated considerable property by a life of industry and frugality. By his first wife there are the following surviving children: Charles, Annie and Verona Schnatterer. His present wife is the mother of Lillie, Emma, Otto and Clement Schnatterer.

1902

Martin Schnatterer's obituary

This is a crucial lesson for any would-be entrepreneur. I often meet or hear about people who only focus on the future, the next big thing. Don't get me wrong: this is immensely important. In fact, every successful business needs to focus on the future, and Papa John's is no exception. We want to anticipate what's next, where we can improve, how we can make our company better and our customers happier. The possibilities are limitless. It's just a matter of us identifying them and figuring out how to get from where we are to where we want to be.

But we also have to be aware of how we got to where we are in the first place. That's why I've spent so much time describing what happened before Papa John's was ever created. Knowing where we came from helps Papa John's figure out where we're going next. If we search hard enough, we find that other people planted seeds that sprouted in our own lives. For me that came from my great-grandfather Martin G. Schnatterer, my father Robert Louis Schnatter, and my maternal grandfather, my Papaw, Louis Erman Ackerson. Once you find those seeds, you can cultivate them into a garden that keeps on growing and giving.

So we dig all the way back to 1867, the Reichstag and Martin G. Schnatterer. The practices and principles modeled by my great-grandfather undeniably influenced Papa John's. Those ideas were passed down by generations of Schnatters (the American customs officials cut off the extra "er," changing his original name. It meant "the goose" or "the gabbler," which was appropriate for a family that liked to talk a lot). Ultimately, those ideas found their way to my Dad and then to me. In fact, I think that the very thing that drew my great-grandfather to America is what ultimately drew me into business myself. Like my great-grandfather, I enjoyed building a business. Like him, I wanted to have a brighter future for myself and my family. In order to do that, I had to create something that made people's lives better and improved my community. I had to match my passion with my talents. I had to make better pizzas with better ingredients—and satisfy millions of people across the world.

That's what we strive to do at Papa John's every single day. We want to be a fundamentally *good* business. We want to be what Martin G. Schnatterer came to America to find.

We have subsequently defined exactly what those virtues and values are that guided my forefathers and still guide Papa John's. We didn't develop any part of the Papa John's philosophy overnight. It's been a slow process that has taken nearly three decades of exploration and refinement. We're still improving our system to this day, which always starts by looking back at where we came from. But in terms of systematizing our philosophy and giving it definition and names, we started doing that shortly after we went public in 1993.

Now, I had always had plenty of ideas about the right and wrong ways to run a business. How could I not, given that both my Dad and my Papaw lived and breathed entrepreneurship? I learned a lot from them just through observation and osmosis. I started to learn even more after I started my first job at Rocky's Sub Pub at the age of 15. The Fondrisis were good, honest, hardworking people who knew how to make a good pizza and treat their team members right. I can say the same thing about Chris Karamesines, who mentored me in the ways of pizza-making while I was in college. I continued refining my own ideas about how to run a business when my Dad and I saved Mick's Lounge from bankruptcy and when we started making pizzas in the broom closet. It was nonstop, on-the-job education that helped me figure out what Papa John's was all about.

My belief system was simple and straightforward when we officially opened Papa John's in 1985: we would take care of our team members, make a better pizza using better ingredients, and never stop trying to get better.

Even though these ideas were already in my head, we never got around to turning them into a formal code. We didn't have to at first. Papa John's was a tight-knit community for our first few years in business. All of our stores were in the same metro area from 1985 until the end of 1988. And we were only in two metro areas by the end of the decade. Up until this point, I was intimately involved with all of our stores, which allowed me to make sure we were acting in accordance with our core principles. Training was simple—it was mostly by observation of the team members who'd been there since the start. It's easy to get everyone on the same page when you only have a few dozen or even a few hundred people. Papa John's was like a good-sized family. We knew all our family members on a first-name basis. That goes a long way towards making sure everyone is rowing in the same direction.

Unfortunately, that got harder and harder to do as Papa John's grew beyond the Louisville and Lexington areas. We had always acted as if we were a small business. At heart, Papa John's is an independent mom-'n'-pop pizzeria. But I could no longer be involved with every store starting in the early 1990s. There were just too many. We had 100 stores by the middle of 1991. We went public in 1993 with 232 stores. We opened our 500th store only one year later—on June 27th, 1994—when I was still 31 years old. We reached 1,000 stores on August 8th, 1996. We hit the 1,500-store mark before the end of the millennium, on June 20, 1997, and it wasn't long after that when we started expanding into other countries. In addition, most of the new stores were no longer officially owned by Papa John's International. They were franchises, which own, operate and manage their stores and their employees separately from Papa John's International.

These two factors—the growth of Papa John's overall and the simultaneous growth in franchisees—made it all but impossible to ensure that we were living up to our as-yet-unstated values.

So we had to state what those values were. We needed a formal code that every Papa John's team member could see, understand and follow. We got to work developing one in 1993. First, we looked back to people like Martin G. Schnatterer, Papaw and my Dad—the people who helped make Papa John's a reality. We had to figure out what made them tick. Second, we looked around at the people who were currently at the company, the people who were making Papa John's a success. To paraphrase Michelangelo, I saw the angel in the marble and I just chiseled until I set her free.

The best place to look was at our best team members. Some of our earliest co-workers were obvious candidates. Denise Robinson, our all-around rock star who had been with us since Mick's Lounge. Her husband Glenn, had also helped out around the bar. Jeff Couch, an early delivery driver—he's still with the company 29 years later, and Albert "Tubby" Parcell, our first commissary truck driver.

(Funny story about Tubby. One day in the late '80s, he forgot to turn on the walk-in refrigerator in the commissary where we kept our dough. Sitting in the wrong temperature for so long, it expanded to the point where we could no longer use it. Tubby knew it, too. He tried to hide it from me by dumping the dough in the dumpster out back. But that backfired on him. It was 100 degrees outside, so the dough kept expanding overnight. I came around the corner the next morning and found the dough had expanded so much that it had overflowed out of the dumpster and started oozing down the road. The river of dough must have been twenty-five yards long—I wasn't sure whether to laugh or be angry!)

We also looked at some of our more recent hires, many of whom had risen through the ranks because of their passion, dedication and skill. Papa John's has a large number of employees who have been with us for more than two or even three decades. Just recently, we recognized two team members, Lawrence Bosco and Ronald Burk, for being with Papa John's for 25 years. As thanks for their stellar service, we gave them Papa John's stock. You don't work for Papa John's for 25 years unless you model our values day-in, day-out. Those people have my eternal thanks. I still see many of them on a daily or weekly basis, so I give them my thanks in person as often as I can.

These are the people who embody everything that makes Papa John's great. And there are many others. I've already mentioned Mike Smith, who started as an hourly shift leader at store #29 in Lexington, Kentucky, where he made $5.50 an hour. Now he's our Vice President of Operations. Steve Ritchie has a similar story. He bought his own pizzeria as a senior in high school. He tried everything he could to mimic the Papa John's product, searching our dumpsters for our recipe and trying to recreate our fresh-packed sauce. Eventually he joined the Papa John's team in his early 20s, starting at $5 an hour. Today, he's the president of the whole company.

I could probably list hundreds of people here who deserve to be recognized. Mike Meche. Rob Porter. Connie Houston. Keeta Fox. Lance Tucker. I'll actually profile a few of them later in the book. I'm sorry that I can't name everyone who deserves to be recognized—I just don't have enough space. Just know that I'm thankful for all that you've done for our great company.

It was these people who we looked at when we started to develop FASPAC. We began identifying their attributes and what they did that set them apart from others. We interviewed them to get a sense of what they thought made Papa John's successful. We went back and forth for months. By the mid-1990s, we had our answer: FASPAC. It stands for Focus, Accountability, Superiority, PAPA (People Are Priority Always), Attitude and Constant Improvement. Each of these six values is absolutely critical to Papa John's continued success.

● ● ● ● ●

Focus

"We must keep *The Main Thing, The Main Thing*. We will consistently deliver a traditional Papa John's superior-quality pizza."

As I mentioned earlier, *focus* is the most important word in the Merriam-Webster Dictionary when it comes to building a business. (The most important word overall is *people*, which is what we're focused *on* at Papa John's.) If you don't have focus, you'll never achieve what you set out to do. You have to keep your eye on the ball at all times. That's the only way you can ever hit it out of the park.

At Papa John's, our main focus is twofold. First, and most important, we must take care of our people. Second, we must use better ingredients to make a better pizza. Both of these components harken back to my original goal to run Papa John's like an independent, mom-'n'-pop pizzeria. This has always been important to me, ever since I came up with the idea for Papa John's in college. The first part is obvious. Papa John's wouldn't exist if we didn't make quality pizzas that satisfied our customers. We're always striving to improve those pizzas so we can make our customers even more satisfied. If we come up with an idea that doesn't somehow give us better ingredients and a better pizza, it's not an idea worth listening to or acting on. Our customers want pizzas, not hamburgers or vacuum cleaners or toothpaste.

But it's not just about pizzas—it's also about people. I've said before that we're in the people business more than we're in the pizza business. Team members won't reach their full potential if they aren't in positions that suit their skills and give them personal fulfillment. It's just not enough to get the right people on the bus—you also have to make sure each person is in the right seat. When our team members are where they're supposed to be, they're more likely to do a good job, enjoy their work and make a good living for themselves. That's true of everyone at the company, from top to bottom. Personally, I contribute the most to the company when I'm doing marketing, promoting quality control and building our culture. Papa John's would fall apart if they put me in charge of the legal department!

The moment we lose our focus on these two things is the moment we start to struggle. Our reputation as a business depends on us keeping our focus. We can't cut corners, use poor quality ingredients, mistreat our team members, hire the wrong people, or get distracted by something other than our core purpose. Falling into any of these bad habits could jeopardize Papa John's existence in the long-term.

You can see from Papa John's early history just how important focus is. When we were in the broom closet, we could not have been more focused. We wanted to make quality pizzas and sell them. Sure, we tried out new things as we started expanding—a broader menu, a dine-in area and more. Yet thanks to our laser-like focus, we quickly cut out anything that didn't work or distracted us from our Main Thing. We even sold Mick's Lounge in 1987 so we could focus 100 percent of our energy on the pizza business. That kind of focus is what enabled us to go from a broom closet to a publicly traded restaurant chain in only eight years.

But that doesn't mean we were perfect. We never were and we never will be. We've struggled to maintain our focus several times in Papa John's history. I've already described what happened with my uncle in 1987 and 1988. He lost his focus on making pizzas and taking care of his team members. Instead, he focused more on making money. We had another crisis of focus in the years after Papa John's went public. Overnight, a lot of our team members became very wealthy. This caused a few of them to turn their attention away from the company. They started focusing on things that didn't matter—boats, houses, cars and so on. As a result, the company started to suffer from their lack of focus. The quality of our pizzas and our customer service began to deteriorate. But more on that episode later.

I can't stress the importance of focus enough. I wake up every morning and immediately start working on Papa John's, and I keep working on Papa John's up until the moment I go to bed at night. I know that I can't lose my focus. The same is true of the rest of the company.

•　•　•　•　•

Accountability

"We do what we say we are going to do when we say we are going to do it. We earn the right to hold others to a higher level of accountability by being accountable to ourselves, our customers and our business partners."

At Papa John's, we make a promise to our customers: *You're going to get a traditional, superior-quality pizza.* We make sure we keep our word through our accountability.

We have to be accountable at every level of the organization, from the boardroom to the pizza delivery folks. We have to be personally accountable. We have to be accountable to our partners and suppliers. We have to be accountable to our franchisees. And we ultimately have to be accountable to the customer, without whom Papa John's would not exist.

What does this mean in practice? It means that we ensure every member of the Papa John's team is living up to the values and ideals that make us successful. Each of us has an important role to play in making sure we make a superior pizza and get it to the customer on time. We hold each other accountable so that everything runs smoothly and the trains arrive on time. We have a saying at Papa John's: "If it isn't required, it isn't required." This means people will only do what they have been held accountable for. When we don't hold each other accountable, errors start to creep in and people begin to lose focus. And when any part of our well-oiled machine breaks down, all of Papa John's feels the pain.

Over the years, we've established metrics to help us keep each other accountable. One of the phrases you hear a lot at Papa John's is "what gets measured gets done." We have to know what good looks like before we can hold ourselves and each other accountable.

Take the example of our "virtues and talent" matrix, which is a graph we use in the hiring and employee review process. The horizontal vector is for talent, with the left representing low talent and the right representing high talent. The vertical vector is for virtues, beliefs and values. It goes from bad values at the bottom to good values at the top. Our ideal team members fit into the upper-right hand corner—they both have talent and act consistently with Papa John's values.

After that, we prefer to hire people who have the right virtues, even if they don't have the right talent. Why? Because you can train talent. It's almost impossible to train virtues, beliefs and values. That's why we try not to hire anyone who has high talent but doesn't model the values that Papa John's stands for. If you don't have the right virtues, talent doesn't matter. We've found that a potential team member won't be accountable long-term if their beliefs and values don't align with ours.

But there's a higher meaning to accountability, too. We believe businesses have a moral duty to improve the world around them. We do that at Papa John's by making a product that people value. They could spend their money anywhere they want. They come to Papa John's because we offer something that's better than the competition. We'll know we aren't making the world better when people stop buying our pizzas. Therefore, we always have to innovate and stay on the cutting edge. If we stay still, we will get overtaken by someone with a better pizza. We are accountable to each other so that we don't let this happen. When we improve, we benefit our fellow team members, our franchisees, our suppliers and finally the millions of people around the world who buy Papa John's superior-quality pizzas.

Finally, we must also be also accountable to our communities. We must take care of the neighborhoods, towns and cities where Papa John's operates. By giving back, we make the world a better place, one person and place at a time. That's what accountability is all about.

● ● ● ● ●

Superiority

"Our customer satisfaction must be consistent, quantifiable and demonstrable. At Papa John's we expect excellence—the 'best in its class' in everything we do."

Every entrepreneur needs three things in order to succeed. You need a passion for what you do. You need a business model that makes a profit. And you need to be best in your class. Put another way, you need to be superior.

We're obsessed with superiority at Papa John's. That's why our slogan is "Better Ingredients. Better Pizza." We mean what we say and we say what we mean. We make pizzas that are better than the competitors', because that's what our customers expect from us. That's one of the key reasons why we went from a broom closet to a company with hundreds of millions of dollars in revenue in less than a decade. It's why the very first Papa John's in Jeffersonville, Indiana had a higher sales volume than the local Domino's after only a few months in business. Customers reward you when you give them something that's superior. They're not going to reward something that doesn't taste good. Why would they? There are plenty of other places to buy a mediocre pizza—Papa John's will never be one of them.

We take pride in the superior-quality pizzas we make. Now I don't mean that we're arrogant—arrogance breeds ignorance, and ignorance breeds arrogance. It's a vicious cycle that has the potential to never end. Once you become arrogant, you risk spiraling down to a bad place. This is especially dangerous in the world of business. Arrogant business leaders believe their product is perfect—no ifs, ands or buts. This can breed complacency and an unwillingness to improve their product or service. When you think you've reached the top of your game, you only make it easier for one of your competitors to knock you off your perch.

A humble business leader, by comparison, always recognizes that they have room to improve. So when I say we take pride in our work, I mean the sort of pride where we enjoy what we do and believe that we're making the world a better place. I see this all the time when I walk around the Papa John's headquarters or one of our more than 5,000 stores around the world. It doesn't matter where I go. I always see the same thing—a belief by our team members that they're doing something that truly matters. Superiority is infectious. We know our pizzas are better. We want to keep it that way. And that's why we always want to improve our pizzas—we want to stay ahead of the game. Superiority demands that we do so. It's a goal that we're always striving to achieve.

It's important to recognize that superiority doesn't happen overnight. Remember: it took me months of making pizzas in the broom closet before we found the right configurations, ingredients and amounts that customers liked. We're still improving those recipes to this day. It's not enough to believe that you're superior—you have to work your ass off to get to the point where you actually *are* superior. That's true whether it's one guy making pizzas in a broom closet or a hundred thousand people making pizzas in stores across the world. It takes time and money to make something superior. If you're too lazy to put in the time, or if you're too stingy to make the investment, you can kiss your dream of superiority goodbye. We weren't afraid of doing either of those things at Papa John's, which explains why we're now what I call a "32-year-old overnight success story."

At the end of the day, you know superiority when you see it. Chick-Fil-A. Texas Roadhouse. Papa John's. These businesses have a reputation for quality and superiority. They earned it by respecting their customers, by making a quality product, and by being better than their competitors. The alternative is to be like Pizza Hut, whose CEO recently said he believes that convenience trumps quality. I don't know about you, but that doesn't sound like superiority to me.

• • • • •

P.A.P.A.—People Are Priority Always

"People Are Priority Always. Our success depends upon our ability, as a team, to work together to achieve our goals and expectations."

Focus may be the most important word in the English language, but people are the secret to Papa John's success. People are our priority, always. Whether it's the customer, our team members, our partners, or anyone else, we need to treat them with respect and fairness at all times. I've said it before and I'll say it again—we're in the people business more than we're in the pizza business. Without good people, we'll never make the traditional, superior-quality Papa John's pizzas that hundreds of millions of people love.

That's why we devote incredible resources to the people who are part of the Papa John's family. We make sure everyone's in the right role. Why? Because that allows them to create the most value and find the most personal fulfillment. When our people are happy, their work reflects it. When they're in the right role, they can exercise the independent critical judgment that moves the company forward and makes us all better.

We also want to make sure every member of Papa John's understands the principles that guide us. Why? Because once they understand what we're about, they can take pride in the fact that they're contributing to a better world. Papa John's is more than just a job—it's a place to learn a new way of looking at the world. We want to train people to make the world a better place, one pizza at a time.

Most importantly, we take care of our team members, paying them well and giving them the opportunity to grow both personally and professionally. There are two reasons for this. First, everyone deserves to be treated with dignity and respect. When we take care of our team members, they'll take care of our customers and everyone they come in contact with. Second, our customers won't have a good experience if our employees aren't also having a good experience. The two are directly related. That's why we take care of our employees as well as we do. We want them to be happy and fulfilled and to achieve their potential. We'll lose good talent if we don't do that, and our customers will suffer from it.

There are many businesses that enrich the people at the top while taking advantage of the people at the bottom who actually do the heavy lifting. Not Papa John's. We treat every team member with respect, no matter who they are or what they do. Our team members make me proud because they show the dignity of labor in all they do.

Three things we do stand out in my mind.

First, I underpay myself compared to my peers at other multinational restaurant chains—I make a fourth to a fifth as much as most of them, and I'm proud of it. Second, we have a rule where the executives cannot take a bonus unless the team members across the rest of the organization also get a bonus. Everyone is aligned from top to bottom. This means the janitor, the accounts receivable clerk, the store manager and everyone in between has to get a bonus—so long as they earned it, of course—before the leadership team gets so much as a penny.

That's how it should be. Whether you're in the boardroom or doing heavy lifting in the commissary, everyone is judged by the same standards. This is an extremely powerful way to motivate everyone to play at the top of their game. Finally, we give about 30 percent of our annual profit back to our team members in the form of merit raises, bonuses, stock options and cold, hard cash. In 2015, this totaled about $60 million. And *every* team member at our headquarters gets at least one raise a year. In 2016, we had over 800 raises at corporate—and that's for only 563 people.

Think about what it would mean if every business in America followed Papa John's lead. If every CEO in America took a 50 percent or higher cut in pay, used the same compensation philosophy for everyone in the company from the top to bottom, and gave even 10 or 15 percent of their profit back to their employees, profit would no longer be seen as an evil by younger generations. We as business leaders have an incredible opportunity to protect our economic system for future generations—more of us just need to step up.

Instead, we see news story after news story of CEOs who run companies into the ground and then get paid tens of millions of dollars anyway. Others seek to enrich themselves by manipulating the government into giving them subsidies or crippling their competitors. They don't care if they make their profit in a good or bad way—they just want the profit regardless. We all recognize that these problems are rampant in the modern American economy. They are causing millions of people to look at the free enterprise system with disgust, even though these actions represent perversions of free enterprise. If this trend doesn't stop, it will eventually overthrow our country's ability to create the jobs, the opportunity and the prosperity that benefit everyone across society.

We take care of our team members in other ways, too. Papa John's offers a competitive health insurance plan to its team members. We have long recognized that money isn't everything—quality of life is also important. We've built our headquarters to account for this fact. A lot of corporate headquarters are dark, sad places. People work there, but don't enjoy it. They can't wait to go home. Not at Papa John's. We built two gyms for all team members to use. We put in a restaurant that serves traditional Papa John's pizza, salads and more. We added on a doctor's office, with a doctor on call no fewer than five days a week. We offer yoga classes. We have a drug store and a Starbucks. We built walking trails and an outdoor park with two lakes and a waterfall. We've invested in top-of-the-line security so our people can feel safe at all times. The list goes on.

I enjoy going to work in the morning because I know I'm going to be surrounded by people who want to be there. When I talk to any of the roughly 560 team members who work at our headquarters, I almost always hear them say they're happy, they're fulfilled and they love Papa John's pizza. None of them have ever worked at a company that treats them as well as Papa John's does. If they did, they would've left Papa John's to go work there again. They don't.

We see the difference on a daily basis. We're in a competitive industry in which people start and leave jobs very frequently. Not at Papa John's. Our turnover rate is incredibly low—about 30 to 50 percent of what it is at the average fast-food restaurant. Our team members *want* to work at Papa John's. They want to stay at Papa John's because it's a career, not just another job. They want to be part of the Papa John's team, precisely because we operate as a team. Many even say we work together like a family.

That's an incredible thing. Treating your team with dignity and respect makes a world of difference. I just wish more companies did it.

• • • • •

Attitude

"If you think you can or you think you can't—you're right! The difference between winners and losers is a positive mental attitude. Our attitude is a reflection of what we value: successful team members must be upbeat, proactive and passionate about everything they do."

In Chapter One, I told you about when my Dad hired Denise Robinson to be the cook at Mick's Lounge. She couldn't cook. I went ballistic when he told me that—a cook who can't cook? It sounded like the dumbest thing anyone could ever do. That's when he told me, "Hire for attitude, train for aptitude."

Dad was right. Attitude is everything. Denise had a phenomenal attitude, even if her cooking wasn't quite up to snuff. She probably has the best attitude of anyone who's ever worked for the company. When people ask me what kind of attitude is best for the workplace, I tell them to look at Denise. She's kind, focused on the customer, loyal and positive. Her good work reflects her good attitude. She's a winner.

I can't stand people who have a bad attitude. We're in the customer service business, which means that everyone needs to have a positive attitude at all times. It doesn't matter if you never interact with the customer yourself. Emotions are contagious. Happy, sad, angry, depressed, ecstatic—everyone around you is affected by what you're feeling. This is true at both the top of the company as well as the bottom. One person with a good attitude can make a world of difference. The opposite is also true: one person with a bad attitude can bring a company crashing down. That's why we go to such lengths to hire people who are passionate and have a positive outlook on life. They're the type of people who will try to be more productive, improve themselves and find new ways to innovate and experiment.

That's what we look for. Of course, it goes without saying that we don't always find it. We've all encountered people with bad attitudes in our life. We've had quite a few at Papa John's over the years, although none of them have lasted very long. Attitude is everything when it comes to customer service.

• • • • •

Constant Improvement

"We never stop trying to surpass our previous best. We constantly 'Raise the Bar'. No matter how good we are, we will always get better."

I wake up every day wondering how I can make Papa John's better. That's why I tinker so much. Consider just a few examples. I spend time every week in the kitchen and the lab, trying new recipes and seeing how we can improve the Papa John's pizzas that millions of people love. We're always working on our technology to make it better. That's true whether it's the rounding machine in the commissary or the electronic system we use to link every store together. Every single thing we do, we can do better. There are no exceptions. There never will be any exceptions. We can—and will—improve.

Every entrepreneur has to think this way. It doesn't matter how high you fly—you can always go higher. When you rest on your laurels, you do a disservice to your customers, your co-workers, your investors and, above all, yourself. Your company will not be long for this world if you think you've already reached the top of your game. Sure, you make plenty of mistakes when you're trying to innovate—we've definitely done that at Papa John's. But the path to success is paved with mistakes—they show a willingness to take risks and try new things. That's what constant improvement is all about.

Two related concepts may help explain what constant improvement means on a day-to-day basis. The first is intrapreneurship. The second is optionality. Both are equally important to Papa John's success.

Intrapreneurship is a simple concept. It means acting like an entrepreneur within an existing organization. This is especially important at a major company like Papa John's. Everyone has entrepreneurial ideas and instincts, regardless of whether they're a janitor or the CEO. In fact, many times the people at the lowest levels of an organization have the best ideas of how to improve it. They see inefficiencies and opportunities on a daily basis. It's my job, and the job of every manager at Papa John's, to encourage them to share their insights. No one should be afraid to propose a new and better way of doing things.

The people who have done that in Papa John's history often rise to the very top of the organization. Case in point: all 12 members of our Executive Leadership Team actually started out making minimum wage in their first jobs. All of their stories are different, but they each share one thing in common: they're as dedicated as I am to making Papa John's better with each day on the job. It doesn't matter where you start—it's where you finish.

Optionality is just as important as intrapreneurship. By optionality, I mean the sort of innovation where you start off trying to improve one area only to find an improvement for something else. It is the ultimate trial and error. And it can revolutionize a business. Unfortunately, entrepreneurs often fall into a sort of tunnel vision where they focus on one thing to the exclusion of everything else. They get so obsessed with trying to fix one problem that they miss an easy opportunity to fix another. You have to be able to recognize when you've discovered something that can make you better, even if it isn't what you're expecting. Quite simply, the key to optionality is keeping your options open. A good result is one that benefits the company, even if it wasn't the result you were originally looking for. You also have to be willing to discard something that's already working when you find something that works even better. No business can become wedded to the way it currently does things.

Consider this example. A while ago, I visited the University of Kentucky to learn more about growing organic vegetables. While on a tour through a nearby field, we came across a bright red plant. The academics who were with me explained it contained a natural red dye. This immediately set off my internal optionality alarm. I had gone to the University of Kentucky looking for insight on organic vegetables. Instead, I found something that Papa John's could use down the line. If we ever needed anything with red dye, here was our all-natural solution. I wasn't even sure if we actually used red dye when I found it. But that didn't matter— what mattered is that we found something we didn't expect.

That's optionality in action. I have similar stories from across the rest of the company. Thanks to the improvements that come through optionality, our traditional, superior-quality Papa John's pizza now tastes better than ever. Optionality has also played a role in improving how we do things at the commissary, our customer service and countless other things. Papa John's is better off for optionality.

Ultimately, constant improvement is crucial to a business' success. The business world is a fast-moving place. The customer's wants and needs are always changing. At Papa John's, we have to stay one step ahead. We have to constantly improve.

• • • • •

We developed FASPAC at the perfect time. The mid-1990s saw the most explosive growth at any point in the company's history. We basically couldn't do anything wrong from 1993 until 1997—Wall Street loved us and America loved us. We were adding hundreds of stores each year, going from 232 in June of 1993 to 2,000 stores only six years later. By this point we were a truly national company with stores in almost every state. We were also now an international company, having opened our first foreign store in Mexico City in 1998.

Our unprecedented growth was a result of three key things. First, we had a dramatic influx of capital that came from going public. Second, we had a business model that benefited our customers, our employees, our suppliers, our franchisees, our investors and society as a whole. Finally, for the first time, we had a defined and easily understandable set of guiding principles that united every Papa John's store and team member, no matter where they were.

At this point we also started to get national recognition like never before. Until the mid-1990s, the biggest award we ever won was *Louisville Magazine*'s "Best Pizza" award in 1989. Don't get me wrong—that was a huge deal that allowed us to expand across Kentucky, Indiana and Ohio like wildfire. But it was small potatoes compared to where we were in the '90s.

First came the awards for our out-of-this-world growth. In 1994 we won two such accolades from major national publications. First, *Inc. Magazine* ranked us the 51st "hottest public company" in America—an incredible honor given that we were competing with literally thousands of other businesses. More impressively, *BusinessWeek* named us No. 1 in its annual list of Hot Growth Companies.

And the awards kept coming. In 1995, *Forbes Magazine* ranked us as one of the Top 10 "Best Small Companies" in America. As a 33-year-old, I felt that this validated my vision for Papa John's in a whole new way. We were a major national company in our own right.

Yet *Forbes* saw through this growth to figure out what Papa John's was all about. At heart, we were a small business. Paradoxically, that's also why we were growing so fast. We acted like an independent, mom-'n'-pop pizzeria, whether we were in Jeffersonville, Orlando, Raleigh or anywhere in between. Now the national media was starting to pick up on this critical fact.

And the *Forbes* award was just the start. In 1997, we went even bigger. *Restaurants & Institutions*, the premier trade magazine for foodservice professionals, ranked Papa John's #1 in overall customer satisfaction and product quality among national pizza chains. We were on cloud nine. We were now at the top of the pizza-making field, beating out much larger chains that had been around for two or even three times as long as us. Our unerring focus on making a better pizza with better ingredients was now being recognized across America.

These awards, and others like them, proved definitively that we were on to something. Our guiding principles, expressed in FASPAC, empowered us to do incredible things. The most incredible things we did were take care of our people and make traditional, superior-quality pizzas.

INC. Magazine Award

Restaurants & Institutions

BusinessWeek

A McGRAW-HILL PUBLICATION

THE BEST SMALL COMPANIES

PAPA JOHN'S
....

FROM A BROOM CLOSET IN A BAR TO 485 PIZZA RESTAURANTS

John H. Schnatter always felt he knew how to make a better pizza. As a teenager, he worked at a number of pizzerias, learning a lot about the art of creating a magnificent pie. So a decade ago, after graduating from Ball State University with a business degree, Schnatter, then 21, decided to put his knowledge to use. While running Mick's Lounge, a bar co-owned by his father in their hometown of Jeffersonville, Ind., he tore down a broom closet, installed an oven and began selling pizza. From such humble origins was born Papa John's International Inc., the Louisville pizza chain that is No. 1 on BUSINESS WEEK's 1994 list of Hot Growth Companies.

From its start at Mick's Lounge, Papa John's has grown into a 485-strong network of company-owned and franchised stores across 19 states from Michigan to Florida. And in an industry dominated by Pizza Hut, Domino's, and Little Caesar's, it has carved out a profitable niche. Last year, Papa John's earnings rose 60%, to $4.9 million, as its sales climbed by 80%, to $89.2 million. Even Frank L. Carney, who founded Pizza Hut with his brother in 1958 and sold it to PepsiCo Inc. in 1977, recently signed a deal to open 62 Papa John's outlets in Houston. "I think it's a very, very competitive product," he says.

What's Papa John's secret? For starters, it appeals to value-conscious households. It includes a small tub of garlic butter and two hot peppers with each pie—a little lagniappe that helps give the "perception of more bang for the buck," says Gerry Durnell, editor and publisher of *Pizza Today*, a trade maga-

SCHNATTER STARTED PAPA JOHN'S WHEN HE WAS JUST 23

zine. Another reason for success: "You have to keep things simple and focused," says Schnatter, now 32. For Papa John's, that means no salad bars that add to costs. Its menu is limited to pizza, breadsticks, cheesesticks, and soft drinks. And in-store dining is rare. Papa John's specializes in takeout and delivery.

BOUNCY STOCK. To hold down costs even more, Papa John's has three centralized commissaries that provide fresh dough and sauce mix. Each Pizza Hut prepares its own dough. And because they sell ingredients to franchisees, the commissaries produce revenue. They accounted for 46% of the chain's sales last year.

Despite its growth, the pizza chain's stock has bounced around since Papa

John's went public in June at 13. It's now trading at 25¼, down from January's high of 33¼. Some of the drop had to do with the severe winter weather that held down restaurant traffic.

A bigger question for investors, however, is whether the company can continue its torrid growth. Schnatter has ambitious plans to open 215 stores this year and 220 more in 1995. Analyst Steven A. Rockwell of Alex. Brown & Sons Inc. estimates that Papa John's earnings could increase 45% this year, to $7.1 million, with revenue climbing by 67%, to $149 million. There aren't too many pizza parlors that can make their dough rise like that.

By Zachary Schiller in Cleveland

BusinessWeek Award

THE WORLD'S BEST SMALL COMPANIES

November 6, 1995

$4.00 (Canada $4.50)

Forbes

		Company	average	12 mos	growth rate	($mil)	($mil)			change	($mil)		EPS
1	1	**Lone Star Steakhouse & Saloon** steak restaurants	100.0+%	22.1%	122%	$278	$39.4	0%	39%	98.1%	$1,457	$1.09	36.4	$1.67
2	■	**US Delivery Systems** same-day local delivery services	100.0+	31.7	40	198	8.6	51	26⅞	95.5	297	0.83	32.4	1.23
3	■	**Brightpoint** wholesales wireless telecommunications devices	91.0	25.8	53	232	4.0	0	16¾	35.3	109	0.66	25.4	1.02
4	■	**Nu Kote Holdings** manufactures office & home printing products	75.9	12.9	15	261	11.7	100	20¼	55.8	435	0.61	33.2	1.11
5	■	**Marisa Christina** Marisa Christina women's clothing & Flapdoodles children's clothing	66.5	26.2	26	79	9.5	0	15⅞	47.7	134	1.21	13.1	1.41
6	■	**Quality Dining** operates Burger King, Chili's & other fast-food & casual dining restaurants	54.3	19.9	13	95	5.3	31	19¼	55.5	130	0.80	24.1	1.06
7	■	**NN Ball & Roller** manufactures precision steel ball bearings & rollers	51.3	34.4	36	69	10.5	0	18¾	48.5	181	1.08	17.4	1.33
8	■	**Roper Industries** pumps, valves & controls	45.1	25.9	49	164	21.4	20	37	46.5	552	1.43	25.9	2.58
9	■	**Semitool** designs, manufactures, markets & services semiconductor-mfg equipment	42.6	87.4	62	95	10.2	52	18¼	NA	237	0.91	20.1	1.54
10	6	**Papa John's International** operates & franchises pizza delivery & take-out restaurants	42.5	14.3	82	202	8.9	1	43½	51.3	502	0.83	52.4	1.43
11	5	**Landry's Seafood Restaurants** casual dining seafood restaurants	40.8	12.4	52	84	7.7	1	15¾	10.5	284	0.49	32.1	0.72

Stock prices as of Oct. 6. ■ Not on last year's list. NA: Not available or not applicable. ¹Includes all share classes.
Sources: William O'Neil & Co.; IBES Inc. via OneSource Information Services.

Forbes Magazine Award

On that note, we actually trademarked and started using "Better Ingredients. Better Pizza." in 1996, when I was 34. This slogan, which we still use to this day, conveys exactly what Papa John's is all about. The most successful independent pizzerias are known for the quality of their product. I wanted Papa John's to be no different, starting with our first pizza in the broom closet. My goal has always been to run a national chain restaurant that acts and thinks like a small independent pizzeria. That's why we always have to seek out better, fresher and more natural ingredients. If we do this, I believe we will always make better pizzas than our competitors.

Now we had to bring this message to a broader set of customers. Starting in 1996, we launched one of our first major television advertising campaigns, highlighting what made Papa John's different. One ad in particular stands out in my mind. The imagery was drawn from Papa John's stores, with shots of me interacting with our team members and all of us working together to make pizzas. Providing the voiceover, I said: "I learned a lot about making pizza from my grandpa—and he didn't even cook! But he taught me always to do my best. So we use the best ingredients. We won't skimp. We use only fresh-packed tomatoes for Papa John's sauce, like you'd find at the finest Italian restaurants and real mozzarella cheese and lean meats." The ad concluded: "Grandpa was right. You've got to do your very best. It's that simple. Better Ingredients. Better Pizza. Papa John's." This ad perfectly captured who we were as a family-friendly, mom-'n'-pop pizzeria with independent roots.

Still shot from television ad *1996*

We also started doing more to highlight just how fast we were growing. We always linked our growth to our dedication to using better ingredients. Take the example of another television ad we released. The camera focused on the ingredients we use to make our pizzas. The voiceover did the same: "Cheese. Some say it's the heart and soul of a perfect pizza. That's why Papa John's uses real mozzarella. It costs us a little more—us, not you—but the taste is definitely worth it. That's one reason why Papa John's is now the fastest growing pizza company in America. Call and we'll deliver all the delicious reasons right to your door."

Sure enough, people did just that. Papa John's continued to grow, reflecting that we were doing something different, something right, something better.

Still shot from television ad

● ● ● ● ●

We weren't the only ones who recognized this, either. One day in 1996 I got a call from Jack Laughery, the former CEO of Hardee's restaurants and the best of Papa John's board members. He asked me something unexpected: whether the founder of Pizza Hut could start a Papa John's franchise. His name was Frank Carney.

I can't overstate just how unbelievable this was. In the mid-to-late 1990s, the chain pizza business was dominated by Pizza Hut and to, a lesser extent, Domino's. Pizza Hut was definitely the company to beat. The company had started in 1958, so it had been around nearly 30 years longer than us, and reached its 4,000th store in the late 1970s— right around the time I started making my first pizzas at Rocky's Sub Pub. I really respect what Pizza Hut did in its early years. It brought pizza to every corner of America, paving the way for companies like Papa John's down the road. But somehow along the way, Pizza Hut lost sight of what had made it great. The quality of Pizza Hut pizzas slowly started deteriorating in the late '80s and early '90s. Frank explicitly said this to the media. In his words, "There isn't anything in Pizza Hut that is the same as when I left except the logo." He specifically singled out his old company's desire to replace quality with variety.

Papa John's doesn't do this. We make traditional, superior-quality pizzas. This helps explain why we grew as fast as we did in the mid-1990s. We were filling a void for customers who wanted "Better Ingredients. Better Pizza."

Frank saw this clearly. He left Pizza Hut in 1980 in order to invest in several other businesses around the country. Many of his friends and colleagues urged him to get back in the pizza business, but he resisted for well over a decade and a half. He thought he'd had enough. Then, one day in Memphis, Tennessee, he had his first taste of Papa John's pizza. He loved it. He said that our hand-tossed crust tasted like "the best bread stick you ever ate." He also said "the place was clean" and "the people were doing a great job." He now wanted to be a part of our team.

This by itself was a serious vindication of everything we'd accomplished at Papa John's—our business model, our attitude and, above all, the pizzas we made and how we treated our people. To me, this proved

Papa John's quality beyond the shadow of a doubt. The founder of the largest pizza chain in the world—a company more than three times the size of Papa John's—now wanted to become part of the Papa John's team.

He saw in us something better. And I saw in him a huge opportunity. When Jack Laughery asked me if Frank could start a franchise, I only had to think for less than a second. I told him, "Sure, he can become a franchisee. But first he has to agree to shoot some commercials with me." Jack took this back to Frank, who promptly agreed. The founder of Pizza Hut had officially converted to Papa John's.

We didn't waste any time. Frank and I met up a few weeks later and started filming the ads shortly after that. Now, we'd released several commercials over the previous few years targeting Pizza Hut. The most memorable featured customers doing a blind taste test where they had to choose between Papa John's and Pizza Hut pizza. The ad started: "Pizza Hut dares anyone to find a better pizza." Then I show up on screen, smile and say, "Oh really?" The narrator continues, "It was a challenge Papa John couldn't resist. So he commissioned independent taste tests, and Papa John's won—won big time." The ad went on to list some of the many differences in the ingredients we use. "Maybe that's because Papa John's sauce is made with fresh-packed, vine-ripened tomatoes," while "Pizza Hut uses remanufactured paste." I close out the ad by saying, "Anybody can claim to make a better pizza, but it's you, the consumer, who decided." Another ad made fun of the anti-Papa John's toys that Pizza Hut gave to its franchisees—they said "sock it to Papa John's." Our ad pointed out how ridiculous this really was. Why spend money on toys when your pizza isn't that good?

1997

Still shot from television ad

These were already some pretty aggressive ads—but they had nothing on the ones we started making with Frank.

I still look back fondly at those ads. We started running them in the spring of 1997. They were simple, 30-second ads. The hardest-hitting one showed a fictional Pizza Hut convention featuring all of the company's franchisees. The convention announcer kicks it off, saying, "As a highlight of our franchisee meeting, we have our visionary, the co-founder of Pizza Hut, Mr. Frank Carney." Then the narrator kicks in: "Recently, the co-founder of Pizza Hut did something surprising. He bought a Papa John's franchise." Frank steps up to the podium wearing a Papa John's polo. He looks out at the audience, then says, "Sorry, guys. I found a better pizza." Our dedication to making those words a reality is what drew Frank to Papa John's in the first place.

The second ad featured a construction crew tearing down a statue, while the narrator says, "They've had to do a little remodeling over at Pizza Hut headquarters since their co-founder came out of retirement to become a Papa John's franchisee." The next shot shows them taking down Frank's portrait from the Pizza Hut boardroom. The narrator keeps going: "See, he thinks Papa John's makes better pizza than even the company he helped found." It ends with Frank and I making a pizza. Frank closes it by saying our slogan—"Better Ingredients. Better Pizza. Papa John's."

Ad with Frank Carney 1997

And Frank really meant what he said. He loved being a part of the Papa John's team. After starting his first franchise in the Houston area in 1994, he had expanded to well over 100 stores by the early 2000s. He even built several Papa John's in Wichita, Kansas, the city where he founded Pizza Hut.

Papa John's was rising faster than ever, while Pizza Hut was declining. Between May 1996 and May 1997, Papa John's same-store sales increased by 11 percent, while Pizza Hut's declined by 8 percent. The competition between us was really heating up. It was like David versus Goliath, and David was definitely winning. I was a 34-year-old who was beating a company that was older than me.

Of course, we were also competing with Domino's during this period as well. They were, after all, the second largest pizza company in America, smaller only than Pizza Hut. They were founded in 1960, only a few years after Pizza Hut. By the mid-1990s, Domino's business model was focused on delivery, much like Papa John's. But we were rapidly catching up to them. At one point we released a television ad that summarized our growth. It showed a fleet of pizza-delivery cars, all with the Domino's logo on top. The narrator chimes in: "Used to be, there was only one big guy out there delivering pizzas. Then an upstart came along." At that point a Papa John's delivery car pulls up, prompting one of the Domino's drivers to burst out laughing. The narrator keeps going: "And with each passing year, you saw more and more Papa John's cars. Perhaps that's because Papa John's uses better ingredients, and better ingredients make a better pizza. It's made us the fastest-growing pizza chain in America. Have one delivered, and find out why." The ad closes like it started, with a fleet of pizza delivery cars stopped at a stoplight. This time, however, only one of them is Domino's.

Lighthearted ads like these are par for the course in advertising. Domino's responded with ads of their own. They also tried to increase the quality of their product—I'll leave it to you to figure out whether they succeeded. That's how businesses are supposed to respond in a competitive market. When the competition gets fierce, the principled entrepreneur will do everything they can to increase the quality of their product and their service. That's ultimately the key to succeeding in America's economy. Customers go where they can get the best product for the best value and served by the best people. More and more Americans were choosing Papa John's with each passing day.

Why? Because we provided the quality product and customer service that people wanted.

Pizza Hut was angry as this unfolded But unlike Domino's, Pizza Hut didn't respond by trying to leapfrog us in terms of quality and service. Instead, they responded by suing us in federal court.

I can understand why Pizza Hut was mad. Once I heard about the lawsuit, I called my brother Chuck to get his take on it. I asked him, "Chuck, can you believe they sued us?" He responded, "John, you've been poking that bear pretty hard." He was right. We were poking the bear, especially once we started using Frank in our ads. Sure enough, the bear eventually woke up—and boy, was it mad. Now it was out for blood.

In 1997 Pizza Hut started complaining to the Better Business Bureau that our slogan was misleading and unfair. They argued that "Better Ingredients. Better Pizza." simply wasn't true. They also argued that their pizza was the best, even though they had no proof whatsoever. Of course the BBB refused to act. There was nothing to the case. It was just one business trying to handicap another using any means at their disposal. Yet in response to the BBB's decision, Pizza Hut filed suit in the Dallas Federal District Court in 1998. This was an attempt to gain home court advantage—Pizza Hut is based in Dallas and probably hoped that a Dallas jury would be more sympathetic to their case. In any event, Pizza Hut asked the court to rule that "Better Ingredients. Better Pizza." was intentionally misleading and therefore violated federal law.

Once the case got to court, Pizza Hut tried to make it all about "science"—or, at least, their version of science. They paid experts to come to court and testify that our ingredients didn't really matter. They claimed that customers couldn't really taste the difference between fresh and frozen ingredients. Yet this was and is bogus. You can't scientifically prove that grandmother's homemade apple pie is better than the frozen apple pies you buy at the grocery store. But it is better and everyone knows it. There's just something about the fresh, never-frozen ingredients that makes them come alive on your tongue. You can break it down to the molecular level all you want—you're always going to think your grandmother's homemade apple pie tastes better.

The same is true of Papa John's. The proof was in the pudding—or rather, the proof was in the pizza. A growing number of Americans wanted Papa John's pizzas. A shrinking number of Americans wanted Pizza Hut's.

We were confident that both the law and the facts were on our side, yet the district court ruled in favor of Pizza Hut. The judge also ordered us to stop using our slogan altogether, a change that would have cost tens of millions of dollars to implement across the whole company. I wasn't prepared for this to be the end of the matter, though. We knew we were in the right. So we appealed the decision to the Fifth Circuit Court of Appeals, headquartered in New Orleans. That's where we were vindicated. The judge reversed the lower court's decision. Pizza Hut was furious. They petitioned the Supreme Court of the United States to take up the case next. But the highest court of the land refused, handing Papa John's the ultimate victory.

To this day, we use "Better Ingredients. Better Pizza." as our slogan. Why? Because that's what Papa John's is all about. And it's true.

It still baffles me that Pizza Hut tried to sue us rather than beat us in the open market. I'm not the only one. One media analyst called this whole episode "one of the stupidest cases to ever be heard by the judiciary." It's true. Pizza Hut spent millions of dollars trying to get the government to force us to change our slogan. They should have spent those millions of dollars improving their pizzas and their stores. That isn't good business—it's bad business. Our job as entrepreneurs is to give customers something they want, something that makes their lives better. You have to build their trust through consistency practiced over many years. But you betray that trust when you try to use the power of government to undermine your competitors. You're not doing anything that benefits the world around you. You're actually harming your customers, your employees, your franchisees and society at large. Even if you win, you lose.

Fortunately, Papa John's doesn't play that game. Our slogan isn't "Better Lawsuits. Better Pizza." It's "Better Ingredients. Better Pizza." If that ever changes, we'll really be in a dark place.

• • • • •

Papa John's CEO John Schnatter faces a class of children in a spoof of the original court ruling against the company's "Better Ingredients. Better Pizza" slogan. Crossed out is the repeated sentence "I will not say Better."

Print ad following the lawsuit

Looking back on the Pizza Hut debacle, I can't help but think of why Martin G. Schnatterer came to America in the first place. He left Germany precisely because the wealthy and the well-connected could use the power of government to enrich themselves and cripple their competitors. Instead, he sought a country where people could get ahead through honest and hard work. He found what he was looking for in Jeffersonville, Indiana. From there, he proved that the best way to get ahead in America is to help yourself by first helping others. Until the day he died, he built and ran businesses that made people's lives better.

Papa John's should always seek to do the same, every day and without exception. We reaffirmed our commitment to this ideal in the mid-1990s when we developed FASPAC. It enabled one of the most rapid periods of growth in the company's history. This happened for one simple reason: we preached the gospel of Better Ingredients. Better Pizza., and then we practiced what we preached. This took us from a broom closet to a nationwide phenomenon in just over a decade. Anybody can talk the talk, but Papa John's walks the walk.

This wouldn't have happened if we didn't identify the principles that my Dad, my Papaw and even my great-grandfather practiced. Now it was up to me and the rest of the Papa John's team to live out those principles on a daily basis. We had to Go Left, we had to keep our focus, we had to remember and practice every single virtue that made us so successful. If we did this, we would be prepared for anything that came our way. Even then, I knew that there would be many storms on the horizon. It's never a question of whether those storms exist—they always have and they always will. The real question is how you deal with those storms once the wind starts blowing, the rain starts falling and the thunder starts booming. In those dark moments, you have to remember your past, because if you don't, you'll cut short your future.

CHAPTER FIVE

—— • ——

FIX IT

Some of my earliest and fondest memories are from visiting my Papaw's house when I was a kid. When my Dad was out of town on business and politics, my Mom would drive me, my younger brother Chuck and my sister Anne across the Ohio River to spend time with Papaw. He had a decent-sized property that was a wonderland for two young boys under the age of 6. We spent countless hours playing, horsing around and acting like the rambunctious kids that we were.

Papaw encouraged us to have fun when we visited him—that's what grandfathers do, after all. But he also wanted to teach us valuable life lessons. Starting when we were 7 or 8, Papaw began to give us chores to do around the property. That's when he started to say the two words that I will forever associate with the most important man in my life. Those two words were: "Fix it."

I can't tell you how many times I heard Papaw say this. The circumstances were usually similar. We were spending time together on his property, which was like a safe haven to me when I was growing up. It had plenty of old machinery scattered around. He had a tractor, a

1964

1971

Chuck and me
in a wagon &
dune buggy

lawn mower, a tiller, a mulcher and a dozen other things that we used together on a regular basis. Unsurprisingly, each piece of machinery broke down every now and then. Papaw used this as a learning opportunity for me. Whenever anything broke, he would look me straight in the eye and tell me those two words: "Fix it."

So that's what I did. I dragged the broken equipment down a ramp that Papaw built into his basement. That's where he kept his workbench and all of his tools. It didn't matter if it was the tractor, the tiller, the mulcher, or anything else—I would tear it apart to figure out what was wrong and how I could make it right.

I spent hours—and sometimes days—down in that basement. It was an inquisitive kid's paradise. No piece of equipment was too small for me to rip apart, examine, fix and put back together. Papaw encouraged me to do this. He didn't just want me to get the machinery working again. He wanted me to figure out how every single thing worked. Then he wanted me to improve it so that it wouldn't break again—or so that, if it did break again, I'd be able to fix it faster the next time.

Sometimes I figured out the problem and fixed it. Sometimes I didn't. It didn't matter to Papaw whether I succeeded or not. He would check in on me every few hours to see if I was making any progress. If I wasn't, he would help me out and explain what he was doing along the way. It quickly became obvious that Papaw was teaching me to *tinker*.

Tinkering was always a big deal for Papaw. For him, tinkering meant constantly improving whatever you were working on. It meant finding a new and better way of doing something. It meant figuring out what to expect from your surroundings. Papaw spent his own business career tinkering and he expected others to do the same. He rightly believed that tinkering prepared you for whatever problems might come your way. It helped you figure out how things worked. Ultimately, Papaw wanted me to figure out how tractors worked, how business worked, how people worked, how life worked, how *everything* worked.

My Papaw taught me many lessons, but this is ultimately the most important. You can't be a successful entrepreneur if you can't figure out how something works, as well as how something doesn't work. You can actually learn as much, if not more, when something doesn't work. Whatever problem you're facing, you have to be able to tear it apart, fix it and put it back together. That's why we constantly tinker at Papa John's. We call it the "Six P's"—"perfect preparation prevents piss-poor performance."

Thanks to my Papaw, I understood this concept intuitively even before I made the first Papa John's pizza. I practiced what he taught me, which helped me as a young entrepreneur in my early 20s. By the mid-1990s, when I was in my early 30s, Papa John's had already faced its fair share of challenges. You can't be in business for 10-plus years and not encounter some hurdles you need to overcome. Yet no matter what we faced, we tinkered, figured out how stuff worked, made things better and moved on to the next challenge—a pattern we still follow to this day. We hadn't met a problem we couldn't fix. It almost seemed as if we never would.

The mid-1990s was when we really hit our stride. As I mentioned, we reached 500 stores in 1994. We opened store #1,000 less than two years later in August, 1996. The company had grown fourfold in only four years. At the same time, we were recognized in unprecedented ways by the rest of the business community and society at large. The awards we received from 1994 to 1997 seemed to prove that Papa John's was an unstoppable force. It seemed that the only place we could go was up.

Store #500

Store # 1000

Even I started to feel good about how Papa John's was doing. This was a huge change in my personal outlook on life. Ever since I started making pizzas in the broom closet, I was terrified that the company would fail. In the back of my mind, I thought that somebody, somewhere, was going to turn the lights off. Maybe it was the result of my mother's influence. I will never forget her telling me that I would be worthless if I couldn't provide for my family and my loved ones. That's why I was always so afraid of Papa John's going under. I was still afraid in 1996, three years after we went public. It didn't matter how well we were doing. I look back at pictures of myself from this time period and I see my fear written all over my face. I wasn't enjoying Papa John's success. In my mind, we were still on the verge of someone turning off the lights.

My high-school baseball coach, Travis Nay, was the one who made me realize I didn't need to feel this way anymore. Travis has been a huge help to me throughout my life. To this day, we still work out together at least once a week. He's always been full of wisdom, too—the lessons you learn in sports often apply in other areas. Sure enough, we were talking one day in the middle of 1997. That June, we opened our 1,500th store, meaning we'd grown by 50 percent in only ten months. Travis had been aware of my faults and my personality ever since I played ball for him in high school. He could read me very well. Specifically, he could tell that I feared that Papa John's was about to fold, even though it was doing better than ever. So in the middle of our conversation, he asked me, "John, why are you acting like a soldier?"

I didn't understand what he meant. He kept going. "You're acting as if you're fighting a war." He was right: that's actually how I felt. We were in a serious battle with our competitors, after all, and we still had incredible room for growth and expansion. That goes with the territory in the world of business. However, I was acting as if we were fighting for our lives—like we were still trying to turn a profit in the broom closet. Deep down, I was literally afraid that Papa John's was on the verge of collapse.

But my fears didn't reflect reality. No one was going to shut off our water or our electricity—far from it. We were a thriving company that made better pizzas than our competitors. As a result, we were expanding faster than ever. Our franchisees loved us. Our suppliers loved us. Our shareholders loved us. And most importantly, our customers loved us. I didn't need to act like we were still making pizzas out of a broom closet in the back of a run-down bar in Jeffersonville, Indiana. Travis summed up that sentiment up perfectly: "If you don't want a war, don't act like a soldier. John, Vietnam is over."

That stuck with me. He was absolutely right. Papa John's was thriving. We were growing faster than ever. We were winning awards left and right. The company was on the right track. I just had to recognize and appreciate what was happening all around me.

Travis Nay (back right) and my high school baseball team, I'm in the back row, third from the left

Unfortunately, this realization came at the worst possible time. Papa John's story was one of more-or-less constant improvements between the broom closet in 1984 and our 1,500th store in 1997. But the good times couldn't last forever. Right when it seemed like we were on the verge of greatness, we started to plateau, then we started to decline. If Papa John's wasn't in a war at the start of 1997, we definitely were by the year's end. Little did I know it was going to be a war for the company's soul.

· · · · ·

Like every war, the warning signs were there well in advance. Unfortunately, neither myself nor anyone else at Papa John's recognized them until it was too late. We were on top of the world when 1997 started. We were expanding incredibly fast, more and more customers were visiting our stores and we were getting recognized for being at the top of our game. The *Restaurant & Institutions* award in particular was a real achievement—we were #1 in overall customer satisfaction and product quality among national pizza chains. We were beating all of our competitors, and everyone knew it.

Yet as so often happens, our success started going to our heads. We started to get fat and happy.

The problems began to manifest themselves shortly after we received the *Restaurants & Institutions* award. It wasn't a dramatic shift—far from it. I started to see little things here and there. Small comments from company leadership and franchisees. A lack of attention to detail from team members at our stores. A few pizzas that weren't at the level we demanded. A few other things.

At first I didn't think much of it—everyone has some bad days, after all. But the little things didn't stop. Whether you're getting better or getting worse, it always happens the same way: incrementally, one step at a time. Sure enough, that's what happened at Papa John's through the rest of 1997. The problems started to get bigger, slowly but surely. By the end of the year, I started to fear that we were losing our focus as an organization. I was absolutely right.

At this point I had to figure out what was happening. Over the following months, I toured the country to visit Papa John's stores. This has always been an important part of my role as the company's founder. I've always known what makes Papa John's Papa John's—how we should operate—down to the smallest detail. This is especially true when it comes to two things: the quality of our pizzas and how we treat our customers. The pizzas have been an obsession of mine ever since I made my first one at Rocky's Sub Pub. I've always had an intuitive grasp of what makes a good pizza, but it still took me two to three months of constant tinkering before I finally got the Papa John's recipe right. I could tell it was right when the customers at Mick's Lounge cleaned their plates and asked for seconds. Similarly, I've always gone to great lengths to make sure we treat our customers with respect and courtesy. If you talk to a rude Papa John's team member on the phone, or if the delivery guy is 15 minutes late, chances are you're not coming back to Papa John's. It's our job to give the customer what they want, when they want it. Actually, it's our job to exceed our customers' expectations. Customer loyalty is won—and lost—one customer at a time.

It was clear to me that we weren't paying attention to either of these things at the end of 1997. We weren't making traditional, superior-quality Papa John's pizzas. Nor were we giving good customer service. We were acting more like a true chain restaurant than the independent pizzeria we aspired to be. We had the principles, but we weren't practicing them. We were talking the talk, but we definitely weren't walking the walk.

Once I realized this, I started to search for an explanation. Papa John had to figure out what was wrong with Papa John's. After some investigation and reflection, I discovered two different but related problems.

First, some of our leadership weren't acting like the leaders they were supposed to be. This was a byproduct of Papa John's incredible success over the previous few years. Some of our executives and franchisees grew complacent as they became successful. They also got distracted by the trappings that came along with success. Instead of focusing on Papa John's, they focused on boats, vacations, golf club memberships, fancy cars and so on. As a result, some of Papa John's so-called leaders were no longer leading. Put another way, they were no longer preaching the gospel of using better ingredients to make a better pizza. But if we weren't preaching the gospel, we weren't making any new converts. And the converts we already had—whether they were customers or our team members—were starting to lose their faith.

The second problem was potentially even worse. I could tell that Papa John's was struggling, but we didn't have any way to measure anything we did. We weren't measuring either the quality of our pizzas or the quality of our customers' experience. This was also a byproduct of Papa John's recent successes. Early on in the company's history we measured everything through personal involvement in every store. In fact, I was personally involved in the founding of every Papa John's site up until store 1,500. After that point I simply couldn't keep up with our expansion. Neither could anyone else. In such an environment, our quality began to slip. We weren't making the traditional, superior-quality Papa John's pizzas that our customers knew and loved. Nor were we delivering the superior-quality customer service that millions of people had come to expect.

Store #1,500 in Dallas/Ft. Worth, TX
Opened on June 20, 1997

Let me explain what I mean when I say our quality was slipping. I don't mean that we were making pizzas that didn't taste good or were inferior to our competitors. That was never the case, which explains why we kept growing and why more and more people wanted to try Papa John's. However, we weren't making pizzas that were up to *Papa John's* quality. We were neglecting what made a Papa John's pizza so unique, so different and so wildly popular. We had always held ourselves to a higher standard, whether it's the pizzas we made or how we treated our customers. We always focused on surpassing our previous best. Now, for the first time, we weren't doing that.

At first I didn't understand why. I thought we had a sound measurement system in place. In fact, we had a pretty good ranking system that we used to evaluate our pizzas. We started developing this system in the mid-1990s, around the time we began developing FASPAC. This decision reflected the six values that made up our code of ethics. You can't have "superiority" or "constant improvement" or "accountability" or "focus" or "attitude" or "People Are Priority Always" if you don't also have some way to measure what you're doing. I'm a firm believer that "what gets measured gets done" and "what gets rewarded gets repeated." In fact, you'll find these exact words throughout our Papa John's facilities. In our headquarters, for instance, they are right above the doorway into our quality assurance kitchen. That's where we tinker with new recipes, analyze and improve the quality of our traditional Papa John's pizzas. We're always fine-tuning. We're always refining. We're always getting better. If we aren't, we're in deep trouble, which is where we found ourselves in the late 1990s.

The scale we developed was simple. We still use the basic format today to measure our pizzas, although we've made a lot of improvements over the years. It goes from 1 to 10. The three key sections are the crust, the cheese and the toppings. Each of these three parts contains various items that need to be measured, and then we measure each individual slice. For the crust, we make sure it's the right size and that cheese and toppings don't spill over onto it, which would make each slice difficult to pick up. Next comes the cheese. Each slice needs to have good "edge lock," meaning the cheese is patted down at the crust to make sure the tomato sauce doesn't spill out. This also prevents air bubbles from developing between the crust and the cheese. Each slice must also have the correct amount of cheese to begin with,

Sign above quality assurance lab

and it must be fully cooked and not burned. Finally, the toppings must be properly distributed across each slice. We have specific measurements for literally every topping we have. Remember: what gets measured gets done, and what gets rewarded gets repeated.

Whenever any item is missing or insufficient, we deduct points from a pizza's score. Our rule has been the same ever since we first introduced this grading system: if a pizza is less than an eight, we shouldn't serve it. No exceptions. A pizza that's below an eight is insulting to our customers, who expect better from Papa John's. Our slogan, after all, is "Better Ingredients. Better Pizza." A better pizza isn't just an okay pizza. We demand and expect excellence. That's why when a store makes perfect-10 pizzas, I send them a personally-signed thank-you note. The people who practice what we preach at Papa John's deserve to be recognized.

But excellence is exactly what we *weren't* getting by the end of 1997. I was 36 by the end of that year, but my unerring focus on quality hadn't diminished at any time since I founded Papa John's. It didn't take me long to figure out what kind of pizza each store was making when I visited. My routine is always the same when I step into a store to see how it's doing. To this day, the first thing I do is give every team member a high five. Then I make a beeline for the boxing station so I can see what kind of pizzas we're making.

The original "Ten Point Perfect Pizza" scale

Picture of a perfect-10 pizza

Imagine my surprise when I arrived at stores to find they were churning out fives, sixes and sevens—and sometimes even fours. By the middle of 1998, it was clear to me that we weren't making a pizza worthy of the Papa John's name. We had the better ingredients, but they weren't translating into better pizzas.

Worst of all, our stores were making these low-quality pizzas even when they knew I was coming to visit. This was shocking. I thought to myself, "If this is what they're making when I'm here, then what are they making the rest of the time?" As soon as I left the store, I knew they would go back to making fives, fours, or maybe even worse. Those are the types of pizzas the customers don't finish—and why those customers sometimes don't come to Papa John's again. I'd learned what customers wanted in a pizza from my time washing dishes at Rocky's Sub Pub as a 15-year-old. The sink where I washed dishes was directly across from where the Fondrisis made the pizzas, so I had a good view of how customers reacted to our pies. If a pizza was an eight or above, the pizza pans came back empty. If it was a five or below, the plate would come back with half the pizza still on it. They didn't even want to take it home. At age 15 I already had an intuitive grasp of what the customer wanted on his or her pizza.

This lesson was reinforced to me when I started making my own pizzas in the broom closet. The customers at Mick's Lounge were my focus group. If I made a nine or a ten, they devoured the pizza. If I made a four or a five, they sent it back half-eaten.

Yet by late 1999 and early 2000, fours and fives were exactly what we were making at many of Papa John's stores. At first I was baffled. We had a system to measure our pizzas. So why weren't we making good ones? I slowly began to learn an important lesson. It isn't enough to just have a measurement system. We had one, but it didn't seem to make much of a difference. It turns out that's only half of the puzzle. Just as important is a system for *implementing* that measurement system across an entire organization. We needed to start monitoring the pizzas we made—all 200 million each year. If we could start monitoring them, we could ensure that every Papa John's pizza was a traditional, superior-quality pizza.

But we had to figure out how to do that. This was a monumental task—definitely the biggest hurdle Papa John's faced up to that point. In many ways, we were starting from scratch. I asked many of my friends and peers for their thoughts and insight. I distinctly remember talking to Jack Laughery, the late and great CEO of Hardee's restaurants. He was one of Papa John's best and brightest board members. He also had tons of experience and knowledge, considering he had run a restaurant chain that had roughly 3,000 stores when he retired.

One day in 1999, I asked him, "Jack, how do you measure 200 million pizzas a year?" I also asked him how we measured the way Papa John's team members interacted with our customers. I wanted to make sure we were treating them with respect and courtesy. Jack had no idea. No one did. And that included me.

In fact, no one in the Papa John's boardroom or in senior leadership knew the way forward. Many of them had lost their focus. As I mentioned before, Papa John's incredible success in the mid-1990s had gone to many people's heads. Quite a few people became millionaires overnight. Now they thought they could skate by and do a half-assed job. They were willing to put Papa John's on cruise control rather than keep pushing on the accelerator. Rarely have I seen such a disrespectful attitude. It is rude to our team members, franchisees, suppliers and, above all, our customers. Laziness doesn't lend itself to constant improvement. It does the opposite—it leads to a decline that can ultimately kill any business, big or small.

I'm happy to say that not everyone fell into this trap. One such person was our president, Blaine Hurst. He started at Papa John's in 1995 and quickly rose through the ranks. Unfortunately, he presided over the start of our downturn when he became president in 1999. This was a new position for the company. Previously, I had exercised the duties of president under the title of CEO. I still kept my title as CEO of Papa John's when Blaine came on board, but he was charged with running the company on a day-to-day basis.

We made this change for one simple reason. Our quality had been slowly declining for years. I couldn't figure out how to stop it. So I determined that others should have the opportunity to do what I couldn't. Hopefully they'd be able to figure the solutions to our problems. I was still involved with the company, of course. I have always featured heavily in our advertising campaigns, and I continued to visit our stores to check in to see how we were doing. In the meantime, Blaine Hurst was charged with putting Papa John's back on the right track.

I have the highest respect for Blaine. He did a lot of good for Papa John's. He is extremely intelligent, hard-working and a dedicated family man, all of which helped contribute to Papa John's culture.

Blaine's greatest strengths lay in the world of technology. He worked for Boston Market before he joined us in February 1995. We knew we wanted him, so I personally flew out to meet him, his wife and their son. He started showing me all the complex technology and systems he implemented at Boston Market—none of which I understood. Now, I've never been the best at recognizing the need for technology. I remember in 1987 when Denise told me we needed a printer for the office at the Clarksville commissary. I had no interest in what I thought was an extravagant expense. I responded, "The copy machine doesn't make pizzas." I've always been so caught up with our main product that I have sometimes ignored other things the business needs. Fortunately, I've surrounded myself with people who help me overcome my weakness.

Blaine did exactly that. We basically had no computers at Papa John's when he first came on board. His first job was to institute a system-wide technological system that would increase productivity across the company. There was no doubt in my mind that Blaine could do that—he was brilliant. But his initial ideas were all over the place. They were also way too complex for most people to understand. I quickly realized that he needed some guide posts to help point him in the right direction. Specifically, he needed something that showed him the principles and fundamentals he needed to protect and enhance. So on a flight from Denver to Phoenix, I explained to Blaine what I called the "Ten Commandments for Technology." They kept him focused on devising a cutting-edge technological system that complemented Papa John's strengths and improved the company overall.

Using this framework, Blaine designed a point-of-sale system that could be implemented across literally every Papa John's store. That system, which we called PROFIT, was so successful that it lasted for *15 years*. It was simple, it was effective, it complemented store-level operations and our team members easily figured it out. As a result, it improved communications between stores and headquarters. I can't thank Blaine Hurst enough for the system he designed.

Better Ingredients.
Better Pizza.

Information Systems 10 Commandments

Established 1995

John H. Schnatter

1) Thou shalt keep the fundamentals of store-level operations as the number one priority in developing, modifying and improving information systems. *(If it doesn't help our store-level team members do their job better, it isn't an improvement)*

2) There shall be only one in-store system (POS) used by Team Papa John's: The Papa John's PROFIT System

3) The Papa John's PROFIT System shall have no more than three store-level configurations.

4) No other information systems projects shall be put before the system-wide roll-out, support and maintenance of The Papa John's PROFIT System.

5) Thou shalt be held accountable for meeting deadline and budgets.

6) Thou shalt not install any computer hardware or software without also providing proper training. *(To allow our team members to benefit from the installation)*

7) If we install it, we must support it, and do so in a distinctive, unmatched way.

8) Thou shalt not add "bells and whistles" that unnecessarily complicate our systems. (Keep-It-Simple at all times)

9) Thou shalt follow the channels, systems, and processes implemented by the Information Services Group for developing, acquiring, and deploying Papa John's information and technology resources.

10) All information system and technology development, acquisition, improvement, modification, and deployment shall be approved by the Vice President of Information Systems.

My "Ten Commandments of Technology"

But for all the good Blaine did, he wasn't able to stop the decline in quality, much less start to restore things to where they were in 1997. When I handed the reins over to him in 1999, our quality had been slowly slipping for nearly three years. It kept slowly slipping over the next year and a half. Ultimately, Blaine's enhancements to the company couldn't overcome Papa John's substandard quality and customer service. He may have slowed the decline down, but that wasn't nearly enough. A slow and steady decline is still a decline. There's no way around that. I saw this myself as I visited Papa John's stores. The company was still on the wrong track. And the longer you're going in the wrong direction, the harder it is to get back to where you started.

People outside the company slowly started realizing that Papa John's was in trouble. By late 2000 and early 2001, the shareholders could smell that something was wrong. When I stepped aside in 1999, our share price was $43. It fell by half—to $21—by the end of 2000. Papa John's continued to grow during this time, reflecting my belief that even a mediocre Papa John's pizza is better than the competition. But mediocre doesn't cut it. People, from customers to investors to everyone in between, had come to expect excellence from Papa John's.

To be clear: Papa John's problems weren't Blaine's fault. The real problem was that we were selling 200 million pizzas a year but didn't know how to measure their quality. The company was facing problems that were bigger than any of us knew at the time. Even the founder of the company—me, Papa John—didn't know what to do or how to fix things. Blaine did the best he could with the reality he was facing, but he didn't know what to do to fix the company. Again, I can't blame him for this. I didn't know what to do, either. We were all equally confused and concerned.

Understandably, he couldn't stay in that situation forever. Blaine Hurst abruptly left Papa John's on December 22, 2000—Christmas week. Personally, I was very sad to see him go. He did a lot for Papa John's during his five years on our team. He was unfortunate to be where he was when the dark years began. But now he was gone. I had to step back up and take the reins again.

I knew I was facing a real crisis. Over the previous four years, I watched the company's decline as if it were a slow-motion disaster. It seemed to me like we'd lost the trust and confidence of everyone, from our investors to our customers. Once you lose that trust, it's incredibly difficult to gain it back.

But we had to regain it somehow. Papa John's was struggling for one simple reason: we weren't doing what we were supposed to be doing. We weren't walking the talk. We weren't practicing the principles that took Papa John's from a broom closet to 2,000 stores in 15 years. We had lost our way. Now we had to find it again. In some ways, I felt like I was an 8- or 9-year-old again. It was as if I was sitting next to my Papaw on the broken tractor. He was telling me to "fix it."

There was definitely a lot to fix. The stock had plummeted. Our pizza quality wasn't up to Papa John's levels. Customer service was awful. Morale was falling. If we didn't get back to the fundamentals of quality pizzas and customer experience, Papa John's was on the path to becoming nothing more than just another mediocre national chain.

But here's the thing: I knew what to fix, but I didn't know how to fix it. I kept asking myself and others the same question over and over: "If what gets measured gets done, then how do we measure 200 million pizzas a year?"

I simply didn't have an answer. Nothing I tried or thought or came up with between 1997 and 2001 worked. I felt utterly helpless when I came back to take the helm at Papa John's after Blaine left. I looked around the company and I looked inside myself, but couldn't figure out the path forward. Without anywhere else to turn, I looked outside the company for help. There was only one man on the planet who could help me turn Papa John's around. He was a very tough and smart businessman from out West—a modern day gunslinger. His name: Dino Cortopassi.

●   ●   ●   ●   ●

Dino Cortopassi is a man who defies explanation. But let me give it my best shot.

Dino is an authentic Italian who loves homemade, high-quality food and lives by traditional Italian values. He's well over six feet tall, with broad shoulders. He has an intimidating presence to him. Even when he's in the best of moods, he's still the toughest guy I've ever met. Yet despite his rough edges, Dino Cortopassi is honest, brilliant, and wildly successful. He understands intuitively that what gets measured gets done and what gets rewarded gets repeated. In fact, Dino Cortopassi has the most brilliant strategic and business mind I've ever encountered.

Dino grew up as a farmer's son in the central valley of California. His family farmed grains, beans, tomatoes, orchard crops, and more. He started helping his dad out on the farm at the age of five. In 1978, he bought Stanislaus Food Products. (He has since retired and his nephew Tom is now president.) The company was originally founded in 1942 by traditional Italians living in California. During World War Two, Italians were viewed as collaborators with the Nazis, so the founders named the company after Stanislaus County where the business was located. Years later, they would run an ad campaign that explained the origins of its name. The ad asked, "Why does the 'Real Italian' Tomato Company have a Polish Name?!" That ad has always made me chuckle.

I first learned about Stanislaus when I worked at Rocky's Sub Pub when I was 15 years old. Rocky's exclusively used the company's fresh-packed tomato sauce. From the moment I tasted it, I knew it was the same sauce I would use if I ever started making pizzas myself. Sure enough, the first pizza I made in the broom closet was made with Stanislaus fresh-packed tomato sauce. Simply put, Stanislaus Food Products makes the best tomato sauce I've ever had. I have admired the company since I first tasted their sauce in 1976.

Why? Because Dino Cortopassi built a major company that has always behaved like a small, independent one. I realized we shared the same vision from the moment we met in 1995. Since our founding, Papa John's has been dedicated to making traditional, superior quality pizzas ever since the broom closet. Stanislaus Food Products looked for similar values in the companies they supplied their products to. If a Stanislaus customer didn't have a commitment to superior quality, Dino didn't think twice before turning around and walking away. He's too principled to compromise on the things that really matter, and has a set of fundamental beliefs that will never change. Nor should they.

Yet while we first bought Stanislaus fresh-packed pizza sauce in 1984, I didn't actually meet Dino until a decade later. We hit it off right away. This was actually surprising in many respects. In between 1984 and 1994, Papa John's experienced rapid multi store growth, and Dino became concerned that Papa John's was becoming "Chainy". Stanislaus didn't sell to national chains, pure and simple. Dino told me as much when we met. He said that as chains evolved they developed a "production mindset" rather than a "quality mindset." Businesses that are run under this mindset will focus on price, efficiency, etc.—none of which are as important as food quality. As Dino described it when we met, "chainy restaurants aren't for Stanislaus, we want quality-oriented customers"!

I had to convince Dino that Papa John's wasn't a "chainy restaurant"—we were the opposite. We may have been a national chain, but our explosive growth could be chalked up to the simple fact that we emphasized quality over everything else. We were no different than the small, independent shops he loved selling to. The only difference was we had a business model that allowed us to expand around the nation while still making traditional, superior-quality products. I urged him to rely on our promise to make a better pizza using better ingredients.

So Dino Cortopassi made an exception. So long as Papa John's maintained its dedication to quality, Stanislaus would keep selling fresh-packed tomato sauce to Papa John's for three reasons. First, because we started working with Stanislaus when I was dead broke making my first pizzas in a broom closet at the back of my dad's bar. Second, because he believed I was sincere about Papa John's commitment to quality; and third, because he liked me. It doesn't matter how much money you have—if you don't have those three things, Dino Cortopassi wouldn't do business with you.

Dino Cortopassi and John Schnatter

That's why I knew I had to talk to Dino after Blaine Hurst left Papa John's on December 22, 2000. On the one hand, I was afraid he would see what was happening at Papa John's and pull out. After all, Papa John's was no longer living up to the quality-first promise that I had made to Dino in 1994. But on the other hand, I felt he would appreciate that we'd been with Stanislaus for 16 years. Even though Papa John's was struggling, we still had the same values as Stanislaus. We were going to turn the company around. We just needed his help to do that. I desperately hoped that he would see my point of view.

These thoughts were going through my head as I called him. He picked up after a few rings. I cut straight to the chase—"Dino, I need your help." After briefly explaining my situation, he was quiet for a few moments. Then he said what I needed to hear: "I'll take a look at it."

I immediately breathed a huge sigh of relief. In retrospect, we were actually lucky that Papa John's problems all involved quality. I've subsequently learned that Dino goes out of his way to help customers improve their quality. Now I just needed to get in the same room as him. Dino agreed that we needed to meet in person in order to get on the same page. Unfortunately, he said that he and Stanislaus president, Bob Ilse, were on a fishing trip in the Florida Keys. So I told him, "Great, I'll meet you down there and we'll try to figure this out."

My sense of urgency showed Dino just how desperate I was. Papa John's had spent the past four-plus years making our problems worse. I wasn't going to waste another day.

I quickly made my way down to Florida and picked them up in my white Chevrolet Suburban. Right after I got them, Bob asked me why I didn't have a fancier car. My answer to him was simple: I bought it because it had a 350 Chevy engine. That's the kind of engine you can tinker with. The more expensive cars aren't like that—they're mostly computers nowadays. I'd rather have something I can mess with, something I can work on, something I can fix, something I can improve. Bob and Dino liked that.

Dino, Bob, and I laid out our game plan as we drove. We agreed that they needed to see first-hand what was happening at Papa John's stores. It wasn't enough for me to tell them—they had to touch and taste our pizzas to see how far our quality had fallen.

This is another characteristic of Dino's. He doesn't take anyone's claims at face value, but wants to see for himself. That's a good trait for any entrepreneur to have. You can't tinker—you can't improve—unless you're willing to get your hands dirty. You have to roll up your sleeves regardless of your job description.

I've tried to cultivate that same mentality at Papa John's. I expect all of our team members to exercise what I call "independent critical judgment." Here's what I mean by this: If you don't challenge my judgment, you weaken me. On the flip side, if I don't challenge your judgment, I weaken you. We must constantly challenge each other if we hope to constantly improve. This is a crucial lesson for long-term success.

We made our way to the closest Papa John's in Naples, Florida. Sure enough, the pizza was a four or a five at best. Then we went to a second store nearby. The same thing happened. The last Papa John's store we went to was off of Pine Ridge Road in Naples. Sure enough, the pizza wasn't Papa John's quality, making it three for three. As we left the store, I turned to Dino and said, "We have a quality problem." Dino looked at me, shook his head slowly, and said, "I think you're right. You've got a quality problem. Now let's find a way to strategically fix it."

So that's what we did. We piled back in my Chevy and drove to my condo in Naples. We sat down at my kitchen table and started talking through alternatives. Dino and Bob started throwing out ideas—and they had a lot of them. Dino in particular is one of the best strategic thinkers I know. He had actually designed a comprehensive quality management system for Stanislaus years before, which gave him a unique perspective on the challenges we were facing at Papa John's.

We stayed up into the wee hours of the night. But we weren't going to stop until Dino figured out a path forward. We finally got there—it must have been close to sunrise.

Dino and Bob provided me with a bullet-proof framework to systematically measure quality across all of our stores. Bob expressed the idea behind their strategic framework with a simple, pithy phrase: "It's the food, stupid." He meant that we had to focus on the food, and nothing else. In order to accomplish this, Dino said unequivocally that Papa John's needed the equivalent of a bureau of internal affairs. He put it this way: "You need good cops looking for bad cops."

At first I didn't understand what he meant. He explained it another way. We couldn't measure all 200 million pizzas we made, he said. Instead, we needed to get a picture of the average pizza by randomly sampling pizzas at Papa John's stores across the country. Put another way: We had to "take a poll," similar to how political campaigns poll a small number of people to determine how a broader group feels about a candidate or issue.

We needed an army of "secret shoppers" whose job was to buy Papa John's pizza everywhere. Then we would build a dedicated team at our headquarters whose sole job was to measure the secret shopper scores. By randomly analyzing enough pizzas over time, we could get a mathematically accurate average of quality at each and every Papa John's store. And finally we would fundamentally alter our bonus system so it was tied to these store-by-store metrics. Dino pounded home the message that "what gets measured, gets done"!

Dino and Bob were certain the system would work if we didn't stray from the strategy. They convinced me that if I followed through on the secret shopper program, I could finally get a solid grasp on the customer's experience at every single Papa John's store—from Louisville to Timbuktu. And then I could use that data to turn Papa John's around.

It seemed so simple the way Dino and Bob explained it. Once I understood the strategy, me and my team went to work developing the tactics in accordance with our mission and strategy. We spent the next few weeks filling in the blanks. By the end of the month me and my team hammered out a workable system that I was sure that Dino and Bob would approve of.

It's difficult to express just how much I owe Dino Cortopassi and Bob Ilse. It took them less than a week to solve a problem that had bedeviled Papa John's for more than four years. If it wasn't for them, Papa John's would be just another national chain restaurant that was synonymous with mediocrity. Instead, they helped us get in a position to get lucky—luckier than we'd ever gotten before. If I could build the system they sketched out, I could finally put Papa John's back on the path to becoming a powerhouse global brand. Dino Cortopassi and Bob Ilse basically saved my ASS!

• • • • •

Once Dino, Bob and I finished up in Naples, I called up the rest of the executive leadership team to let them know what we were going to do. They agreed immediately—they were nearly as desperate to fix Papa John's as I was. Within hours of stepping off the plane in Louisville, we were already working to build and implement the secret shopper system. It took us less than a month to implement the system we developed while sitting around that kitchen table. By the end of February 2001, we were ready to start measuring. After four years of deteriorating quality, we were finally on the way to fixing Papa John's.

It cost a sizable chunk of money to create our own department of internal affairs in such a short amount of time. Fortunately, the team itself didn't need to be that big. We hired roughly half a dozen people at our headquarters. Their sole job was—and is—to sample and measure Papa John's pizzas.

Here's how the system works. The team at headquarters works with several vendors around the country. The vendors' job is to hire average people to go in to Papa John's stores to buy pizzas—the "secret shoppers." The store team members have no idea who these people are, when they're coming, or what they're going to order. They order a small, medium, or large pizza with either one or two toppings, since the vast majority of our pizzas fall into these categories. They vary the order every time to make sure we're looking at a representative sample of pizzas. Once they have the order in hand, which they either pick up themselves or have delivered, they take pictures of it and send it back to headquarters. They also fill out a questionnaire that details the quality of the customer service they received. In a business built on delivery, quality service is just as important as the pizzas themselves. A rude deliveryman is liable to stop a customer from ordering Papa John's again.

The measurement starts once the pictures and data arrive back at headquarters. A team member uses a sophisticated program to analyze the pizza. They identify each slice to see how the crust, the cheese and the toppings stack up against the perfect pizza. We also measure the cross-section of each pizza to make sure it's cooked evenly. Once everything has been measured, we get the final score—hopefully one that's an eight or above.

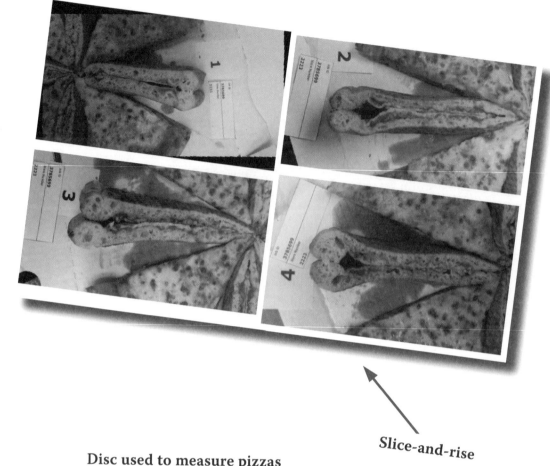

Slice-and-rise

Disc used to measure pizzas

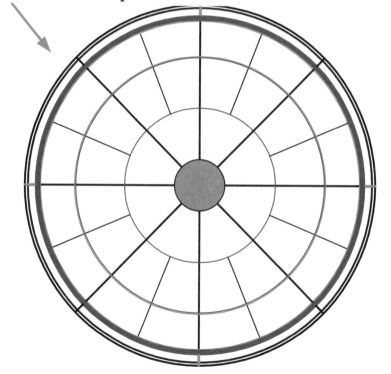

The Snapshot team does some of the most important work in the whole company. Every single Papa John's team member is affected by pizza scores. Our entire brand is built on the promise of "Better Ingredients. Better Pizza." This team helps us figure out whether we're keeping our word to our customers. If we aren't, our investors, our franchisees, our suppliers and every single one of our team members suffer.

That's why we're so relentless about measuring. After all, we believe that "what gets measured gets done," a phrase my co-workers hear me say constantly. We don't just measure a store's pizza once and call it a day. We go back time and time again to make sure they're making what they're supposed to make. The Snapshot team measures hundreds of pizzas a day—one of our team members holds a record of measuring 384 pizzas in one day. Papa John's corporate stores—those owned directly by the company—get measured four times every quarter. Franchise stores get measured three times a quarter. Finally, our international stores get measured between two and three times a quarter. The reason we measure corporate stores more often is because we're held to a higher standard. If we can't make a traditional, superior-quality pizza at our stores, what right do we have to hold our franchisees accountable?

This program has become increasingly sophisticated since we first introduced it in early 2001. Today we call it "Snapshot," because it gives us a snapshot of the pizzas made by each Papa John's store around the world. It's also a large part of corporate expenditures, costing us between three and a half and four million dollars per year. Yet this is a price worth paying in order to quantify and guarantee quality across over 5,000 Papa John's stores around the world.

Issues with quality were clear as soon as we flipped the switch and officially turned the system on. Within a few days, we began to get data back from Papa John's stores around America and the dozen or so foreign countries where we had a presence. That's when we found out just how bad things really were. Remember: our rule at Papa John's is that if it isn't an eight or above, it ain't worth serving. In the spring of 2001, the average Papa John's pizza was a 5.1. We were barely clearing 50 percent. That's an "F" grade any way you slice it. It's a wonder we were even slicing our pizzas the right way.

A 5.1 Pizza

I still cringe when I think about seeing that result for the first time. This meant that half of our pizzas were sixes and sevens, while the other half was threes and fours. We were lucky if even 10 percent of our pizzas made it to eight, to say nothing of nine or ten. I was doubtful we even made a single ten at that point. I believed that our competitors would have no problem serving the pizzas we were making. But we didn't take the country by storm in the mid-1990s because we served the same pizzas as our competitors. We spread like wildfire because our pizzas were *better*. Yet only a few years later, it was abundantly clear that we were no longer making Papa John's traditional superior-quality pizzas. We had truly lost our way.

Yet realization is the first step towards finding a solution. We had the numbers that proved we were on the wrong course. The next task was starting the long, hard task of getting back on track.

I knew that job now fell to me. As the founder of Papa John's, it was incumbent upon me to take the lead in fixing the problem. That process officially started at our Operations Convention in April of 2001 in Orlando, Florida. This event—which we hold annually—brings all of the Papa John's team together. By this time, Papa John's was closing in on 3,000 stores around the world. The event was attended by over 1,200 of our franchisees, senior management and key team members. About 50 percent more people attended compared to the year before. Anyone who was anyone in the Papa John's world was there.

Put another way, these were the people who set the example for the rest of the company to follow. As we had seen over the previous four years, a good number of them were no longer living up to FASPAC. The lack of focus in particular was incredibly obvious—and incredibly dangerous.

I had a fire in my belly when I took the stage to give the keynote speech. The whole room fell silent almost immediately. Everyone looked at me like I was some kind of miracle worker. For the first time in two years, the founder of Papa John's was back at the helm. This automatically inspired people and gave them hope that things would get better. They trusted that I would act in their best interests. You could feel the excitement in the room.

At the same time, everyone knew there were going to be some big changes. They were right. They just didn't realize how painful it would be—for all of us, including me.

I started off my speech on a casual note. I said I appreciated every-thing everyone was doing, their hard work meant the world to me, we would fix the company together, and so on. Then I made a statement that got everyone's attention. I said, "If you want to know the truth, this is going to be an easy fix. You guys just need to get your heads out of your asses."

Well, that didn't go over too well.

The crowd immediately started getting restless. This wasn't what they expected. But I kept going, full steam. I explained that we were no longer practicing the principles that made Papa John's successful and that our quality had completely deteriorated as a result. Then I told them about the new "secret shopper" program we had implemented only a month and a half before—a program almost no one knew any-thing about. Then came the data points—the 5.1 average pizza in par-ticular. The details were gruesome. The crowd was completely silent. It wasn't the uplifting, exciting speech most of them thought I would give.

Then I got really blunt. I said that everyone in the room was re-sponsible, starting with me. I told them what we had to do: get the product right. For the first time in Papa John's history, we would know if we succeeded in doing this. We would have the data to prove it thanks to the secret shopper program. Any store manager or franchi-see who failed to get their store and their team moving in the right direction would be held accountable. No one—at any level of the or-ganization—would have an excuse not to do so any longer.

The convention quickly turned tense—actually, that's an under-statement. Very few people wanted to recognize the problems that had festered over the previous four years. Even fewer wanted to fix them. There's a pattern that repeats itself in situations like this, not just at Papa John's, but at companies big and small around America. It starts when a company is doing well. Everyone's awake and dealing with reality. Then they start to fall asleep. They're asleep, but they think they're awake, even though they aren't. Eventually they wake up to the nightmare that grew while they were sleeping. They don't like what they find, so they try to go back to sleep. But the fact of the matter is that sooner or later you have to recognize the nightmare and deal with reality. You can't stay asleep forever.

That's where we were in April of 2001. We'd been asleep for four years straight by this point. No one wanted to wake up. But we had to. The future of Papa John's depended on it.

It was already clear that it would take a *lot* of work to fix our quality problem. We had to go from a 5.1 to an 8 or higher—a more than 50 percent jump. That was no easy task. Every member of the Papa John's team had to reaffirm their commitment to FASPAC. Every member of the Papa John's team had to Go Left.

It all started with me. I had to lead by example. If we were going to turn Papa John's around, I had to work harder than ever before— harder even than when we saved Mick's Lounge or built the broom closet and the first Papa John's. I had to model our principles and inspire others to do the same. As I've said before, a leader's attitude and outlook affect an entire organization. If I was asleep, or if anyone else in leadership was asleep, then the rest of the company would go to sleep, too. We had to be awake, we had to be energized and, above all else, we had to be focused.

• • • • •

The question now was, where should we start? Close to home, of course. The first Papa John's store we fixed was the one in our headquarters. How could we make traditional, superior-quality pizzas around America and the world if we couldn't even make them down the hall from my office?

Right after OpCon 2001, I went to Terri Lewis, the head cook at the pizzeria in Papa John's headquarters. Sadly, Terri passed away in September of 2016, although her husband Dave is still with the company in research and development. They're like family to me. Back in 2001, Terri was one of the first lines of defense when it came to quality. She knew how to make a good pizza. To her credit, she wasn't making the sub-par pizzas that I'd seen in other Papa John's stores. They weren't fives. But they also weren't eights. They were close, even if they still needed work.

This is where the Papa John's comeback was going to start. One day, I gathered up Terri and her team members to tell them what we were going to do. I said, "We're going to get a bunch of baby wins on the way to the grand victory." Then I pointed at Terri and said, "We're going to get it right here, then we'll get it right in Orlando, then we're going to get Lexington right, then we're going to get the eastern seaboard right, and then we're going to fix the whole damn thing. It starts here!" The team members cheered. Then we got to work. I spent hours with them in the kitchen. We went over the fundamentals. We smoothed out the rough edges. And we re-learned how to make a traditional, superior-quality Papa John's pizza.

It worked. Within a month, the Papa John's headquarters was cranking out eights, nines and even tens. Looking back, I still can't believe we ever made anything other than traditional, superior-quality Papa John's pizzas.

The time I spent in that kitchen helped me realize what I had to do for the rest of the company. If I was going to fix Papa John's, I had to find the problem stores and fix them myself. The other members of the leadership team had to do the same. It wasn't enough to tell franchisees and store managers what to do—we had to show them ourselves. If they saw how we did things and learned from our attitude and focus, they would follow our lead. We had to start a quality revolution from top to bottom.

We had our work cut out for us. Like I told the team members at The Hub (the central gathering place at our headquarters), Orlando was the next place we had to fix. Orlando has been one of our biggest and most important markets ever since we opened our first store there in 1993. Unfortunately, it was also one of the places where our quality had sunk the lowest. I recognized that as soon as I got there in summer 2001. I went store by store, checking out pizzas and training team members as I went. Some of my conversations with franchisees and store managers were unpleasant, even painful. They pushed back against everything I said—they didn't want to admit that any problems existed. But I wasn't going to accept that. If a store backslid after I left, I flew right back down. I must have returned to some stores seven or eight times in the first two months. It was hard. But we had no choice. We had to turn around our most important market.

It took us about six months before Orlando started showing some progress. It was exhausting. This was taking much longer than I originally anticipated. When we started down the road to recovery in April 2001, I figured it would take us less than a year to turn Papa John's around. I couldn't have been more wrong. Orlando made me realize just how many bad habits our team members had picked up over the previous four years. Those bad habits were rampant in Orlando, and they were rampant everywhere else, too. Unlearning those habits—and replacing them with new ones—was going to be a multi-year project. We had 3,000 stores to fix—and we had to fix 'em one by one.

The numbers backed this up. While I was in Orlando, the rest of the executive leadership team was fanning out over the country on similar missions. We gathered back together in late 2001 to see what we'd accomplished. We turned to the secret shopper program for answers. I expected us to be well on our way to an eight. To my shock, we'd only moved from a 5.1 to a 5.9. Yes, we were improving, but a 5.9 was still an "F."

I resolved then and there to spend as much time as was needed to fix Papa John's. I wasn't going to watch my life's work unravel. Winning is a habit—a habit that we had unfortunately lost between 1997 and 2001. We had replaced it with a different, and much worse, habit: losing. This bad habit had pervaded the entire company. Habits are already hard to break, but they're even harder when you have about 3,000 stores and roughly 65,000 team members spread between corporate stores and franchises. But I had to break the bad habits, no matter how hard it was, and no matter how long it took. I had to make sure every member of the Papa John's team had the right focus, the right mindset, the right priorities and the right understanding of the fundamentals that make Papa John's great.

So that's what I did. I hit the road again to visit stores and talk with managers and franchisees. Some cities were easy—usually those where we only had a few stores, or where my personal relationship with the leaders was strongest. Lexington, Kentucky was a good example. It only took us a few months to get those stores to a good place. Unfortunately, Lexington was the exception that proved the rule.

Worst of all, we kept finding more places where we were failing. In 2002 we also discovered that our customer service itself was becoming unacceptable. Later that year we began measuring how long it took between when a customer ordered a pizza and when it was delivered to their door. A staggering 23.4 percent of all orders took longer than 50 minutes—an eternity in the delivery world. (If it's 50 minutes, the consumer rounds up to an hour, and so do we.) If we wanted to fix this new crisis, we had to come up with a better way to measure the quality of our customer service.

So that's what we set to work doing. We created a system that now measures a number of different items. For instance, it looks at how many times the phone rings when a customer calls to order a pizza, whether the team member offers them any promotional deals and the quoted delivery time compared to the actual delivery time. Our goal is for every pizza to arrive before the quoted time—"under-promise and over-deliver," as we say. The main caveat is that any delivery over 50 minutes, even during the ultra-busy Friday and Saturday dinner rush, is completely unacceptable. We also started measuring how the delivery drivers acted once they got to a customer's house. The best team members thank customers for their business, smile and address the customer by name, wear the correct uniform and do more.

Ultimately, the driver is graded on a similar scale as the pizzas. And just like the pizzas, the customer service numbers were abysmal when we first started measuring. Papa John's had fallen a long way from the 1980s, when our slogan was "Fine People Serving Great Pizza." By the early 2000s, we still had fine people, but we didn't have great pizza. We had to have both in order for Papa John's to flourish.

Fixing these problems required immense effort. We quickly realized we couldn't turn the ship around by just telling store managers what was wrong. We had to go to the stores ourselves and show them the right way to do things. This meant going store by store, over and over, to make sure they were practicing what Papa John's preached. I personally visited hundreds of stores a year starting in mid-2001. Every time a major problem arose, I dropped what I was doing, hopped on a plane and flew out to fix it. So did other members of our executive leadership team. Of course, we couldn't spend all day every day doing this—we had a multinational company to run. We needed dedicated team members who could go to underperforming stores and help them out. Today, we have "Directors of Operations" and "Franchise Business Directors" who fill this role. Their job is to train team members to make a quality pizza and model excellent customer service. In the early 2000s, they certainly had their work cut out for them.

When I gave that first speech at OpCon 2001, I didn't realize how entrenched some of our franchisees were in the way they operated. I knew there would be pushback. But I got much more than pushback.

Some of the franchisees bitched and moaned every step of the way. They wanted easy fixes, which meant they weren't willing to make hard choices. They were very much asleep. The next few years were going to be a constant battle of wills between me and anyone who didn't want to wake up. But I had to wake them up and save Papa John's.

One specific story sticks out in my mind. Shortly after we introduced the "secret shopper" system, one of my most outspoken franchisees gave me a call to discuss the company's direction. To my surprise, the person told me we were focusing on the wrong thing. I respect this individual very much and appreciate their contribution to Papa John's, so I won't mention any names. Yet at this point we were very much in disagreement about what Papa John's needed to do. The franchisee told me that pizza quality wasn't the problem. Instead it was the lack of diversity on our menus. To fix this supposed problem, the person thought Papa John's needed to introduce a line of chicken wings and nuggets to round out our menu. Specifically, the person told me, "Chicken wings are the key to our success."

My jaw probably dropped to the floor when he said this. It's difficult for me to explain just how bad this idea was. Papa John's had grown like wildfire between 1984 and the late 1990s because we had stayed on strategy. We'd made better pizza using better ingredients. By the late 1990s we had forgotten our motto, which meant we had to remember it and live by it. That's what we had to do—preach the gospel and live by it.

Yet now this franchisee was telling me we needed to preach a different gospel. He wanted a pizza company to focus on *chicken wings*— something that had nothing to do with the pizza that made Papa John's such a success. Instead of focusing on what was most important, they wanted to focus on things that didn't matter.

I told this to the franchisee. I explained to him that we needed to focus on our core competencies rather than branch out into new ones. I thought that would be the end of things. But the individual in question had no intention of giving up on this idea. They kept bringing it up over the next few months, refusing to let it go no matter how many times I said it wasn't going to happen.

The situation came to a head at our 2002 Operations Convention—a year after I first called the whole Papa John's system on the carpet. The franchisee and one of their store managers came to talk

Examples of pizzas that are not up to par (each is a '5' on our scale)

to me at the start of the multi-day event. A few days later they were supposed to give a speech to the rest of the company. The person said they were going to get everyone else to see things their way. They were going to get chicken on the menu, whether I liked it or not.

I had no intention of letting that happen. It wasn't a matter of pride; it was a matter of principle. We had already lost our focus once as a company—that's why we were in such a bad place by 2001. We couldn't lose our focus again. If the franchisee got up in front of 1,200 people and told them we needed to focus on chicken wings, they could undo all of the work we'd done over the previous year. This could take us back to square one. It could also embolden others to come up with similarly stupid off-strategy ideas. Once that dam broke, who knew what damage the resulting flood could do?

I had to stop that from happening. I immediately called up the secret shopper program at headquarters. At my request, they spent the next two days getting data from the franchisee's stores. My hunch was that they weren't making pizzas worthy of the Papa John's name. How could they, since they were exerting all their energy on chicken wings rather than pizzas?

My hunch was correct. The average pizza score at the stores was a four. Some of the pizzas reached a six, while some reached as low as a *two*. A pizza that bad enrages me. It's insulting to the customers, to the suppliers, to everyone who helps make Papa John's tick. If you make that pizza, you're actually hurting all of us.

With this information in hand, I approached the franchisee and one of their store managers right before their speech at OpCon. I gave them an ultimatum. If they brought up chicken wings in front of the rest of the company, I would respond in my own keynote speech at the convention. Specifically, I would show everyone a slide with the person's average pizza scores at his or her stores. My goal wasn't to be vindictive. It was to show them how serious I was about fixing Papa John's quality. If we staked our identity on the claim that we make better pizzas with better ingredients, then the company's leaders better live by these words. That's basic accountability.

The franchisee turned white on the spot. We both knew the scores weren't good—they were usually between a three and a four. In fact, the franchisee had some of the lowest pizza scores in the entire company. Now I had the upper hand. Neither of us wanted for that information to go public, but I was willing to do it in order to keep everyone focused on improving the quality of our pizzas. The stakes were high.

Fortunately, the franchisee backed down. Later that day, the person stepped on to the stage and gave a rousing speech about staying the course. This particular franchisee had significant sway in the company. I needed them to publicly agree with my vision in order to inspire others. Further dissension would only worsen the serious problems we already had.

This was far from the only obstacle we had to overcome, although it was definitely one of the most memorable. Another one worth mentioning is from the Franchise Advisory Council meeting in 2002. Most of the attendees came to play the blame game. They were willing to point the finger at anyone if it took the focus off of them. They claimed food service profits were too high, saying that we had violated the gentleman's agreement we'd made years before that corporate would never make more than 3 percent profit off of the ingredients it sold to franchisees. They complained our technology wasn't good enough. They said our marketing was terrible. They raised hell about a dozen different things, none of which were true. After everyone had aired their grievances, I put my foot down. I said, "You need to fix your own stores before you blame anyone else." I continued, "Until you get your quality and your customer service right, don't tell me to fix anything." Again, you can't solve a problem by pointing fingers at others. Obfuscation only makes things worse.

Similar fires kept breaking out all over the place. Nor were they contained just within America, where most Papa John's stores are located. At one point I traveled to the United Kingdom, which was one of our fastest growing markets outside of the United States. I wanted to see for myself how our stores were doing there. Our domestic stores had made good progress, so I assumed that our international ones would also be on an upward trajectory. I couldn't have been more wrong.

The quality problem was even worse in the United Kingdom. The team members weren't even using the right ingredients, which prevented them from making a traditional, superior-quality Papa John's pizza, no matter how hard they tried. Even worse, they didn't seem like they *wanted* to try. I remember tasting one of those pizzas on my first day in the country. It was infuriating. It was like we were starting all over. You better believe I raised a big stink to the leadership team over there. We needed to make some changes in order to get them on the right track. As a result, two people rose to the top: Jack Swaysland and Gareth Davies. They have inspired the entire United Kingdom operation to get back to basics and start making pizzas worthy of the Papa John's name. They have heavily invested in quality control and measurement, as well as training so their team members knows what's right and what's wrong.

The proof is in the pudding—or, rather, the pizza. Thanks to them and the vision they've imparted to their team, the United Kingdom is one of our most important markets outside America. It went from one of our worst to our best, which shows what's possible when people preach—and practice—what Papa John's is all about.

No matter where I went during these four years, I saw the same situation repeated over and over. When we identified a problem, we talked to the team members responsible for creating it and laid out a plan for them to fix it. Yet more often than not, they didn't want to admit any problems existed. They wanted to avoid taking responsibility for making quality pizzas and delivering quality customer service. They used different tactics. They had different excuses. Some of them tried to rally others to their cause. A few franchisees actually jumped ship. They weren't willing to do what needed to be done. They were more comfortable asleep than they were awake.

It's always sad to see team members and partners leave in the midst of crises like this. But Papa John's was ultimately stronger for it. We had to separate the wheat from the chaff, no matter how painful it was. It didn't matter if they were making money hand over fist for the company—they still weren't making quality pizzas or treating the customer with respect. That's not the Papa John's way. And the Papa John's way is the best way to succeed in the long-term.

We weathered some serious storms as we tried to turn Papa John's around—literally. In the winter of 2003, the upper Midwest experienced a freak snowstorm that disrupted the delivery of ingredients to stores in the region. The store managers and franchisees were understandably upset about this. About 50 of them rented U-Haul and pickup trucks and drove down to the Louisville commissary to get what they needed. When they arrived, they were shocked to find me in the warehouse loading trucks with a dolly. I personally loaded all the dough into their trucks, taking only one sleep break over the next

48 hours. This showed them just how serious I was about fixing Papa John's. I was willing to do everything I could. From that moment on, they were definitely on my side.

Some weeks it seemed like there were too many fires to put out. But no matter what happened, I stayed on message. I wouldn't budge an inch. Papa John's needed everyone, at every level, to stay focused. That was the only way we could fix our sub-par customer service and our pizzas.

Keep in mind: Papa John's didn't stand still while all of this was happening. We were still growing during this period, for the simple reason that our pizzas were simply better than our competitors'. That never changed even when our quality dropped. We also kept innovating to stay ahead of the game. In 2001, for instance, we became the first pizza chain to offer online ordering at all of our corporate-owned restaurants. We recognized the revolutionary potential of the internet early on. Sure enough, our customers loved that ordering option. Online ordering took off and hasn't stopped since.

Meanwhile, our pizza quality was going up slowly but surely. In early 2002, shortly after I turned 40 years old, we finally cleared 6. By the middle of 2003 we were getting close to a 7. But that still wasn't good enough. An average of seven means that half the pizzas were still fives and sixes, which was unacceptable.

During this process it often seemed to me like we were backsliding at worst and making no progress at best. Many of our franchisees and managers fought me every step of the way.

I don't have time for people with that mindset. You *have* to focus on the customer ahead of yourself. You're supposed to help yourself by first helping others. It doesn't matter whether you're the manager of a store or the owner of a hundred franchises—the customer is still your boss. Sam Walton, the founder of Walmart, put it best. He said the customer "can fire everybody in the company from the chairman on down simply by spending his money somewhere else." These words are true for literally every business in the world.

It was my job to make everyone at Papa John's understand that. In all that I did between 2001 and 2004, I relentlessly focused on improving our quality and customer service. My life's work depended on it.

And it worked. In late 2004, we *finally* got to the point where Papa John's pizzas were averaging a score of eight or higher. Similarly, our customer service was doing much better across the board. The percentage of pizzas delivered over 50 minutes had dropped to below 5 percent. It goes without saying that we still had room to grow—constant improvement is one of our guiding principles, after all. In an ideal world, every pizza should be a perfect 10 and every delivery should be made in less than 30 minutes. Yet while we may not have reached perfection, we were finally back to a good place in terms of quality and customer satisfaction. Papa John's was back to being Papa John's.

I can't explain how this felt. The "dark years"—eight years total—were finally over. But this victory had come at an incredible cost. Between 2001 and 2004, we hadn't given an inch to anyone. My mantra to every Papa John's employee was, "We will make the product right, we will fix the customer service, we will smile, we will care about our fellow team members, and we will win together." Then I worked with franchisees, store managers and other team members to make sure we did just that. It was a painful process for all of us.

Many of the people who worked with us through this period are still with Papa John's. Some of them remember what happened like it was yesterday. Just recently, I was visiting some franchisees down in Miami, Florida, named Manny Overton and Ricky Warman. I asked them what it was like when I came down to their stores in 2004 to check on how they were doing. Manny took a deep breath before he answered: "We weren't making eight pizzas, that's for sure. But you gave us the wake-up call that we all needed."

Sure enough, Manny and Ricky recognized where they were falling short and they vowed to fix things. They believed in Papa John's mission: they wanted to make a traditional, superior-quality Papa John's pizza. So they focused on what they were supposed to do, and they did it through hard work and determination. They turned their stores around and then didn't stop. They haven't looked back ever since. They believe that Papa John's makes "a common thing uncommonly well," and they try to do that every day.

It shows. Their stores do almost double the national franchise average. That's only possible when you're living by the gospel of Papa John's—better ingredients, better pizza. Manny, Ricky and their team are real Papa John's heroes. They were actually the Papa John's franchisees of the year in 2015—that's how impressive they are.

But not everyone was like them. For every franchisee who saw the light, someone else wanted to keep living in the dark. I was relentless about calling them out. This naturally angered them. Some of our franchisees got downright angry with me. They resented my tenacity. I didn't just ruffle their feathers—I made serious enemies who wanted to take me down. It got especially bad as we got close to finally reaching our goal of eight-grade pizzas. It was like I was a personal trainer helping people lose weight. The goal was to get them to lose 60 pounds. Once they got to 50, they wanted to be done. They thought they'd gone far enough. But it was my job to get them all the way to 60. Losing those last 10 pounds required a lot of kicking and screaming. It was worth it, though. I wasn't going to let us settle for pizzas that were only a 7.5. We needed eights and better.

Sure enough, we eventually got there. Papa John's was finally back on track by the end of 2004. Yet the previous three years—especially at the very end—had taken a toll on the relationship between me and some of our franchisees. They were on edge after the previous few years, when I had come to their stores and reminded them how to make a traditional, superior-quality Papa John's pizza. A small number of them wanted to get back at me. It didn't matter to them that they were doing better in 2004 than they were only a few years earlier.

It would be wrong for me to name names. All I'll say is that they did everything they could to undermine me. They complained to their peers, they complained to the board, they complained to anyone who would listen. My personal favorite was when they said they didn't like my "style." I've always gotten a kick out of that. Does Wall Street or the customer care about my style? No, they care about the quality of customer service, whether we make a traditional, superior-quality Papa John's pizza and whether we're growing the business for the long-term. That's what matters to our customers and our investors. Therefore, that's what should matter to every member of the Papa John's team.

Unfortunately, a few of the disaffected franchisees were out for blood. They actually started attacking me in the media—saying that Papa John was a threat to Papa John's. I'd be lying if I said this wasn't incredibly hurtful. I had given everything to save Papa John's between

Examples of pizzas that score at the top end of our scale

2001 and 2004. Now I was being repaid with stabs in the back—and when it came to the public attacks in the media, stabs in the front.

This actually threatened to undo the progress we made over the previous four years. A company has to present a united front to both the outside and the inside world. A house divided against itself cannot stand. Internal disagreement is fine—it's actually necessary, because it strengthens you and causes you to confront things you may not have thought of. But it crosses a line when that disagreement spills into the open. That's when a company becomes endangered. Papa John's was now running that risk. People in the media and on Wall Street could tell there were serious tensions throughout the company. This led them to ask a valid question. Was Papa John's going to be torn apart by internal dissent?

I would never let that happen. Papa John's was my life's work—I couldn't stand by and let it die. Something had to give. I eventually realized that something was me.

I realized in late 2004 that I had to step down. That fall, I called up Bill Street, the chairman of our Governance Committee and the retired CEO of Brown-Forman Corporation, a major Louisville-based company that makes Woodford Reserve, Jack Daniel's and other high-quality liquors and wine. He definitely didn't expect me to say what I did. I asked Bill if he could help replace me as the head of Papa John's.

My reasoning was simple: a company can't survive very long when its founder is under attack by some of his own team. I understand that the price of being successful in America is getting attacked by the media and by your own government. That's just the country we live in. It's fine. I accept it. What I don't accept is getting attacked by some of the people who are supposed to be on my side. That can be fatal. If the founder gets attacked, the whole company could get hurt. Bill saw where I was coming from and promised to help. Over the next several months, the board and I figured out a way out of this predicament. I agreed to step down from my role as president and CEO. We would hire a new team to take my place. Although I would still be involved on the board and in marketing, I would no longer be calling the shots on a day-to-day basis. That would be the new team's job.

We brought in a new professional management team in early 2005. A number of new faces joined the corporate team. This immediately defused the franchisee tensions that were threatening to tear Papa John's apart. Everyone was happy—the few rebellious franchisees were happy that I was no longer at the helm, the board was happy that internal tensions were dissipating and I was happy that Papa John's was back to being the best. It seemed to everyone that Papa John's was poised for another period of tremendous growth and success. We had finally gotten back to fundamentals. Our foundation was finally strong. We had a huge runway ahead of us—the sky was the limit.

· · · · ·

A huge weight was lifted from my shoulders the day I stepped down as CEO. For the previous four years, I had worked even harder than I did when I was first making pizzas in the broom closet. I had worked seven days a week from 2001 to 2005, doing everything I could to save my life's work. It needed to be done. We climbed to incredible heights from the time we went public until the dark years started. That meant we had much further to fall. The bigger you get, the easier it is to learn bad habits and the harder it is to break them. Papa John's had well over 2,000 stores by the early 2000s, with tens of thousands of team members. As I learned firsthand, getting back to the fundamentals is an incredibly difficult task for a company that large. It was the hardest thing I've ever done in my life.

But it had to be done. I did what my Papaw would have wanted me to do. I had to "fix it," just like he told me to fix his old tractor when I was just eight years old. It took me four long, painful, torturous years to do that. Now, finally, Papa John's was fixed. Not only that, it was healthier than it had been since the 1990s. We were building new stores in America and internationally. We were bringing in new customers and keeping old ones. The balance sheet was strong. Overhead was low. The business model was proving its worth once again. And above everything else, we were making traditional, superior-quality Papa John's pizza. Looking at the business when I stepped down, I thought I'd never have to fix it again.

I was wrong.

CHAPTER SIX

— · —

HEAD COACH

A day doesn't go by where I don't think about the two men who made me who I am today: my Dad and my Papaw.

Robert Louis Schnatter and Louis Erman Ackerson were two very different men, as I described early on in this book. Everyone who knew them can attest to this fact. They treated their families differently. They ran their businesses differently. They used their money differently. They interacted with their communities differently. Even when I was very young, I could tell that their lives didn't look very similar. I say that as someone who learned valuable lessons from each of them. Maybe I learned so many lessons *because* they were so different—they each showed me different strengths and weaknesses.

Yet despite their many differences, they both seemed alike in my mind. They shared *something*—I just didn't know what it was.

It took me years of thought and reflection before I finally put my finger on it. I definitely didn't know what it was when my Papaw passed away in 1984. I hadn't figured it out when my Dad died a year later. And I still didn't have a name for it by the time we went public almost a decade later. It wasn't for lack of trying. Like I said, a day didn't go by where I didn't think of the two of them and the lessons they taught me. They were a constant source of help and guidance during the hard times we faced. When I had to Go Left to build the first Papa John's, when we developed FASPAC, when I had to "fix it"—in these and many other difficult situations, my Papaw and my Dad were a source of inspiration, comfort and hope.

But the mystery remained through all of this. Despite years of trying, I couldn't describe that strange something that they both shared. That changed after I stepped back from Papa John's in the late 1990s.

This was a new experience for me. I'd been working pretty much nonstop for roughly 15 years by that point. I had been putting in between 60 and 70 hours a week nonstop—often more. Now I was able to take a step back and look at Papa John's from a different angle, from the outside. This gave me a whole new perspective on the company and our incredible success. It also gave me ample time to reflect on my Dad, my Papaw and the principles, values and beliefs that they shared.

I collected and organized my thoughts over the next three years. It finally dawned on me: my Dad and my Papaw were each a "Head Coach." This was—and still is—one of the most important realizations of my entire life.

● ● ● ● ●

What do I mean by "Head Coach"? My Dad and my Papaw each gave me different answers to this question based on their lives, their words and their actions.

A Head Coach is a leader. More than that, he or she is a leader whose ultimate goal is to bring out others' potential. They want to help their team members become the best they can possibly be. In order to do this, a Head Coach has to preach—and practice—a specific set of virtues and values. It's a long and specific list, and it can change the world for the better when it's lived out.

A Head Coach has focus. They keep their eye on the ball. They emphasize the fundamentals because they recognize that the fundamentals are exactly that—fundamental. Just as important, they have a vision, and they share it with those around them. They want to build a team to make that vision a reality. Ideals are never enough for a Head Coach. They have to be used and applied in daily life to improve yourself and those around you.

Head Coaches refuse to lose, no matter what their odds are. They naturally want to win, but they also want to win fair and square. Why? Because playing by the rules—playing fair—is the single best way to inspire their team members and achieve long-term success. That's why Head Coaches lead by example. They don't let themselves become an exception and they treat people with dignity and respect—not only their team members but others as well. There's another word for this: integrity.

A Head Coach makes the tough choices. They have a good grip on reality and seek solid, factual data to inform their decisions. They ask for help when they need it, recognizing that they don't have all the answers. They build teams that overcome weaknesses and play to their strengths. They are willing to confront problems head-on rather than cover them up. They recognize their own shortcomings and take steps to overcome them. They have a "solid sense of self," as I call it. They also take responsibility for their actions and their mistakes—what I call "taking the hit." They self-confront, constantly analyzing how they can improve and how they can better help others around them. When they see a problem, they first look inwards and ask, "Does the problem start with me?"

A Head Coach never stops looking for ways to improve, because they recognize that everything can always get better, no matter how good it already is. There are absolutely no exceptions. Yet regardless of whether things are good or bad, a Head Coach has a positive attitude that inspires those around them. They know that their attitude affects everything around them, which is why they keep it positive at all times. And when they see a problem, they roll up their sleeves, get their hands dirty and fix it. No job is too small for a Head Coach.

This is crucial: a Head Coach does everything in order to help their team. They want to see their team members grow, both personally and professionally, and they take steps and develop systems to make that happen. That includes building "collaborative alliances"—the mutually beneficial relationships where people get ahead together, instead of one person getting ahead at others' expense. On that note, Head Coaches share in everyone else's ups and downs. They constantly communicate with their team members in order to understand them and help them achieve their potential and find fulfillment.

That's also why Head Coaches practice "collaborative confrontation." The meaning of this is simple. If I don't challenge your judgment, I weaken you, and if you don't challenge my judgment, you weaken me. The Head Coach both challenges his team members and wants to be challenged by them so that everyone can grow together. A Head Coach also gets their team members to be open and honest about what they're seeing and experiencing. I'd rather not hear, "I was going to say something, but I didn't". We can only fix the problems we know about.

Head Coaches are fair. They treat everyone with the respect they deserve, regardless of whether they're chairman of the board or the company janitor. They build trust between themselves and their team. They model what they're looking for, inspiring others to rise to the occasion. They genuinely care about others and want them to succeed. They try to put people in the positions where they're most able to contribute and grow. They try to bring out the best in people and spur them to improve and become even better. They pat people on the back rather than tear them down. They feel a responsibility to take care of their team.

Head Coaches also give team members a chance to learn from their mistakes. When someone falls down, the Head Coach comes alongside and asks, "Are you okay?" Then they help them get back on their feet and try again. They want the team to win together and lose together with no exceptions.

I could keep going. A Head Coach manifests the critical qualities of heroism, courage, humility, kindness and mutual respect. Ultimately, a Head Coach knows success is a team effort. They know they aren't the one on the field winning games—the entire team does that together. The Head Coach humbly recognizes that the team as a whole, rather than any one individual, is responsible for success. And that's why they work so hard to help every team member, regardless of their role, reach their full potential.

At the end of the day, a Head Coach gives you intangible assets that are far more important than money, power and winning. A Head Coach gives his or her team members a sense of pride and dignity. They feel like they're part of something special, something bigger than themselves, something that makes the world a better place. Money can't buy that kind of feeling.

There's so much more to say about what a Head Coach is and why they're so important. If you're living a Head Coach model in the business world, your company can become a people-growing machine. These are the companies that truly change the world. It really is a beautiful thing.

A few recent examples of specific individuals may help illustrate what I mean. My Dad and my Papaw are the obvious candidates, even though they both had shortcomings. (All Head Coaches do.) But they are far from the only ones.

For example, I have huge respect for Dabo Swinney, the head coach of Clemson University's football team for the 2015 season. He led his team to the national championship game—an impressive feat in and of itself. But that isn't what makes him a Head Coach. Right before the Orange Bowl, three of his players were caught violating the team's behavior policies. This presented Swinney with a choice. He could have tried to cover it up. He probably could have pulled a few strings to keep them around. Why not? It could have helped his team win. But he didn't do that. Instead, he did the right thing. He sent them home right before the big game. That took guts. Head Coaches have the guts to do the right thing.

This is only one recent example—I could name dozens more. You've probably met a number of Head Coaches in your own life. Maybe it was one or both of your parents. Maybe it was a teacher in school. Maybe it was an actual coach. Maybe it was a boss at your first job. Head Coaches are sadly rare, but most people are fortunate to find one or two throughout their life.

I certainly was. My Dad and my Papaw both modeled the Head Coach mentality in different ways. That tremendously influenced me—I was on their team, after all. Their influence helped me become the entrepreneur I am today. In their own unique ways, both of them went to great lengths to help me reach my full potential. I have met others who I would describe as Head Coaches, yet none of them were as important to me as my Dad and my Papaw.

The world of business is a natural place for Head Coaches. When you think about it, the best businesses are usually led by someone who fits this description. The traits that define the Head Coach are the same traits that make a good president or CEO. They build up their teams and they make tough choices. When a business leader acts like a Head Coach, their company can do truly amazing things. These are the businesses that truly make people's lives better through customer focus and innovation. They're fundamentally good businesses—the type of business I've always wanted Papa John's to be. We will always have more to do, but I intend to wake up every day with that goal in mind.

This realization awoke something in me—something intense. I suddenly wanted to spend more of my time figuring out what makes a good business, as well as what makes a good business leader. Around this time, I began working with several other key members of the Papa John's team to identify other businesses that were run by Head Coaches. We didn't have a name for it at the time—I wouldn't start using the term "Head Coach" until 2005—but we knew what some of their characteristics were. We were looking for clean businesses, honest businesses, businesses that were very intentional about making the world a better place through entrepreneurship and innovation.

We identified quite a few. Over the years I've met a large number of entrepreneurs and executives who are Head Coaches of the finest kind. (Sadly, I thought I'd meet many more Head Coaches than I have. I also thought, foolishly, that everyone at Papa John's was a Head Coach. But we'll get to that in the next chapter.)

A few come to mind pretty quickly. Scott Colosi, the president of Texas Roadhouse, is a good example. He's an honorable guy who runs a good business. So is David Jones, the co-founder of Humana Insurance. He's in an industry in which it's very easy to be something other than a Head Coach. But he hasn't abandoned his principles, and I respect him for it. Jerry Richardson, the owner of the Carolina Panthers, is a Head Coach for similar reasons. It's easy to cheat and try to win by underhanded means in professional sports. Jerry doesn't do that, though, because he's a Head Coach. And to be clear, you don't have to be the CEO or the owner to be a Head Coach. Take the example of

Charlotte Anderson, an executive at the Dallas Cowboys. She's a great example of someone who does the right thing and builds up her team.

The last person I'll mention is the late S. Truett Cathy, the founder of Chick-Fil-A. His company's continued success is a testament to the fact that he was a true Head Coach. The company is renowned for making quality food and for treating its team members well—a hallmark of a Head Coach.

We also identified some Head Coaches in the long list of Papa John's suppliers. I'm very proud that Papa John's partners with men and women who focus on their teams' well-being and success.

All of these businesses share one thing in common: they're fundamentally good businesses that focus on quality and treat their people right. Those are the same principles that I founded Papa John's on, even going back to when I was coming up with recipes and menus in LaFollette dorm at Ball State University. It turns out a good business is a business that can be tremendously successful in the long run. Amazing things can happen to the companies that follow this model and to the people and communities they touch.

Looking at these companies—and the men and women who ran them—inspires me. I wake up every morning and ask myself what I can do to be a Head Coach like them. I will always have a long way to go, but every day, I hope and pray I'm getting a little bit closer.

Let me tell one quick story before we go any further. It shows how the Head Coach model has been around a lot longer than I have. A few years back, I flew over to the United Kingdom to check on some restaurants and meet some franchisees. We arrived in the middle of what I thought was a light snowstorm, but it turns out that even light snows can disrupt the entire country. We ended up having to divert to Ireland, where we stayed in a town that had an ancient castle that had been converted into a hotel. It was really something. The day after we arrived, I asked the hotel manager: "Why aren't there more castles like this?" He responded: "The peasants burned them all down." My next question came quick: "Well, why didn't they burn down this castle?" The manager smiled and said, "The owner was a fair landlord who took care of the community."

That's what a Head Coach is all about. (It also hints that there's a different model that leads to disaster—just wait for Chapter Seven.)

If you don't take care of your team, your castle's gonna get burned down. But if you do take care of them, you can thrive. It's a powerful thing. Ironically, my interest in the Head Coach model began right as Papa John's quality was starting to decline in the late 1990s. When I came back to the company's helm in early 2001, I knew I had to act in a very specific way in order to turn the company around. I had to act like a Head Coach, even though I didn't yet have a name for it. In the context of Papa John's, that meant I had to practice our guiding principles—FASPAC—and Go Left on a daily basis. Fortunately, these paradigms are entirely consistent with the Head Coach model.

That's because the principles that make for a good, clean business are the same principles that make Head Coaches tick. Head Coaches Go Left and do what needs to be done, no matter how hard it is. They understand that "what gets measured gets done." And they exemplify and practice every component of FASPAC. They have focus. They have accountability—both with themselves and with their team members. They want superiority, because they want to be the best. They know that People Are Priority Always—they care about their team members' well-being. They model a positive attitude and are passionate about what they do. And last but not least, they understand that constant improvement is the name of the game. You'll never go to the next level if you aren't always getting better. That's just Business 101.

As I told you earlier, it took every ounce of my energy to turn Papa John's around from 2001 to 2004. It worked. Papa John's was getting back to its best by the end of 2004. After years of hard work, our stores were finally making the traditional, superior-quality Papa John's pizzas that they should have been making all along. Our customer service was also better than it had been in years. In the span of three years, we went from plummeting downwards to skyrocketing upwards. This turnaround was a testament to what is possible when people practice the Head Coach model.

But I couldn't have done it alone. I already told you about Bob Ilse and Dino Cortopassi, whose unparalleled strategic thinking helped me turn Papa John's around. They weren't the only ones who helped get the company back on the right track. Starting in early 2001, I did everything I could to inspire the Executive Leadership Team to join me in my righteous crusade. If Papa John's had any shot at getting back to its best, we needed a whole team of Head Coaches who could go out and guide their teams to victory. They got on board. The next three years saw all of us traveling around the Papa John's empire inspiring others and calling them to their full potential.

That's what the Head Coach model is all about. As the founder and CEO, it was my job to inspire those around me. Then it was their job to inspire the people around them. Remember: a Head Coach-run company is a people-growing machine.

I learned during this period that it's absolutely critical to get people at every level of an organization to contribute to success. That's at the heart of collaborative alliances. It's also mutually reinforcing: everyone at every level of the organization is holding each other accountable because they *want* to be held accountable themselves. If a company's executives can inspire the people who report to them, it can create a chain reaction that permeates an entire organization down to the store level. And once the people at the store level are on board, they can turn around and show their superiors exactly what it means to have a team mentality and a customer-focused attitude. This points to a simple lesson: a company should never be top-down. Instead, it should lean towards bottom-up. You have to strike the right balance in order for an organization to be successful in the long term.

There's one crucial ingredient I haven't really touched on so far: good people. They are absolutely crucial for an organization that's run on the Head Coach model. If you don't have good people at every level of an organization, it's very difficult to achieve your goals. You all have to be rowing in the same direction if you want to get to where you're supposed to go.

On that note, I have had the pleasure of working with great men and women throughout all of Papa John's history. Some of my team members have been among the best Head Coaches I've ever met. So have some our suppliers, franchisees, investors and others we've been able to work with over the years.

That was true even before Papa John's was around—the Fondrisis at Rocky's Sub Pub and Chris Karamesines at Greek's were excellent people who taught me so much. I practice lessons I learned from them to this day. Similarly, the people who worked alongside me at Mick's Lounge, and then in the broom closet, did an incredible amount of work to get Papa John's officially underway. Every chapter in Papa

John's history has been filled with people who woke up every morning, came to work, made pizzas and served customers with smiles on their faces, and helped take Papa John's from a broom closet to a bona fide pizza empire. They truly instill a sense of dignity into labor. Even the basic things we do on a daily basis are incredible when you see them in this light. My dream became the dream of so many people I've worked with, and we worked together to make it into a beautiful reality.

Here's what I'm trying to say: Papa John's story is one of team-work. The company has always done best when our team members are working to advance our common goal of making traditional, superior-quality Papa John's pizzas. That's how we grow. Papa John's should never be a one-man show, nor should it be run by a small group of self-interested people sitting in the corner suite. If we're ever heading in that direction, it means we're heading into a dark, dark place. Just wait until Chapter Seven . . .

Before I get there, I'd like to tell you about a few of the men and women in Papa John's history who have consistently practiced the Head Coach model.

These are the people who inspire me to be a better person. They make me want to come to work every morning, because I know I'll be surrounded by good people who are working to make the world a better place. They come from every time period in the company's history. I've already mentioned a number of them in the first five chapters. Over the next few pages, I'm going to tell you a little bit about each of them: where they came from, what they did, what they do now, and how they model the principles that make Papa John's great. I've listed how long each has been involved with me or the company below their names. Most of all, I'm going to show you how they're each Head Coaches in their own unique ways, and why they mean so much to me.

•   •   •   •   •

Denise Robinson
(32 years)

I already introduced you to Denise Robinson in Chapter One. If you recall, my Dad hired her as the cook at Mick's Lounge, even though she didn't know how to cook. He told me that it didn't matter that she couldn't cook—she had a great attitude. Although I doubted it at the time, it turned out that he was exactly right. Denise has been with us ever since, and Papa John's wouldn't be the same without her.

It's now been over three decades since I first met Denise. Over the years, I've seen her model Head Coach in more ways than I can count. I knew she had qualities worth emulating years before I even came up with the Head Coach model—if you remember from Chapter Four, Denise was one of the people we based FASPAC off of. She embodies so much of what we look for in a team member. When a member of the Papa John's team asks me what I'm looking for in an employee, my answer is simple: look at Denise Robinson. There's a reason she's the longest-serving member of the Papa John's team, other than myself. We're the only two original team members who are still with Papa John's today.

If I had to sum Denise up in just a few words, I'd put it this way: she's resilient. She's scrappy. She's street smart. She's loyal. She's committed to Papa John's. She's willing to put in the time to make herself and those around her better. She cares about them, too. She builds long-term relationships, which are absolutely crucial for long-term success. She sees opportunities and vulnerabilities that others don't. She doesn't compromise her principles. And she knows that success requires personal sacrifice. Her own sacrifices literally helped take Papa John's from a broom closet to a worldwide phenomenon.

I could tell Denise was a Head Coach even before Papa John's existed and long before I knew what a Head Coach was. In addition to cooking, she also helped bartend at Mick's Lounge. That's when I learned she was tough as nails. Denise Robinson does the right thing, no questions asked, and she has no time for anyone who doesn't do the same. If someone was getting out of line at the bar, she'd tell them to shape up or get out. She has always been a "no nonsense" type of person. Put another way, she has *focus*.

That's a huge part of why she and I have made such a good team over the years. We are both dedicated to making Papa John's the best it can be. Every single Head Coach shares this trait. They keep their eye on the ball, no matter where they are on the field. That's actually the only way to get the ball down the field and keep it there. Thanks in no small part to Denise Robinson, we've come an incredibly long way in Papa John's relatively brief history. I can never thank her enough.

● ● ● ● ●

(L-R): Karen, Roger, and Scott Roalofs, and Peyton Manning

Karen, Scott and Roger Roalofs
(29 years)

Today, roughly 75 percent of Papa John's stores are run by franchisees. We go to great lengths to identify talented, principled people to be our franchisees. This is immensely important. They represent Papa John's to millions of people, even though they don't actually work for the company. Having the right franchisees is make-or-break for our company. They are the types of small business owners who make America run.

Luckily, our first-ever franchisees are the very model of what we look for. Their names are Scott, Karen and Roger Roalofs, who you briefly met in Chapter Three. They opened Store #10 in Fern Creek, a suburb of Louisville, on June 1, 1987. They still run that same store—along with one other—today. Their stores are easily among our best-performing, and have been for many years. Consistency and the Roalofs go hand in hand.

That fact alone tells you that Scott, Karen and Roger are Head Coaches. But here are some other facts that prove it even more. You'd be hard-pressed to find three more loyal people. They've been through almost every up and down in Papa John's history. Yet through all of that, they have kept their focus on making traditional, superior-quality Papa John's pizzas. They always want to get better and will make investments to help them do that. They're also real community people—they take care of their team and their town, from the little league to their church to the area schools. They're pillars of their communities.

If more business leaders were like Scott, Karen and Roger, every college student in America would want to follow in their footsteps. Instead, they're the exception that proves the rule.

●　●　●　●　●

Jeff Couch
(30 years)

In the game of life, there are some people who want to rise all the way to the top, and some who find their niche and stick with it because they love it. These are often some of the best, most humble and most hardworking people you'll ever meet—the kind of people who wake up every day, go to work and make this country great. That's Jeff Couch for you.

Jeff Couch has been a Papa John's delivery driver since 1986—that's *30 years ago.* Why? Because he loves delivering pizzas. Every member of the Papa John's team—including me—could learn something from Jeff's dedication and hard work. He inspires those who know him and makes them better people by his example. He may not be a leader in the traditional sense, but he's a true Head Coach in my book.

• • • • •

Tim O'Hern
(43 years)

Cards on the table: Tim O'Hern is my oldest best friend. Maybe that makes me biased, but I'd stake my name on the fact that he's a Head Coach. I really saw this firsthand in the late 1980s, when I sold Mick's Lounge to him. He bought a business that was doing really well—and then he made it even better. This happened for the simple reason that Tim O'Hern knows how to run a fundamentally good business. He focuses on the long term. He helps his people grow and become the best they can be. He sticks to his guns and demands excellence from those around him.

Those are the type of people you want on your team. Now he works at Papa John's as our Chief Development Officer, which means he's in charge of opening new stores. He excels in this role, just like he excelled at Mick's Lounge. In a good year, Tim will oversee the construction of 400 stores, always with an eye towards sustainability and long-term success. I'd say this even if he wasn't my best friend—any company would be lucky to have a Head Coach like Tim O'Hern.

• • • • •

Mike Smith
(30 years)

One of the things that sets Papa John's apart is the fact that a large percentage of our senior leadership started off as delivery drivers or pizza makers at one of our stores. One of the best examples of this is Mike Smith.

Mike Smith is the Operations Vice President and is responsible for all of the corporate-owned restaurants in a particular region. He's come a long way since he started with Papa John's in 1990, making $5.50 an hour at Store #29 in Lexington, Kentucky. If you remember, Lexington was the second major city that Papa John's expanded into, and it quickly became one of our best markets. A lot of that success can be chalked up the Mike's influence. Today he's on our corporate team.

One of the things that impresses me most about Mike is that he never forgets what Papa John's is all about: making a traditional, superior-quality Papa John's pizza. Mike also realizes that we can't make these pizzas if corporate headquarters is calling all the shots. He goes to great lengths to inspire and empower the general managers that run individual Papa John's stores. Why? Because he knows that success for Papa John's starts at the store level. Mike has developed more profitable store operators and managers than anyone else in Papa John's history. Every Head Coach should aspire to inspire their own teams like Mike has at Papa John's.

● ● ● ● ●

Todd Jenkins
(25 years)

Todd Jenkins is what Papa John's is all about. Today, he's the General Manager at Store #64 in Shelbyville, Indiana. He started his career with us as a delivery driver in 1991. He didn't start out as a full-time employee. He was actually working two jobs beforehand—one at a local factory and another at a local restaurant. He was working so hard because he and his wife had recently found out that she was pregnant. He needed to supplement his income somehow, so after he got laid off at the factory, he applied for a part-time job at Papa John's before it even opened. He got the job, meaning he was working for us part-time while working for another restaurant full-time.

Todd showed dedication and commitment from the get-go. After his shift ended at his main job, he'd drive over to Papa John's, pick up pizzas and start delivering them around town. He worked on nights and weekends, doing everything he could to bring in enough money to provide for his growing family.

His hard work didn't go unnoticed. About a year after he started, Todd was offered the position of assistant general manager at the store—a role that paid more than his other job. So he packed up over there and came to work full-time for Papa John's. He kept improving and showed incredible leadership potential. About six months after he was promoted, he got promoted again. Now he's a general manager at the store where he started some 25 years ago. One of his best qualities is that he has made Papa John's an integral part of the Shelbyville community, sponsoring activities and events that draw the whole town together. That's why Todd is a Head Coach. Papa John's needs more people like him. *Everywhere* needs more people like him.

• • • • •

Kim Seebold
(18 years)

If you've learned anything in this book, I hope it's that quality is the name of the game at Papa John's. It's my personal obsession and has been since I was a teenager. We promise quality to our customers every day, which is why our slogan is "Better Ingredients. Better Pizza." If I had to single out one employee who's just as zealous about quality as I am, it would be Kim Seebold, the chef in charge of the pizzeria located at Papa John's headquarters.

Kim gets it. She knows that you have to make a "Perfect 10" pizza and serve it with a smile on your face. She expects and ensures that the pizzas her team makes are worthy of the Papa John's name. Few people make a better pizza than she does. Kim's belief in Papa John's mission is also infectious. She welcomes every person who walks into her restaurant with a smile and an excellent pizza. Everyone at headquarters knows her and loves her. She's also inspired no fewer than five members of her family to join the Papa John's team, including her husband and her daughter. And her team has incredibly low turnover, a sign of how she takes care of those around her.

A Head Coach always believes in what they do. Kim Seebold is a true believer, and a true Head Coach. The proof is in her pizzas.

• • • • •

Michael Meche
(23 years)

Michael Meche has a very important role at Papa John's—he manages all of our more than 650 corporate stores, which isn't a job for the faint of heart. But I don't want to tell you about what he does. What I really want to tell you is who Michael Meche *is*.

For starters, he's a phenomenal pizza maker. He can walk into any store and show the team there what good looks like. A Head Coach needs to be able to do that. If they can't, they'll find it very difficult to convince others that they know what they're doing. You can't inspire if you can't practice what you preach. Michael also has one of the most infectious personalities you'll ever encounter. He is upbeat and positive and makes the job fun in even the most challenging of situations.

I should also note that Michael wants to make sure that Papa John's keeps its small-business feel, no matter how big we get. That speaks volumes about who he is as a Head Coach. He gets what Papa John's is all about, and he works to make sure we stick to our roots. We'll keep growing so long as people like Michael keep us grounded in what really matters.

● ● ● ● ●

Keeta Fox
(23 years)

I have a special place in my heart for the people who have been with Papa John's for more than 20 years. Keeta Fox is a good example. She first joined our team in 1993, right after we went public. She's filled a number of roles for us since then, all of them on the finance team. Now she's our Senior Vice President and Controller—a position that gives her responsibility over a vast swath of Papa John's finances.

I was impressed with Keeta from the moment I met her. Even though she's not in a position where she's interacting with customers buying pizza on a daily basis, she knows that Papa John's depends on quality customer service in order to succeed. That's obvious in how she interacts with everyone around her—she is respectful, courteous and kind, even when she's holding others accountable. This naturally makes her a good Head Coach. She recognizes the value of her team members' input and strives to get them to contribute their ideas and use their talent to the best of their ability. She also knows that you can accomplish more as a team than as an individual—a key realization for a Head Coach. Her team won Papa John's prestigious "People Are Priority Always" award in 2005. To date, this is the only time a *team*, rather than an *individual*, has won this award. That's because Keeta works so hard to advance her team rather than herself.

There aren't many people you can say that about.

• • • • •

Sean Muldoon
(17 years)

When we say "Better Ingredients. Better Pizza.", we're making a promise to our customers. Sean Muldoon makes sure we keep our word.

Sean is our Chief Ingredient Officer. If that sounds like an incredibly difficult job, that's because it is. I would honestly say that he has the toughest job in the entire company. He's stuck between a rock and a hard place. On the one side, he has to deal with me, a founder who is an absolute fanatic when it comes to quality. On the other side, he has to deal with the franchisees, who put more emphasis on what their ingredients cost. How do you balance these two competing—and incompatible—desires? Sean Muldoon does it, and he always errs on the side of quality. The man with the unenviable job makes it look easy.

Here's why. Sean knows that you can't make good wine from bad grapes and that you can't make good dough from bad water. He also knows that ensuring quality takes time and costs money. He works with me to put in the time and spend our money in a way that improves our ingredients and keeps our promise to customers. When I try one of our products—whether it's upcoming, new or tried and true—and it doesn't seem right, I head to Sean's office and let him know. Then he fixes it, guaranteed. With him on our team, we'll keep finding even better ingredients to make even better pizzas.

• • • • •

Simon Smith
(10 years)

Simon Smith came to Papa John's right before the start of "the Dark Years"—you'll hear more about those in Chapter Seven. Without giving too much away, let me just say that Simon was one of the few bright spots during the mid-to-late 2000s. Papa John's was fighting for its life. But thanks to Simon and others like him, we survived and have since soared to new heights.

I admire Simon. He encourages those around him, which makes them feel they can accomplish things they never thought were possible. In his role of overseeing North American franchisees, he sets very clear expectations for his team and his franchisees and has extremely good listening and interpersonal skills. He is never afraid to admit when he is wrong and always strives for the right long-term outcome. Rare for people in his position, Simon has the uncanny ability to remain calm in the most challenging of situations, which gives others confidence and security when things aren't going well. You want Simon in your corner when there's a crisis.

More than anything else, Simon understands the power of relationships. A Head Coach creates an environment in which people grow and thrive. If you could talk to Simon right now, you would sense in him a deep desire for you to succeed and reach your full potential. You can't be a Head Coach without that. You can't be a Head Coach unless you care about the well-being of your team. You can't be a Head Coach unless you're like Simon Smith.

• • • • •

Jack Swaysland
(10 years)

Papa John's is an American company through and through, but our international presence is becoming more important with every passing year. In fact, most of our growth these days comes from beyond our borders, because people across the world want a taste of a traditional, superior-quality Papa John's pizza. Jack Swaysland helps make that happen.

One thing's for sure: Jack has had a heck of a ride. He first started with Papa John's in the mid-2000s, right when Papa John's was experiencing its crisis of quality in America. Yet while things were bad in America, they were actually *worse* in the United Kingdom. But Jack, along with his team, basically turned the United Kingdom around. One of the things a Head Coach does is learn and study what they need to do in order to win. Jack did that. He devoted himself to the Papa John's way. He made a point of understanding the ins and outs of "Better Ingredients. Better Pizza." Once he had a good grasp of what Papa John's does and why we do it, he began implementing it in the stores and areas he oversaw in the United Kingdom at that time.

That kick-started a renaissance in quality. Customers responded and growth began to take off. Thanks to Jack's influence, the United Kingdom went from one of our worst-performing markets to one of our best. Now his portfolio includes everywhere Papa John's operates except the United States. What more do I need to say?

● ● ● ● ●

Lynn McQuillen
(14 years)

Papa John's and the Louisville metro area are pretty much synonymous in my mind. So much of our history is wrapped up in our hometown. Our first dozen-plus stores were there. Our first franchisees were there. I still live there. So you can imagine that I have high expectations for the people who oversee the stores in this area. Fortunately, I don't actually have to worry about it because we have a real Head Coach in that role—Lynn McQuillen.

As an Operations Vice President, Lynn makes sure that the corporate stores in his area are doing a good job. His area includes not only Louisville, but also Lexington and Indianapolis, which, as you know by this point, are also among our most important markets. Lynn does an excellent job of making sure the stores in these three cities are fulfilling Papa John's promise to deliver a better pizza made with better ingredients. I believe his success comes from the combination of trust and accountability he uses with his team. He doesn't believe in telling people what to do. Instead, he communicates what needs to be done and lets them figure out the best way to get there. His team responds to this freedom by rising to the challenge—even when they make mistakes, they learn from them and do better the next time.

This is at the root of Lynn's success, which explains why he's able to do such a great job in such a demanding role. He reminds me of a saying I once heard: "Real leaders are ordinary people with extraordinary determination." That sums up Lynn McQuillen pretty well.

• • • • •

Dennis Gerstner
(15 years)

Dennis Gerstner is one of only a few Papa John's franchisees that I've named in this chapter. You might be asking yourself, what makes Dennis so special considering he's one of well over 700 franchisees? Well, how's this for starters: he's one of the *best* franchisees—and one of the best Head Coaches.

Dennis started at Papa John's about 15 years ago as a corporate employee. Today he owns and operates about 33 stores as a franchisee in Minnesota. Very few people have made this jump—from corporate to franchisee—over the years. It can be a difficult transition. But Dennis was always up for the challenge. He brought with him a lot of wisdom and knowledge about how to run stores worthy of the Papa John's name. He is serious about our company's culture. He makes sure that his team understands what Papa John's is all about. That sounds like something that every franchisee would do, but the sad fact is that they often don't. That's what makes Dennis so special—that's what makes him a Head Coach.

● ● ● ● ●

Rich Butler
(17 years)

As I've said many times throughout this book, Papa John's is in the people business more than we're in the pizza business. As I also said at the start of this chapter, a business run by Head Coaches is a people-growing machine. Rich Butler is the man who makes sure that Papa John's is growing its people, no matter who they are or what they do. Plus, he rocks.

As Senior Director for Global Training and Development, Rich is in charge of Papa John's people development around the entire world. That's an enormous task, but Rich is definitely up to the challenge. He is an inspirational leader who recognizes and helps people realize their potential. Rich often says that "you should never accept what is," and that you should "always dream big and know that reality is what you make it." He builds trust with those around him, giving them the courage to have candid conversations that enables personal growth and self-actualization. Rich also builds self-confidence within individuals so they feel they can conquer the biggest challenges.

Papa John's recently celebrated its 30th anniversary, and one of the biggest challenges we face is building and strengthening our culture as we continue to grow. We're already ramping up our efforts to bring FASPAC, Go Left, and the Head Coach model to every level of the organization. I believe this is critical for our continued long-term success—the more team members who know Papa John's principles, the more team members who can help take us to new heights. Rich Butler is crucial to this process, and I can't think of a better Head Coach to head it up.

● ● ● ● ●

(L-R): **Manny Overton and Ricky Warman**

Manny Overton and Ricky Warman
(20 and 14 years)

Here's what you need to know about Manny and Ricky. They were Papa John's franchisees of the year in 2015. Why? Because they practice what Papa John's preaches.

I already told you about them briefly in Chapter Five, but it's worth reiterating just how impressive they are. Their Florida stores are some of the best-performing in the whole company. A hallmark of the Head Coach is sustained long-term success. Manny and Ricky have a strong track record of delivering just that, along with traditional, superior-quality Papa John's pizzas. They also supported me when the chips were down. They're great.

• • • • •

Caroline Oyler
(17 years)

Lawyers have a bad reputation for a good reason: a lot of them are unprincipled and use unethical business practices, just like a lot of so-called business leaders. Not Caroline Oyler. She does the right thing.

As our legal General Counsel, it's her job to make sure we're following the law and acting with integrity on a daily basis. A lot of people in this position wouldn't have a problem fudging the numbers here and there or skirting the law when it makes you a quick buck. Caroline Oyler has no time for that. She does the right thing and doesn't think twice about it. She keeps Papa John's on the straight and narrow. A good Head Coach always does—they know that winning isn't winning if you break the rules along the way. Caroline Oyler understands that better than most.

•   •   •   •   •

Nadeem Bajwa

(22 years)

Have you ever met someone with a truly inspiring story? I've been lucky enough to meet quite a few. But one of the best comes from Nadeem Bajwa.

Nadeem was born in Pakistan. He came to America in 1991 to pursue an education in Fort Wayne, Indiana. Along the way, he picked up a part-time job as a delivery driver for Domino's Pizza. He liked it, but he didn't love it. So he left Domino's and started working at Papa John's. You better believe he loved what he found.

In 2002, Nadeem set out on his own as a franchisee. He opened up his first store in East Liverpool, Ohio. His goal, however, was to take over the Fort Wayne market where he first started working for Papa John's. Slowly but surely, he started working to make his dream a reality. Now he's the proud owner of well over 150 Papa John's franchises, including in Fort Wayne. He's one of our largest and best franchisees. More importantly, he's one of our best Head Coaches. One thing he told me will always stick with me: "The more success I see, the more humble I should get." Anyone can say that, but only a Head Coach can say it *and* live it. Nadeem Bajwa does just that. Talk about inspiring.

• • • • •

Scott Durigg
(23 years)

It's a sign of Papa John's success that so many of our best employees came from other pizza companies. These people—and there are hundreds of them—recognized that Papa John's is something different, something better. Take the example of Scott Durigg, who joined our team from a rival local pizza company in 1993.

Scott has achieved more with Papa John's than he would have anywhere else. He helped us expand into the western United States in the late 1990s and early 2000s. If you ask him why he's been so successful, he'll give you a simple answer. "I always chalk up success to two things," he says: "Make good, common-sense decisions and treat people right." He'll also tell you about the importance of having fun while still holding people to high expectations. Scott proves that you don't have to be a hard-ass to be a good Head Coach—something a lot of would-be leaders should learn.

• • • • •

Edmond Heelan

(15 years)

It doesn't take long to explain why Edmond Heelan is a Head Coach. Sometimes it's just obvious when someone fits the bill. In Edmond's case, we recognized it early on. He started in restaurant operations about 15 years ago. Now he's the Senior Vice President of North American operations —one of the most important roles in all of Papa John's.

Here's what sets Edmond apart. He has a passion for doing things the right way. Just as important, he has a passion for helping *others* do things the right way. He challenges those around him to get to the root cause of a problem so they can fix it right the first time. Best of all, he does this with a smile. He has a unique way of engendering loyalty and camaraderie with the people he works with. That's rare. But so are Head Coaches. We're lucky to have someone like Edmond on the Papa John's team.

• • • • •

Dougie and his wife, Ieasha

David "Dougie" Allen
(11 years)

People with a background in sports often learn the Head Coach model pretty quickly. That's the case with Papa John's franchisee Dougie Allen. He's been involved with sports his entire life and has a special love for football, which he started playing at age eight. He learned early on that the Head Coach model is extremely important for anyone who wants to take their team to the next level.

Dougie has definitely done that with his own team. He started as a Papa John's franchisee in the Lexington area in 2005. Since then, he has expanded into five other markets and has 53 stores. He just *gets it*. He knows what Papa John's is all about and he's focused on implementing the Papa John's model and vision everywhere he goes. That explains why he's always moving the ball forward, which is what the best Head Coaches always seek to do.

• • • • •

Lance Tucker
(22 years)

Lance Tucker's story is a story of two halves. The first half isn't that great. He came to work for Papa John's in 1994, but it really wasn't a good fit. He didn't buy into my vision for the company. He left shortly thereafter. Unfortunately for him, his new employer went bankrupt pretty soon after that. Having learned some hard lessons, he came back to Papa John's.

That brings us to the second half of his story. It was like a light switch went on in Lance's head once he came back. Things suddenly clicked. He established himself as one of my closest advisers during the mid-to-late 2000s. Now he's head of the company's finance department, and he does an amazing job. Remember what I said earlier: Head Coaches turn their businesses into people-growing machines. Lance has done just that with our finance team. It's one of the best-performing teams and regularly churns out some of our best team members who are the most promotable. That's an incredible testament to who Lance is and how he leads his team like a true Head Coach.

• • • • •

Steve Ritchie
(20 years)

Steve has one of the best and most inspiring stories of anyone at Papa John's.

Papa John's has been different and special ever since the broom closet. Our ideals—our *ethos*—set us apart from all of our competitors and explain our unprecedented and unmatched growth. Naturally, we've had a lot of people try to mimic what we do, but none of them have been successful. Steve Ritchie was one of those people back in the early-to-mid 1990s. He started his own pizzeria as a senior in high school. He tried everything he could to do what Papa John's did, even to the point of searching our dumpsters for our recipe. Eventually he decided that he simply couldn't beat us.

As the saying goes, "if you can't beat 'em, join 'em." Steve joined the Papa John's team in 1996 as a customer service representative making $5 an hour. Long story short: he's now the president of the entire company.

276 · HEAD COACH ·

How does someone rise from minimum wage to company president and chief operating officer of a company with $3.7 billion in system-wide sales in less than 20 years? The answer is that Steve Ritchie is one of the best Head Coaches I've ever had the pleasure of knowing. In fact, I don't think I've ever met anyone who better fits the description. He's the first one in the building every day and the last one out. He's a model of what a leader should be, and plenty of people look up to him for that reason. His single greatest asset is his ability to put others before himself. Steve wants others to succeed and will go to great lengths to help them get ahead. The team is everything for him, and it shows.

His focus on growing his team has had amazing results. His stores prospered when he was a franchisee in the mid-2000s. Now the company prospers with him as president and chief operating officer. And despite everything that he's achieved—rising faster and farther than anyone else in Papa John's history—he's still one of the most humble and unassuming guys you'll ever meet.

Here's the bottom line: Steve Ritchie is a stand-up guy. I firmly believe that Papa John's will thrive so long as he's our president. He gets me and I get him. He gives me great confidence—something not all of our company presidents have done, to put it mildly. So long as we have Head Coaches like him at the helm, there's no limit to what Papa John's can do.

● ● ● ● ●

John Himler with his wife, Kerry

John Himler
(23 years)

John Himler is the last Head Coach I'll mention. I saved him for last because he's the *ultimate* Head Coach.

John isn't someone you'd expect to be on this list. He never worked in a Papa John's store. He never worked at corporate. He was never a franchisee. As far as I know, he never even made a pizza in his entire life. Yet he was still immensely important to Papa John's success. He was my chief pilot for 23 years.

You get pretty close to someone when you spend 23 years flying around the world with them in a metal tube. I personally approved all of the first 1,500 Papa John's store locations, and John Himler was the guy who got me to nearly all of those sites. We had a simple relationship: I was the boss when we were on the ground and he was the boss when we were in the air.

Here's a story that illustrates our relationship, as well as what type of man he was. One day, while we were flying to a new store opening, I thought I'd have some fun with John. I told him, "Barrel-roll this thing." He glanced back at me with a look that said, "Shut up, John." I kept pressing him—"Seriously, barrel-roll this thing." I was trying to get a rise out of him. So imagine my surprise when he barrel-rolled the plane. He scared me half to death. That was the last time I ever gave John Himler an order—even jokingly—when we were in the air.

Over the years I learned to trust John implicitly. He pursued excellence every day, and never stopped trying to get even better at what he did. You can't say that about a lot of people. He was also an inspiration to his fellow pilots and every member of the Papa John's team who knew him. We had a saying about John—he was "Himler ready, Himler tough." Everything was extremely organized and disciplined. He was always on his game. He never took any crap from anyone.

I came to rely on John Himler more than most. In fact, I couldn't even conceive of running Papa John's without him on my team. One morning in June of 2014, I was sipping my coffee when I got a text on my phone. It was from his wife, Kerry. I picked up my phone and couldn't believe what I was reading: "John, this is Kerry Himler. John Himler died last night of a massive heart attack. Please keep him in your prayers." I put the phone back down, consumed with shock. It probably took me a full 10 minutes before I moved. I picked the phone back up and read the text again. Then I called Kerry and asked her a simple question: "Is this true?" She told me it was. We sat on the phone for what seemed like an eternity, completely silent. Eventually I just said, "I'm sorry." I was gutted by this news—I still don't know if I've gotten over his loss.

We miss and think about John Himler every day. Like I said, he was the ultimate Head Coach. Words can't possibly describe someone like that. It was a privilege to know him for as long as I did. I salute him.

● ● ● ● ●

These are only a few of the tens of thousands of examples I could give of the Papa John's team members who are Head Coaches. I have been privileged to work with so many impressive and honorable men and women over the past 30-plus years. Like I said in Chapter Four, I'm very sorry to all of you I did not name. I recognize that there are many, many others who deserve praise. I can never thank you enough for everything you've done. I promise to you that I will do my best to let the people you and I work with know how important you are. Every Head Coach at Papa John's deserves recognition, especially since they don't seek it out. You're too busy taking Papa John's to the next level. From the bottom of my heart, I say thank you.

● ● ● ● ●

By this point you may be asking yourself, *Why did John just take so much space talking about "Head Coaches?"*

The answer is simple. It's the same reason I've told you so much about my Dad and my Papaw—the two most important men in my lives. Papa John's wouldn't exist without them. It also wouldn't exist without the Head Coach model that they first imparted to me during my formative years. I tried to practice what they taught me, even before the broom closet existed, before I even had a name for what a Head Coach was. Thanks to them, I always had the general idea that I needed to act a certain way and live a certain kind of life if I ever wanted to be successful. That idea was only reinforced over the years as I met and saw others who lived and acted the same way. Head Coaches are depressingly rare, and when you see one, it sticks with you. It's definitely stuck with me.

The story of Papa John's is, in large part, the story of our team trying to live out the Head Coach model. It's also the story of how I slowly put the pieces together to find out what, exactly, that model looks like. I have spent the better part of 20 years trying to accurately describe what a Head Coach is and how it looks in practice. I've learned a lot, often through my own failures and shortcomings. The result of this hard work is something I can take to every member of the Papa John's team to help them understand what we believe—and why it makes a world of difference. The Head Coach model is the guidepost we can look to when we get lost.

Unfortunately, parts of Papa John's history show what happens when you don't have that guidepost. We thought we knew what good looked like when I stepped down as CEO in early 2005. We understood two of the three key "frameworks" that were critical to Papa John's success. We had a good grasp on the framework of our business model—the company was booming because our model was so good. We also understood the framework of quality—it always has been and always will be central to Papa John's identity. But we didn't yet have the framework of culture figured out. The idea of "Head Coach" hadn't permeated the entire organization yet—not by a long shot. We simply trusted that Papa John's would always have the right people at the helm, which would prevent the company from going down a dark road.

We couldn't have been more wrong. Papa John's had never systematically focused on our culture in the same way that we focused on our business model and on our quality. But if your culture isn't well established, it's incredibly easy for people to come in and institute a culture of their own—a culture that runs counter to everything you stand for. That's when Head Coaches disappear, and when they fade away, they are replaced by the type of leader who can destroy an entire company.

CHAPTER SEVEN

— • —

KINGSHIP

The opposite of the Head Coach model is the Kingship model.

I didn't know this when we started developing the Head Coach model in the late 1990s. I still didn't know about Kingship (or Queenship, depending on gender) by the time I stepped down from Papa John's in 2005. In the early 2000s, I devoted every ounce of my energy to practicing the leadership model that we were developing. I didn't have any time to figure out if there was an opposite type of leader—the type of leader who runs a business into the ground rather than builds it up.

But I soon learned that this type of person existed. I learned this by watching what some of the new leadership regime did to Papa John's after I stepped down. The leadership model I had learned from my Dad and my Papaw—the Head Coach model—was replaced by Kingship. It is, to date, the most terrifying thing I've ever seen happen at Papa John's.

Let me paint the Kingship model in broad brush strokes before I get to specific examples. But first, an important caveat: the description I'm about to give doesn't apply to any one individual. Rather, I'm painting a picture of what the Kingship model looks like when taken to its logical extreme. The same is true of the Head Coach model I described in Chapter Six—it is an ideal that a good leader must strive to achieve. The portrait of Kingship I'm about to paint should inspire a real leader to do the opposite.

In a nutshell, whereas a Head Coach focuses on helping others recognize and achieve their potential, Kingship is all about the people in charge getting ahead on the backs of those beneath them. A Head Coach builds from the bottom up, while Kingship approaches things from the top down. It's about building a system in which everything revolves around the leader—just like medieval times, when monarchs had their courts and every courtier had to please them. Kingship is fundamentally narcissistic.

This naturally leads to a wide variety of unhealthy and harmful actions and consequences.

In the world of business, Kingship can cause a company to crash and burn. Why? Because Kingship enriches the few at the expense of the many. It focuses on how much the people at the top can make and how they can get ahead at the expense of others. Instead of leading by example, the leader in a Kingship model holds him or herself to a different standard of conduct. They think the rules apply to everyone but themselves and that they can get away with whatever they want.

People aren't willing to recognize their own shortcomings when they're operating under the Kingship model. They sometimes think they don't even have any shortcomings at all—an impossibility for a human being. When something goes wrong, they blame others. And when the going gets rough, they start beheading those around them. Personal responsibility—taking the hit—is a foreign concept under Kingship.

That's a recurring theme: the constant mistreatment of others. Recall that Head Coaches build collaborative alliances. Kingship, on the other hand, builds collusive and combative ones. These are relationships built on conflict, strife and abuse, all of which create anxiety. Kingship-driven people rarely care whether their team members grow personally and professionally. Instead of asking, "How can I make others' lives better?" they ask, "What can others do for me?"

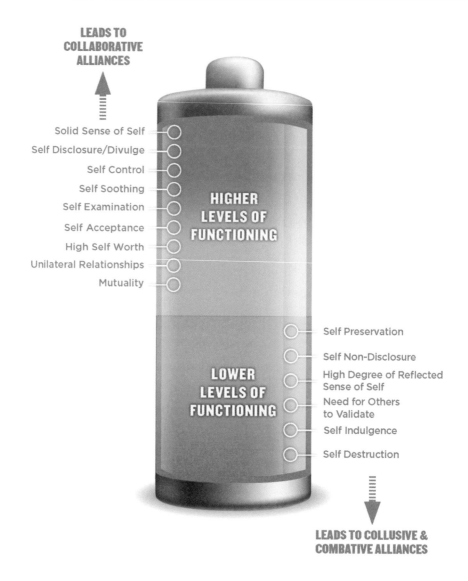

LEVELS OF PERSONAL FUNCTIONING

LEADS TO
COLLABORATIVE
ALLIANCES

Solid Sense of Self
Self Disclosure/Divulge
Self Control
Self Soothing
Self Examination
Self Acceptance
High Self Worth
Unilateral Relationships
Mutuality

HIGHER
LEVELS OF
FUNCTIONING

Self Preservation
Self Non-Disclosure
High Degree of Reflected
Sense of Self
Need for Others
to Validate
Self Indulgence
Self Destruction

LOWER
LEVELS OF
FUNCTIONING

LEADS TO COLLUSIVE &
COMBATIVE ALLIANCES

Under a Kingship or Queenship model, people typically come second to profits—they are seen as objects of self-gain. They talk a big game about the long term, but focus almost exclusively on the short term. By the same token, Kingship causes people to believe that the ends justify the means. There's something deeply Machiavellian about this. They don't treat their team members like team members at all. Instead, they treat them like serfs, minions or ants to be stepped on. They want to milk every ounce of productivity out of people, yet they refuse to give the rest of the team the credit and appreciation they deserve. They pit people against each other, creating collusive alliances. Currying favor is a daily fact of life in the Kingship model.

Leaders who follow the Kingship model go to great lengths to control the flow of information. They place their team members in silos to prevent people from talking to each other—and from finding out that the emperor has no clothes. When presented with data or information that they don't like, they hide it, only use part of it and manipulate it to suit their own ends. This is a pattern that we'll talk about throughout this chapter.

Ultimately, they use and abuse information in order to convince people that what they say is correct, even though it isn't. That's part of what causes people to fall asleep or go back to sleep after they wake up and start to see the nightmare. Someone practicing Kingship thinks they're the smartest person in the room. A Head Coach knows that if they are the smartest person in the room, it's time to get out of that room.

In terms of the workplace itself, it shouldn't be a surprise that Kingship- and Queenship-run companies have a culture characterized by stress, mistrust, paranoia and anger. Anxiety runs high under a Kingship model. These people are not control freaks, they are out-of-control freaks. Burnout becomes a major problem. Everywhere you look, you find discontent. No wonder: the Kingship model causes people to use others for their own enrichment. That's just business as usual for them, because they see people as objects of self-gain. They want to restrict and punish rather than facilitate, create and empower.

Just like we've all seen the Head Coach model in action, we've all seen Kingship, too. Maybe it was the bully at school. Maybe it's a co-worker—or worse yet, a boss—in the workplace.

Kingship can be found anywhere. I've seen it in books—Oscar Wilde's *The Picture of Dorian Gray* portrays the Kingship model better than I could ever describe it. I've also seen it rear its ugly head at colleges and universities, where administrators can easily fall into bad, self-serving habits. Kingship often replaces the Head Coach model in sports, including at some of America's major franchises.

And of course, Kingship and Queenship thrives in the business world, at least in the short run. Corporate America is full of self-serving Kingships, and we all know it. You see headlines about these sorts of people all the time. They pursue short-term gains over long-term success. They're not interested in making a product or service that makes people's lives better—they're mainly interested in enriching themselves. I counted over a dozen examples of people exhibiting such behavior just while writing this book. Kingship is happening every day, all the time. It's incredibly disturbing.

You may be asking yourself, why is Kingship such a widespread problem? The answer is simple. It's powerfully alluring—and it's difficult to detect, because the reptilian brain is extremely slippery.

Think about it. If you're on a corporate board or part of a company's management team, you could benefit tremendously under Kingship or Queenship. After all, the monarch enriches those at the top with short-term gains. Those people are promised bigger paydays and more stock options—an enticing prospect since Kingship often leads to boosting the stock price in the short-term. That's appealing to a lot of people, even if they know in their hearts that short-term gains are coming at the expense of long-term success. When you're making more money, it's easy to forget about everyone else in the company and whether your success comes at their expense. Kingship often causes a company's leaders to forget that the people on the front lines are the ones who are doing the real heavy lifting and make real, long-term success possible.

Ultimately, the Kingship model makes the people at the top fall asleep, which I partially described in the last chapter. Buying people off with higher salaries, bonuses and perks is a tried-and-true way that Kingship puts people to sleep. Another way is to ratchet up the levels of anxiety within the organization. Rather than dealing with issues in a healthy, collaborative confrontation, and making decisions based on facts, those working at the top know that challenging the monarch will result in an explosive, unpleasant reaction—they'll blow up. It's easier to go to sleep and avoid the confrontation, thereby giving the monarch a free pass. No one wants to deal with the alligator in the cage.

On that note, there are two types of sleep: dozing off and a coma.

A lot of companies are in the dozing stage. These are the companies where the nightmare isn't fully developed. They're either growing through simple inertia or are stagnant—in either case, the status quo prevails. They probably don't realize what's happening to them, either because it's happening slowly—think of the classic "boiling a frog" analogy—or because the status quo is so comfortable. Papa John's exhibited some of these symptoms between 1997 and 2001, when our pizza quality and customer service began to decline. Fortunately, we woke up in 2001 and started to turn things around. Many other companies are in a similar state, but haven't yet woken up. That only increases the chances that Kingship will take root—and then take over.

Then there's the coma. This usually happens after the Kingship model is well developed at a company. The nightmare has finally arrived. Profit becomes paramount over everything. The people at the top start fudging the facts and breaking the rules in order to get ahead. Yet thanks to Kingship's influence, there's little to no chance of anyone waking up and realizing what's going on around them. They're comfortable in their sleepy state, not willing to recognize or deal with reality. They may wake up along the way, but they just as quickly fall back to sleep because they aren't willing to deal with the nightmare (although they desperately need to). That would be extremely uncomfortable and difficult, so they prefer the comfort of the coma instead.

Here's where the coma ends up: you refuse to deal with reality even when the U.S. Marshals are walking you up the courthouse steps. Compare that to a Head Coach model, where people are awake and dealing with reality in the moment. That's healthy and responsible; ignoring reality isn't.

By bringing businesses into this deep sleep, Kingship can destroy companies in the long run (although the people at the top usually try to get out before the business hits rock bottom, taking their money and running.) Not only has Kingship destroyed relationships and trust within an organization by this point, it has also destroyed relationships and trust between the company, its customers and the wider world. Failure necessarily follows.

Kingship can destroy both in the long run and in the short term. Again, we need only look at companies in the news to see that this is real. Whether it's Enron, Worldcom, HealthSouth or other corporate failures, history is replete with examples of companies that likely fell prey to the Kingship model. My friend Charles Koch might say that these companies pursued "bad profit." Either way, the result is the same: long-term disaster.

Looking over the many examples, it should make sense why millions of people profoundly distrust the business community and Wall Street. They see Kingship at some of the biggest and most visible companies in America and assume that's how all companies are run. It gives the free enterprise system a bad name. The people who practice Kingship aren't making the world a better place like a Head Coach does. Whether you're the head of a multinational company like Papa John's or a mom-'n'-pop pizzeria in your hometown, your job is to build up your team members, your community and the world around you. Help others before you help yourself. If you aren't doing that, you aren't doing your job. Every business leader needs to try to act like a Head Coach.

I say that as someone who tries to act like a Head Coach every day. I don't always succeed—far from it. I've already explained some of the situations in Papa John's history when I fell short. If I'm not careful, I can easily fall into the category of "benevolent dictator." I've tried to solve this by surrounding myself with talented, principled people. They help me. I help them. Together, we try to run our company under the Head Coach model. If we think we're slipping into the Kingship model in any way, we drop everything we're doing. Then we identify where we fell short and fix it.

In my experience, you can avoid falling into a Kingship mentality by staying accountable, responsible, humble, kind and gracious. If you practice these things, you have a much better chance of dealing with reality in a healthy and constructive way.

Sadly, every person is capable of falling into the Kingship mindset—even the best Head Coach you've ever met. I've spent years trying to figure out why this is. My attempts to find the answer eventually led me to the study of the human brain.

Neuropsychologists have spent much of the last century attempting to discover how the brain evolved and why it works the way it does. It turns out that our brains weren't always as advanced as they are today. Right now, you and I are likely utilizing the "neocortex"—what most of us mean when we use the word "brain." It accounts for over 95 percent of our grey matter and is responsible for most of what distinguishes humans from other animals. Thanks to the neocortex, we have the capacity to learn, to reason, to speak various languages, to think abstractly, to be creative, to develop interpersonal relationships, to love and so much more. Human culture would not exist were it not for the neocortex.

But the neocortex wasn't always there. The first part of the brain to evolve was actually the "reptilian" part. It gives humans many of our most basic—and some of our least attractive—reflexive abilities.

That's why they call it reptilian. Imagine two alligators competing for dominance or defending their territory. They aren't driven by reason—they're driven by the will to win. They feel the need to preserve themselves, no matter the cost. The end result is often violence. We see humans exhibit these same traits all too often. When we act in a reptilian way, we think of ourselves instead of others. We think about how we can get ahead while pushing others behind. We deceive others in order to get our own way. Think of what alligators do: they have no sense of humor and they eat their young. That's Kingship in a nutshell.

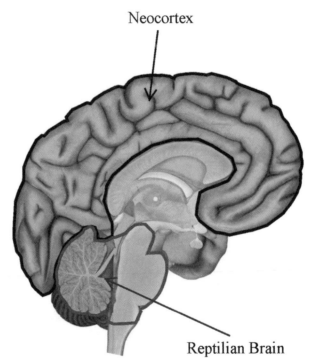

Neocortex

Reptilian Brain

Diagram of brain, showing neocortex and reptilian portions

These feelings exist because these two parts of our brains—the neocortex and the reptilian—are frequently acting against each other. The neocortex may be the largest and most advanced part of the brain, but we can't forget that the reptilian is still there. All of us can slip into the reptilian mindset if we aren't careful. That's why we constantly have to train ourselves to recognize it and avoid its worst elements.

We often succeed, which is why human society has flourished for so long. But deep down, we all still have those reptilian abilities. We see them manifest themselves in war, in conflict, in business and even in the day-to-day of our personal lives.

The bottom line is that all of us are capable of regressing to a reptilian mindset, whether deliberately or as a result of getting overwhelmed. Most of us fight it. Yet some give in and let it rule their lives. In my years of experience and study, the reptilian mind dominates in those who fall under Kingship.

I notice this on a daily basis, both in myself and the people I work with. Every member of Papa John's Executive Leadership Team is familiar with the reptilian-versus-neocortex functioning. Sometimes one of us will get overwhelmed and accidentally slip into a reptilian

Talent and Virtues Matrix

mindset. Fortunately, we each see it as our job to confront ourselves when we do this and to confront each other. Healthy confrontation—collaborative confrontation—is key to combating the reptilian mindset as well as Kingship.

The more I see this, the more I know the company is on the right track. It means that we're following the Head Coach model rather than Kingship. Remember what I said in Chapter Six: if I don't challenge your judgment, I weaken you, and if you don't challenge my judgment, you weaken me. We want to be challenged since we know it makes us stronger. We seek to hold ourselves and each other accountable to make sure that we're always thinking and acting consistently with Papa John's philosophy.

Today, we have combined the Head Coach versus Kingship paradigm with our philosophy of Go Left, from Chapter Two. If you recall, Go Left is the culture that unites every team member at Papa John's. It's a culture of self-determination, living up to one's potential and using a person's gifts and talents to make other people's lives better. It's also a culture of "intrapreneurship," which means we want our team members to have an entrepreneurial mindset no matter what they do for the company. Finally, it's a culture of constantly improving and doing the right thing.

That's the same thing we try to do as Head Coaches. When we Go Left, we choose the path of the Head Coach. The other option is to go in the direction of Kingship—a dark and terrible road.

Papa John's 'Go Left' pamphlet cover: Head Coach vs. Kingship

• • • • •

It pains me to say it, but Papa John's has had its fair share of run-ins with the Kingship model, especially between 2005 and 2009.

As I mentioned in the last two chapters, I stepped down as CEO of Papa John's in early 2005. I firmly believed that my decision was in the company's best interests. Even though Papa John's was back on the right track, tensions were running high between me and a small number of our franchisees. Some of them were furious with me for how I challenged them between 2001 and 2004. They didn't like that I had called them out and demanded that they practice what Papa John's preached about quality.

That can be a painful process because it invites constant attacks at the front end from those who are getting called out. I stepped down to let things settle down. Although I retained my role as Chairman of the Board and principal shareholder, I no longer had any role in running Papa John's on a day-to-day basis.

The board of directors brought in several new professional managers after I stepped down—men and women with years of executive-level experience at major companies. The thought was that they could take a multinational business like Papa John's to the next level. That was a reasonable expectation given the résumés of the new and existing people who were now running the company. We all felt a sense of optimism across the entire company.

After I stepped down as CEO, I still made myself available to the new executives as often I could. I wanted to share my knowledge and perspective with them—I had founded the company, after all. I started meeting with some of the senior folks on a weekly or semi-regular basis. I hoped this would give them some insight into how Papa John's worked and why we did things the way we did. The meetings went well enough. We were all very respectful. It seemed as if we were all working towards a common goal. The outside world believed that, too. The stock began rising faster than it had in years.

But these positive external signs were contrary to my belief that Papa John's was once again heading in the wrong direction. This can't all be chalked up to one person. It was a combination of some of the new folks along with some of those who were already there. The main problem was that not everyone was on board with my vision for Papa John's. They didn't understand the lessons I learned from my Dad and my Papaw—the lessons about the Head Coach model. They wanted to mold Papa John's to their own liking, even if it meant taking the company away from its roots.

The company didn't change overnight. It took about 12 to 18 months. During this time, the company's leadership hired people who thought and talked like them. They also slowly convinced many existing team members to see things their way. (It says a lot about the power of Kingship that many longtime company employees gave in to its allure.) Little by little, the company began to focus on something other than making traditional, superior-quality Papa John's pizzas. Similarly, the culture of "People Are Priority Always" began to slowly disappear. If I had to sum up the new culture in one phrase, it would be this: short-term profits above all else.

I didn't realize this for nearly a year and a half. I'm not sure anyone else realized it either. Like I said, it started small and then grew from there. I believe that winning requires a whole team taking lots of little baby steps on the way to the grand victory. You can't achieve the grand victory overnight. By the same token, losing requires a team that takes lots of baby steps towards the ultimate loss. You don't usually get yourself behind the eight-ball with one large misstep—those are fairly easy to spot. It's the smaller, unnoticed ones that can lead to disaster. Instead of getting in a position to 'get lucky,' you get in a position to lose.

This same lesson applies to a company's culture. You're either building it slowly or you're chipping away at it slowly. Every company is heading in one of these two directions. Even the stagnant ones are heading in the wrong direction through simple inertia. A good culture takes work; it can't exist without deliberate actions.

Unfortunately, we were now heading in the wrong direction at Papa John's. I began to notice the problems from my seat on the Papa John's board. Given my role as chairman, it made sense for me to continue to voice my opinion about the company's direction, even if I didn't have any say in how Papa John's was being run on a day-to-day basis.

I started to see the warning signs in the middle of 2006. I've already told you about collaborative alliances—the types of relationships that

Head Coaches build. In a collaborative alliance, people work together for mutual benefit and the common good. There have to be clear and open lines of communication in order for these relationships to develop and flourish. I tried to cultivate this kind of culture, starting with the broom closet, because I wanted collaborative alliances to develop between Papa John's and our customers, our team members, our suppliers, our franchisees, our investors and our communities. From the outset, our goal was to make people's lives better—the ultimate collaborative alliance.

I became concerned when I started to see collaborative alliances disappearing. I believe this was a result of the lack of communication between the various Papa John's teams. Remember, in a Head Coach model, information flows freely so that it can inform everyone's decisions, from the board members to the janitor. That's what enables a culture of challenge in which steel sharpens steel. Kingships, on the other hand, aren't interested in having others challenge their worldview. Why would they, when their worldview is based on a false reality? They fear that a free flow of information would undermine them and cause others to wake up to the nightmare growing around them.

By the middle of 2006, different teams within Papa John's were essentially cut off from each other. Information sharing between different departments stopped happening, replaced almost entirely with vertical communication up the "chain of command." As collaborative alliances began to fade, so did morale—a sure sign of Kingship in action.

You could tell this even by watching some of the company's executives interact with the rest of the team members—or rather, by watching them *not* interact with team members. Even when Papa John's was just a broom closet in a bar, I understood the importance of getting to know your team members and making sure they knew I cared. That hasn't changed. When I'm at Papa John's corporate headquarters, I make a point to walk around the office and talk to as many team members as possible. I know a lot of the 563 team members at our headquarters on a first-name basis and ask them how they're doing when I see them. I try to learn something about their lives. I encourage our store managers and franchisees to do the same thing. This builds a sense of camaraderie and teamwork throughout the whole building—something a Head Coach strives to build.

In my view, this pretty much stopped after I stepped down. The new executives had little interest in interacting with their team members like I did. Instead, they holed themselves up in their corner offices, demanding information from their subordinates but never sharing it beyond themselves. This slowly started to undermine the team mentality that I tried so hard to build at Papa John's. The team members tell me now that they see me more in three days than they saw the old leadership team in three years.

This hints at another problem that had slowly developed over the previous 18 months: centralization.

Another clear sign of Kingship and Queenship is that the monarchs build up their capital at the expense of the rest of the kingdom. They typically believe that top down is always better than bottom up. Sure enough, some of the people who now ran Papa John's dramatically empowered and enlarged headquarters at the expense of the rest of the company. This was reflected at Papa John's in a number of ways. The number of team members at headquarters started to grow by leaps and bounds. The general and administrative budget got much larger, too—it grew from $50 to $70 million in just a two-year timeframe. These are just a few examples.

It became increasingly clear to the franchisees and the individual stores that corporate was becoming the big man in town. This was a dramatic—and unwelcome—change for Papa John's.

Like many companies in our line of work, a lot of our team members come from other businesses in the restaurant industry. We often get comments about how dramatically different our organizational structure and culture are. If you remember from Chapter One, I founded Papa John's with the understanding that we would have 1 store, 5,000 times—not the other way around. In order to accomplish this, we had to make sure that store managers, the operations team, the franchisees and everyone else in the company was on equal footing. This bottom-up approach builds teamwork, encourages innovation, spurs information sharing between teams and gives our team members a sense that they are part of something bigger than themselves. That's an amazing, unquantifiable feeling. It also drives superior results.

Needless to say, I became concerned when I noticed these two problems—more corporate centralization and fewer collaborative alliances—growing worse. I spoke out at the next board meeting, telling my fellow board members that Papa John's was forgetting the principles that made it great. I also voiced my concerns to some of the executives at the company along with the board. Unfortunately, none of them—not one—was willing to address the company's problems. Who would? They were too enthralled by the rising stock.

This was even more concerning to me. I've already told you how Kingship lulls people to sleep. I hadn't yet fully developed this concept—asleep vs. awake—but it's exactly what was happening at Papa John's. The people at the top were asleep, and the nightmare was starting to grow.

Unfortunately, people who are asleep don't know the nightmare is growing. They're too busy juggling false realities. This manifested itself in a specific way at Papa John's. Some of the company's leadership were focused on the stock price rather than the culture. It had steadily risen during 2005 and 2006, which gave people the impression that Papa John's was in a healthy place. But the seemingly healthy stock growth masked a fundamentally unhealthy culture. You can't keep a successful company on the right path by ignoring the principles and practices that made the company successful in the first place. That may run up the stock in the short term, but it's going to come crashing back down eventually.

I spent the second half of 2006 concerned that we were on this path. Yet I needed something concrete in order to convince the board that I was right. Without proof, no one would listen to me. I was about to find what I was looking for.

● ● ● ● ●

Before I give specific examples, I should make a broader point about how information is sought, shared and used under the Kingship and Head Coach models. They couldn't be further apart.

Head Coaches try to find and use the best data and analytics available to help inform their decisions. They seek out facts, science and analytics. They understand that math is not an option. If they find out that something isn't working, they try and fix it like my Papaw taught me. They also try and improve the things that *are* working. Remember: Head Coaches specialize in self-confrontation, which leads to collaborative confrontation. They challenge others and want to be challenged themselves, because challenge strengthens individuals and organizations. They're always trying to improve themselves and their teams. Dealing with data—especially bad data—in a constructive way is a hallmark of a Head Coach.

But that's not how information works in the Kingship model. They don't like information that contradicts their false reality. As I said before, people do one of three things with information in the Kingship model—they hide it, they only provide parts of it, or they manipulate it. If they're successful, the people around them begin to fall asleep. And that's when the nightmare begins to grow.

In December of 2006, the executive team presented its year-in-review financial overview to the board of directors. The company's finances were painted as if they were a slam dunk. But I wasn't convinced. I flipped through the 170-page document during the board meeting. I wanted to see how the team had closed a $10 million gap in projected income that we'd identified a few months earlier.

Buried in the middle of the document was a major change to PJ Food Service. PJFS is the subsidiary through which we sell the company's superior-quality ingredients to both franchisees and corporate stores. That includes our never-frozen dough, fresh-packed pizza sauce, the delicious toppings that go on every Papa John's pizza and more. This is a critical part of the business. Franchisees run roughly 75 percent of the Papa John's system, and they all get their ingredients from PJFS. Food costs are roughly one-third of their overall costs. If they don't have a good working relationship with PJFS, it can lead to serious problems that ripple throughout the entire company.

I recognized the importance of running food service right from its founding in the early 1990s, right around Papa John's store #100. I realized that our franchisees were already going to assume that we were making too much money off of food service, so I figured I would show them this wasn't true. I came up with a simple rule: we would only make 3 percent profit after tax on all sales to franchisees—not a penny more. Some of the franchisees didn't trust me, so I told them, "Don't listen to what I say, just watch what I do."

Keeping this promise has always been sacred to me. The most important reason was that it built trust with the franchisees, who are crucial to the success of Papa John's. It also helped keep store profitability up, allowing more stores to succeed in the long run. At the same time, the low rate makes our products more competitive, giving franchisees an incentive to purchase everything they possibly can from PJFS. This keeps our product consistent across the country—you don't have to worry whether you're being served a traditional, superior-quality Papa John's pizza. And the final reason is that we still make a very good return at the 3 percent rate. It may be low compared to our competitors, but as the saying goes, "Pigs get fat and hogs get slaughtered."

But I wasn't leading the company in December of 2006. Some of the people who now led Papa John's had no intention of keeping the promise I had made. In their minds, it was a senseless limitation on the company's ability to make money and boost quarterly earnings.

Suddenly I discovered my promise had been broken in the middle of that large document. The company had quietly ended the profit cap. The new rate was verging on 8 percent—well over twice as high.

I was livid when I saw this. First of all, I believed that some of the leadership team had not been totally candid in implementing these critical changes. Second of all, I saw no evidence that the franchisees had been consulted about the change. A few within leadership were taking advantage of the people who ran roughly 75 percent of Papa John's stores. Their thought process was simple and disturbing: the franchisees were a captive audience, so why not make millions off of them without them knowing it? This terrified me. It seemed like every night I woke up in a cold sweat at 2:59 in the morning.

I immediately knew the profit margin change would devastate the franchisees' relationship with corporate. Suddenly they'd be paying more for food than they'd planned for—remember, food costs are a third of their overall costs. With this increase in costs, it becomes harder to open new stores, to hire new people and to give raises and bonuses, all of which are already difficult enough as it is.

When you're a big company, you can play games like this, at least for a while. Small businesses can't—and that includes our franchisees. They're in the trenches every day, taking care of their team members and dealing with reality. Those are the types of hardworking men and women who wake up every day and make our country great. They're my heroes.

That's why I built Papa John's based on a small business mindset. Now I had to restore that mindset if Papa John's was going to survive. Over the next weekend, I put together a 20-page presentation with Lance Tucker, who is now the CFO of Papa John's. Our message was simple: if the management team kept this up, it would irreparably harm the company in the long run. After a few hours of discussion, the board came over to my side. We agreed that the company had to be upfront with the franchisees and communicate exactly what was going on. Corporate had to open PJFS's books so the franchisees could see what was happening. The executives had to be completely candid with the franchisees.

Some executives vigorously disagreed—naturally. But the board had spoken. I thought that was the end of it. I couldn't have been more wrong. Days passed. Weeks passed. Months passed. Still the franchisees were in the dark about how Papa John's had amended its pricing, although some of them slowly started figuring it out over the course of the year. By the end of the year, it was common knowledge that Papa John's had violated the handshake promise I had made to each and every franchisee. They were furious—no surprise there. Profits for corporate were rising, but the trust of the franchisees was plummeting as they gradually figured out what was happening.

That's a lesson that everyone would do well to remember. The sun's gonna come up, the sun's gonna go down and the truth's gonna come out. It always happens. It's just a matter of time.

This entire episode showed me that the Papa John's leadership team had basically abandoned the idea of collaborative alliances. Instead, they were now practicing collusive alliances and combative alliances. Unlike collaborative alliances, in which all parties work together for the common good, collusive alliances happen when one party conspires to get ahead at the other party's expense. Sometimes they know about it; sometimes they don't. Either way, it's not the kind of arrangement you want to have.

The same is true of combative alliances, which usually result from collusive alliances. That's when one party becomes abusive towards others, whether intellectually, emotionally or even physically. These relationships often develop once the losing side figures out that they're in a collusive alliance. That's what happened at Papa John's. Once I started identifying the company's actions in late 2006 and early 2007, the executives turned combative on me fast. You'll see some of that later in this chapter.

Neither of these types of alliances is conducive to long-term success—and that's true whether we're talking about a family, a neighborhood association or a multinational business. When these types of Machiavellian actions are occurring, where the ends justify the means, it's usually a sign that Kingship is alive and well. All I can say is: run!

• • • • •

The PJ Food Service incident put me on full alert. It wasn't the last time the company's actions ran counter to what Papa John's was all about.

What I consider to be the single worst incident happened in February 2007, only a few weeks after the food services fiasco. It involved the company's franchise agreement—the legal contract that outlines the rights and responsibilities of both Papa John's and the hundreds of franchisees who run 75 percent of the Papa John's system. It goes into tremendous detail. It describes what phone numbers stores use, the franchisee's territorial rights, how much the franchisee must contribute to the company's national marketing efforts, what quality standards the store must meet and many other important details.

Bottom line: it's an immensely important document, especially given how critical franchisees are for Papa John's success. It's even more important when you consider that the agreement lasts for *20 years*. If the i's aren't dotted and the t's aren't crossed, a bad franchise agreement can haunt a company for decades. That's why we put so much effort into our initial franchise agreements, most of which were done between 1996 and 1999 when Papa John's was expanding like wildfire.

I believed that a new franchise agreement simply wasn't needed. The vast majority of franchisees had joined the company less than a decade before, which meant they were already covered under the company's existing franchise agreement. That agreement was tried and true. It partially explained why so many franchisees joined the company in the late 90s and early 2000s. They knew that it was a fair deal for them. But some company executives thought the agreement needed to be updated anyway. They brought their proposed revision to the board's attention with little preparation.

You might assume that the Papa John's board of directors would have been given plenty of time to review such a pivotal document. You'd be wrong. The board of directors first found out about the franchise agreement on a Thursday afternoon. We were given until the end of the day to ratify it.

My jaw probably dropped to the floor when we learned this. The board needed time—preferably weeks or even months—to properly review and vet the franchise agreement. That became even more abundantly clear when I spotted several serious problems with the agreement after only a few minutes of looking at it. I convinced the board that we needed at least a weekend to review the changes.

I resolved to spend every waking moment between Thursday and Monday fixing the franchise agreement, however I could. I brought in Kevin Coyne, a consultant who had worked with Papa John's for several years, to help me. The two of us spent the next three days working nonstop, day and night. The deeper we dug into the franchise agreement, the more problems we found. From what I could see, it would have been disastrous for Papa John's had it gone into effect.

The most blatant oversight was that the deal wasn't accompanied by a financial analysis. That would have given the board a year-by-year breakdown of what the new agreement would cost—i.e., what Papa John's was getting versus what we were giving up. It quickly became apparent why this analysis was left out. The agreement contained concessions to the franchisees that would have seriously diminished Papa John's profitability in the long run. I have never been opposed to giving the franchisees a good deal—remember my agreement with them over food services—but the fact of the matter was that Papa John's was already incredibly generous. Further giveaways would have diminished the company's long-term competitiveness, even if it increased short-term profits.

The more I dug, the more problems I found. I slowly started to realize that something bigger was at play here. It came to me over that long weekend: the agreement was the management team's effort to be overly generous to the franchisees in order to offset the backlash that would likely come from the previous months' changes in food services pricing. Management was giving to the franchisees with one hand but taking back with another.

I made more revisions than I could count over the next three days. I wish we'd had more time. But the board had only given me the weekend to review it. As promised, I came back on Monday with a heavily revised franchise agreement. Despite the limited amount of time in which to work, we cleaned up the most egregious problems so that Papa John's wouldn't regret them for the next 20 years. It was better for the company. It was better for the franchisees. It was better for everyone. At the end of the day, my revised agreement was much closer to the win-win paradigm that Papa John's was originally built on. Management's proposed agreement, by comparison, was a win for some and a loss for others.

The board recognized that my version of the franchise agreement was fundamentally better. They passed it after several weeks of serious back-and-forth. We're still bound by this agreement today, and that will be the case for a long time.

After the incidents with PJFS and the franchise agreement, a number of franchisees became understandably unhappy at the way corporate was treating them. They thought they needed to let the board know how they felt, so they joined together to form an organization called the Papa John's Franchise Association. The organization existed to communicate the franchisees' general unhappiness to corporate and the board of directors.

The franchisees began complaining on a semi-regular basis to the company's leadership. They were unhappy with a number of things and wanted to see some serious changes. Under normal circumstances, the company would have welcomed their challenges—we're supposed to be in a collaborative alliance, after all. But that was no longer the case.

At one point, the Papa John's Franchise Association submitted two letters to the company in which they laid out the specific actions taken by corporate that were hurting the franchisees. The letters were brutal. The franchisees complained that they weren't making money, that they weren't happy with PJFS and that they didn't trust that Papa John's had their best interests at heart. Information like this is crucial—it would have helped the board members determine how healthy Papa John's truly was.

But here's the thing: the letters weren't brought to the board's attention. I only found out about them because of my friend, Tim O'Hern, who has been a franchisee since 1993. As a Papa John's franchisee, he received copies of the letters. So did the rest of the franchisees. He showed them to me shortly after he got them. If it weren't for him, the board might never have discovered that a huge portion of our franchisees were furious with Papa John's.

The poor leadership continued. At one point the management team spent $18 million buying up a bunch of stores from a franchisee in the western U.S. The board didn't have the chance to adequately review the data regarding the sale until after it had been consummated. We sure would have liked to have seen it. The company paid way more than it should have. The franchisee was disgruntled with the company, and management decided to buy the franchisee out rather than address the underlying problems. They paid him more than his stores were worth just to keep the peace. If the board had known all of the details, we might have stopped the deal dead in its tracks.

The management team also began to cause damage to the Papa John's cheese fund, which was known as BIBP. We used this fund to ensure that our franchisees were protected from the wild price variations that affect the cheese industry. BIBP would buy cheese at market prices and then sell the cheese to the franchisees (through food services) at a fixed price each quarter, based on a number of factors. Starting in 2007, however, the price of cheese escalated quickly and BIBP began to sell cheese at a loss. This made the franchisees happy and boosted profits and earnings for the corporate-owned restaurants. However, these artificially low cheese prices had to be subsidized by someone, and the Papa John's system was on the hook for it.

BIBP ran up a huge deficit through 2008—a staggering $43 million in debt (the company only earned $37 million in 2008) that would either have to be repaid by franchisees and corporate restaurants through higher future cheese prices or be absorbed by Papa John's corporate. This is one of the most egregious examples of how the company only focused on short-term goals at the expense of long-term success. And even though everything was reported properly in the company's audited financial statements, it's another example of how the company wanted to look good on the surface while actually being underhanded.

The list goes on. Leadership downplayed or avoided presenting data on executive compensation. No wonder. Some were trying to give themselves bigger bonuses while corporate earnings were budgeted to decrease. Elsewhere, the company held a major ceremony for the opening of the 100th Papa John's store in China. I later found out it was actually just the 70th store—another example of manufacturing good news.

I could keep going, but I won't. The pattern should be clear by this point. Papa John's was no longer being run by Head Coaches. It was being run on the Kingship model, in which short-term profits were ultimately more important than the people who made the company so successful.

Yet despite everything that was going on, the board of directors remained convinced that Papa John's was heading in the right direction. As I said before, the increased profits from 2005 to 2007 were intoxicating to some of our board members, causing them to fall asleep. For now, I could only sit and watch as others weakened the company that I had built with my blood, my sweat and my tears. It was heartbreaking.

•   •   •   •   •

So far I've described what I saw from the Papa John's boardroom. It's also important to note that things were changing dramatically at the store level. The company's change in direction began affecting how stores operated on a day-to-day basis, starting in late 2006 and early 2007.

If you remember from Chapters Three and Four, I firmly believe that "focus" is the most important word in the Merriam-Webster Dictionary when it comes to building a business. That's why we made focus the first component of FASPAC. We define it like this: "We must keep *The Main Thing, The Main Thing.*" For Papa John's first 20 years, The Main Thing was delivering a traditional, superior-quality Papa John's pizza to our customers and taking care of our people. We weren't nearly as focused on either of these things by the end of 2006.

By this point it should be clear that taking care of our people wasn't something that some members of our new management team really cared about. They forgot that businesses are supposed to help themselves by helping others, specifically by making a pizza that customers enjoy. Instead, some of the executives were far more concerned with helping themselves even if it hurt others. Instead of trying to create value that benefited the entire Papa John's team, they wanted to boost profits and earnings which might increase the stock price but would in turn also increase their bonuses and the value of their own stock options. The entire Papa John's team suffered from short-term thinking.

So did our quality, for that matter. The company's new focus on profits above all else translated into a much lower emphasis on making a traditional, superior-quality Papa John's pizza.

I mean that in two senses. The first is the obvious one: some of the men and women in the corner suites simply didn't care if our stores made pizzas that weren't an 8 or higher on our 10-point quality scale. In fact, they even changed the 10-point scale we had developed in the 1990s. The new standards were lower so that it was easier for stores to make a pizza that was an 8 or above. I didn't know this had happened, but I could see and taste the difference in our pizzas starting in 2007. The inevitable result was that pizza quality started to decline. Only two years after I had finally gotten our stores to start making quality pizzas again, we were sliding back in the wrong direction. Papa John's was shifting into reverse.

There's a second sense in which the company lost its focus on making traditional, superior-quality Papa John's pizzas. Quite literally, corporate became obsessed with products that weren't pizza. Think about how misguided that is. Papa John's is a *pizza* company. We always—and we always will—sell a number of products to complement our pizzas, but we never make those extras The Main Thing. That's a surefire way to lower quality on the most important product of all: a traditional, superior-quality Papa John's pizza.

Corporate slowly began introducing a bewildering number of products into stores. The goal was to get customers to start buying things in addition to our pizzas. It was like Papa John's was a retail company rather than a delivery pizza company. If you walk into the average retail store and go to the checkout line, you'll see all kinds of snacks, candy, crackers and other goodies. That's what the inside of Papa John's stores started to look like by 2007.

I couldn't keep track of how many different products were introduced. None of them—*none of them*—made sense. The stores were forced to start carrying a wide variety of candies and chocolates. We introduced a line of pizza sauce. That eventually expanded to include barbecue sauce and a few other sauces. Next up were bottles of our famous pepperoncini and shakers of Papa John's pizza seasoning.

The list got longer. At one point, Papa John's introduced a "pizza and a movie deal," which forced stores to start carrying a variety of DVDs. One thing that never got off the drawing board—but came way too close—was a CD of the "greatest hits" from Papa John's commercials. Can you imagine?

At this point you must be asking yourself, "What does any of this have to do with a traditional, superior-quality Papa John's pizza?" Nothing. Nothing at all.

These flights of fancy took away from Papa John's reputation as a multinational pizza company that acted like a small, independent, mom-'n'-pop pizzeria. That's the vision I had for Papa John's when the company was stored in the cardboard box I hid in the back of my clothes closet. Now that vision was being discarded in favor of turning Papa John's into just another company that had no identity, no culture and nothing that differentiated it from the competition. We were on the fast track to mediocrity.

That's what happens when you focus on the wrong Main Thing. Papa John's business model is highly specific, and we developed it through a lot of trial and error in the company's early years. We're not a retail store—we're a pizza company that specializes in delivering delicious, high-quality pizzas. Only between 30 and 40 percent of Papa John's customers actually come to the store to pick up their pizza. Expending so much money and energy trying to get these customers to spend more at the store made little sense—especially if it divided restaurants' focus and hurt the quality of our pizzas. Almost everyone knew it, too. The franchisees didn't like it. Neither did the store managers. They all knew it wouldn't work. They were right: the customers didn't respond to it.

Unsurprisingly, the vast majority of these changes were eventually dropped. They never should have seen the light of day in the first place. The better option would have been to keep The Main Thing, The Main

Thing. Papa John's should have doubled down on constantly improving our quality pizzas. Instead, we were doubling down on a strategy of ever more complexity. Complexity is the enemy of focus. It's already hard enough to run a multinational company with 5,000 stores spread across 40 countries.

That's a lesson that every entrepreneur should know. Why do a bunch of things poorly when you can do one thing well? Your goal isn't to be a wandering generality—it's to be a meaningful specific that sets you apart from your competitors. To put it another way, the ultimate level of sophistication is the ability to simplify. For Papa John's, we had distilled our company's ethos into a single slogan since 1996: Better Ingredients. Better Pizza. Papa John's is the multinational pizza chain that acts like an independent, mom-'n'-pop pizzeria. We lose that if we try to become the jack of all trades but master of none.

Papa John's slogan has been "Better Ingredients. Better Pizza." since 1996. Yet by 2007, we weren't focused on living our slogan out. The quality of our products—especially our pizzas—didn't seem to be that important anymore. Talking to the franchisees and other team members at corporate, I often heard that they could go through entire meetings—and sometimes entire weeks—without anyone even mentioning the word quality. The focus was solely on boosting profits, which I found terrifying.

This change—from quality-driven to quarterly-earnings-driven—was a 180-degree departure from the way Papa John's was run from our founding in 1984 to when I stepped down in 2005. I have always believed that the best way to increase sales was to focus on quality. Customers would then recognize the difference and reward us with their business. That's also why Papa John's includes a pepperoncini and garlic butter with every pizza we make. It's an unexpected extra. Customers remember it. As someone once pointed out, "Customer loyalty is gained one customer at a time."

The flipside is true, too—"Loyalty is lost one customer at a time." If we kept insulting our customers by giving them a pizza that wasn't worthy of the Papa John's name, we were going to start losing customers in droves.

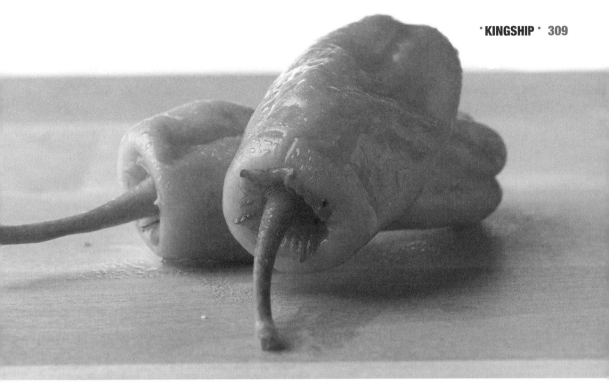

The famous pepperoncini, complimentary with every original crust pizza

It was clear to me by the end of 2007 that Papa John's needed to radically change course. We needed to head back towards the Head Coach model. The company's future depended on it.

Our board meetings were becoming increasingly tense as I tried to make my case. I was on one side, all by myself. On the other side was the rest of the board, along with the management team itself. I was trying to get the entire board to realize that Papa John's needed a new direction. Unfortunately, some of the board had joined with a few executives in a collusive alliance. They wanted to keep the company focused on short-term profits, even if it cost Papa John's in the long run. Some of the directors had fallen into a deep sleep.

I knew it was my job to wake them up. And the executive team knew that's what I was trying to do, too. One thing became increasingly clear: some of them *really* wanted me out of the picture. I first realized this after I pointed out that the changes they made to PJ Food Service weren't a good idea. They were as furious with me as I was with them. Their attempts to get rid of me only intensified as we had further run-ins.

At one point they offered to buy me out of the company. This shows just how much they resented me—they wanted to kick Papa

John's founder to the curb. It also shows just how little they understood me. When they offered me this deal, they assumed I would take it without a second thought. The truth was selling my Papa John's shares would have made me hundreds of millions of dollars. I vividly remember my reaction when they made me this offer: "Do you want my wife and kids, too?" I built Papa John's with my bare hands. I love Papa John's with all of my heart. It didn't matter that they offered me a lot of money—I still turned them down. I wasn't going to turn my back on Papa John's team members, franchisees, suppliers and customers. I believed I owed it to all of them to save what we had built together. I couldn't walk away from my life's work.

When that didn't work, the management team slowly started cutting me out of all of the company's marketing materials. They didn't want me to be in any television ads, radio spots—nothing. By the end of 2007 it seemed as if I was no longer Papa John.

After that, the management team came to me to inform me that, unbeknownst to me, Papa John's owned my image rights. They said they owned my look and could therefore dictate what I said, who I said it to and how I lived my life. I was taken aback when they said this. I was at a loss for words. It simply wasn't true.

When I still hadn't left, some of the executives started to get creative. One day when I showed up for a board meeting, I discovered that my keycard didn't work. I literally couldn't get inside the building of the company that I founded. Of course I got that fixed, but it showed me just how far some in management were willing to go to let me know that I was no longer welcome at Papa John's.

But I truly wasn't prepared for what happened next. One day, while I was at the company headquarters, I got a call from my wife. My daughter had just been to the doctor but was told that she had no health insurance. She had called my wife in tears, wondering why our insurance, which was provided through Papa John's, had been declined. We had received no notification that we were being removed from the company's plan whatsoever. My wife and daughter had just found that out the hard way.

This was the last straw for me. I'd spent the past 18 months being attacked by certain board members and some of the company management. I could take that—I don't back down from a fight. But now they were going after my family. They were trying to hurt me in whatever way they could.

That's when I redoubled my efforts to convince the rest of the board that Papa John's was in a life-or-death struggle. Some of them were starting to come around by the middle of 2008. They were finally waking up to the nightmare that was raging all around them.

Papa John's was really struggling by the middle of 2008. Our pizza quality was once again declining. Customers were starting to order our pizza with less regularity because we were no longer meeting their expectations. Trust between franchisees and corporate had deteriorated to lows never before seen in Papa John's history. The changes made by headquarters were wreaking havoc at the store level. A significant number of stores simply weren't making money and were teetering on the edge of closing. From my seat on the board, it looked to me like Papa John's was entering its death throes.

And then came the fall of 2008. The executive team presented to the board its proposed budget for fiscal year 2009. The budget was a farce, to put it mildly. It relied on wildly unrealistic assumptions. Some of the numbers made no sense to me. With the American economy struggling through the Great Recession, I knew that Papa John's needed to be firing on all cylinders in order to weather the storm. The proposed budget, however, would have only harmed the company at a time when we could least afford it.

My thoughts were confirmed only two days after the board first saw the budget. One of the executives woke up and was finally willing to confront the nightmare. He came to me and told me in no uncertain terms that the budget wasn't going to work. It was, as he put it, "specious."

This caused quite a stir when I shared his analysis with the board of directors. They demanded answers. Even though many bad things had happened over the previous two years, an unworkable budget was simply a bridge too far. The other board members couldn't ignore the situation anymore. It was so jarring that they not only woke up, they finally wanted to fix it.

There was also some luck involved—or maybe it was justice. Papa John's stock started tanking in October and November 2008—it fell roughly 50 percent in a matter of weeks. This hurt me a lot, since I was the company's largest shareholder. But it was the natural result of everything that had happened over the previous two years (with some help from the overall market decline as well). You can only focus on short-term profits for so long before it all comes crashing down around you.

This shook the board even more than the specious budget. Combined, these two things finally convinced everyone that we had to take drastic measures. After talking to every member of the board, we came to an agreement. The company needed new leadership. Even though no one person was at fault for what had happened, Papa John's needed a wholesale change if we hoped to turn from the Kingship model back to the Head Coach model.

I remember talking with another board member who asked me, "What do you think this will do to the company's stock?" My response was simple: "It will most likely hurt us in the short run. But in the long run, Papa John's will be set up for success." I was only half-right—it *didn't* hurt us in the short term, and the company is now doing better than ever, as shown in part by an increase in the stock price of 1,000% since that time.

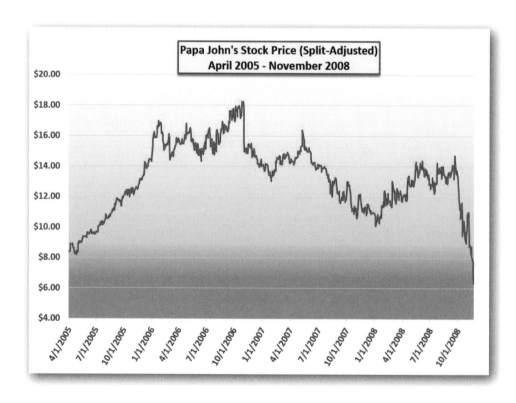

I rejoined Papa John's as chief executive officer on December 4, 2008. I had my work cut out for me. My company was spiraling downwards. All the problems that had been created over the previous two years were now festering in the open. Finances were bad. Quality was suffering. Our team members, franchisees, suppliers, investors and customers felt mistreated. From top to bottom, Papa John's was in a worse place than at any point in our 25-year history. That's what happens when Kingship and Queenship run rampant—chaos ensues.

Head Coaches are the only ones who can turn around a terrible situation like this. As the CEO of the company, not only did I have to be a Head Coach in everything I did, I also needed to build a team that could do the same thing. Then we needed to inspire everyone at every level of the company to start acting like Head Coaches, too. We needed to uncover the foundation upon which Papa John's was built, and then build something bigger, better and stronger than ever before. We needed to practice FASPAC. We needed to Go Left. We needed to be Head Coaches.

So that's what we did.

●　●　●　●　●

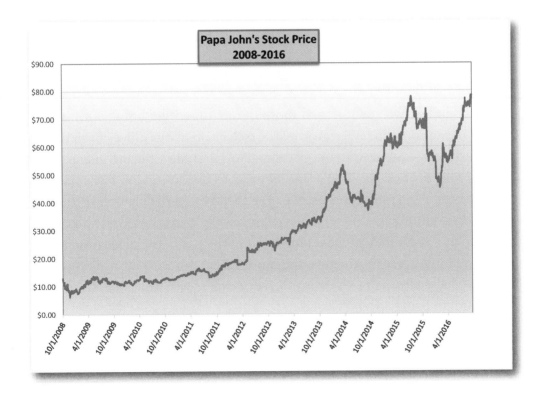

I remember thinking to myself at the time: "Where do I start?"

After giving it some thought, I determined that I needed to do to Papa John's what I had done at Mick's Lounge about 25 years earlier. We needed to clean the place up—literally. Neither headquarters nor stores were up to our high standards in terms of appearance, mainly in small ways. But customers notice the small things, and we are, after all, in the customer service industry. Plus, I figured it would help boost team members' morale if they worked in a place that looked great. If there's one thing I've learned over the years, it's that little things can have a big impact.

The buildings weren't the only things that needed cleaning. We also needed to clean house—especially on the upper floors. You can't turn a ship around if a bunch of people are rowing in the wrong direction—or, worse yet, if the captains and their staff are giving the wrong orders. Starting in 2009, we began to systematically replace every single member of the Executive Leadership Team. There was no way around it. The board and I realized that we had to make drastic changes in order to restore confidence for everyone involved in the Papa John's experience—customers, team members, franchisees, suppliers, investors, everyone.

Today, there isn't a single member of that Executive Leadership Team left. They've all been replaced by men and women who are dedicated to doing the right thing and living the Papa John's way—the Head Coach model.

Together, we spend much more of our time interacting with the rest of the company. We can't hole ourselves up in our offices or in the boardroom—we need to be out talking to, laughing with and inspiring everyone around us. That's true not just at headquarters, but across the entire Papa John's system. We now spend more of our time visiting different cities, meeting franchisees and recognizing the stores and the team members that are knocking it out of the park. The more time we spend building up our teams, the more successful we'll be. This was a *huge* change from the way things were between 2005 and 2008. It's also central to being a Head Coach.

People were skeptical at first, none more so than the franchisees. Who could blame them? The changes made over the previous few years had tarnished their trust in management. They were hurting, too. "Unit economics," as they're known in the business, were in a bad place. In fact, stores were closing in record numbers.

We needed to fix this, pronto. Nowhere was this more important than with food service. Starting in 2009 I determined that we had to make it right with the franchisees. Like good Head Coaches, we needed to take the hit. So that's what we did.

Not only did we renew our promise to not make more than 3 percent profit after tax on food service, we also promised to make *less* than that until we had paid back all the ill-gotten gains that the company had made over the previous two years. We made roughly 2.8 percent profit starting in 2009. It tells you how badly the franchisees had been overcharged when you consider that the price reductions we gave them did not make them whole until 2015. In 2015, we made too much because of rising volumes, so we actually cut each franchisee a check for the money we owed them. We were serious about making it right—a good relationship with the franchisees is crucial to a healthy and happy Papa John's. This may have hurt the company financially in the short run, but it was absolutely critical to making us successful and trustworthy in the long run again.

We also needed to pay off the $43 million debt that had been racked up in the cheese fund. Over the course of my first year back, we started throwing money at the problem to make it go away. We eventually got it down to $14 million by 2010. Despite the company needing this money for other capital needs, Papa John's International bit the bullet and paid off the remaining amounts. We needed to get that monkey off our back, and we did.

Beyond the financial issues, we also began to focus on the innovations and long-term changes that were crucial to Papa John's survival. Some of this had been neglected in the pursuit of short-term profit. Much of the old management team thought it was better to make one buck today than make two bucks tomorrow, or even three bucks the day after that.

My primary focus was making Papa John's the undisputed leader in the online pizza ordering business. Right after I came back, I wrote a one-page memo on the 15 reasons why Papa John's needed to up its online game. This has always been a passion of mine since I saw the internet's tremendous potential. In fact, we had been at the forefront of the internet game since right after the turn of the century: in 2001, we became the first pizza chain to offer online ordering for all of our traditional stores nationwide. By 2008 we were doing $411 million a year in online sales. Now that may seem like a lot, but it wasn't when you consider where we were only two years later—$570 million a year in 2010. We project online sales of $1.5 billion for 2016, proof that a little innovation can go a long way.

The innovations didn't stop there. We created a new executive position to help us stay up to speed in our fast-changing industry. We developed and rolled out a new touch screen point-of-sales system in 2014 that was industry-leading and incredibly easy to use.

We're no stranger to being first in the digital space. Papa John's was also the first national pizza brand to offer system wide mobile ordering with SMS text in 2007 and the first to launch a nationwide digital rewards program in 2010, Papa Rewards. In 2016, we became the first na-

The Papa John's online menu

tional restaurant company to offer online ordering via an Apple TV app.

We also renewed our emphasis on research and development. We completely renovated the R&D lab in corporate headquarters—I describe the lab and the kitchen next door as the beating heart of headquarters. It's staffed with a dedicated team of professionals whose sole job is to figure out how Papa John's can use better ingredients to make better pizzas. They spend their days improving our pizza's flavor, making it healthier, cutting out artificial ingredients—the works. They're always looking for new and better ways to make a traditional, superior-quality Papa John's pizza.

And we created a position that doesn't exist at any other company in the world: "chief ingredient officer." (I told you about Sean Muldoon in the last chapter.) This person's only job is to make sure we're getting the best ingredients for everything we make. In fact, Papa John's spends an extra $100 million per year to buy ingredients that don't contain artificial colors, flavors or additives, as well as antibiotic-free chicken and cage-free eggs.

But keep in mind that corporate isn't the key to the company's success. Every single store also has a critical play a role to play. I challenged every single store in the Papa John's system to start coming up with ways to improve their products and their sales. On that note, we restored significant decision-making power back to the store level because we wanted them to start innovating and finding new and improved ways to serve their customers and their communities. That's almost always going to work better than a top-down, one-size-fits-all mandate. Such a mandate may sound easier in principle, but it usually turns out to be a disaster in practice. The people closest to a problem should be the ones who fix it—they have the best knowledge and the best incentives to get things right.

One of the most important things Head Coaches do is to identify the potential in their team members, and then help them to realize that potential. That's exactly what I started to do from the moment I got back. Some of the earliest changes we made were to our 10-point pizza rating system. We raised the standards higher than they were before I stepped down. I firmly believed that our stores would rise to the challenge and start making truly better pizzas. I was right. Scores began rising.

The Quality Assurance Lab at Papa John's Headquarters

We asked our team members to be the best they could be in other ways, too. At our 2009 Operations Convention—OpCon—I took the stage and issued a challenge to all of our franchisees and store managers. I told them we needed to start thinking big. At that point most of them were making the assumption that a store was successful if it did $15,000 to $18,000 a week in sales. I told them we needed to aim higher—$25,000 or more a week. Once we freed them to start coming up with ways to do this, many stores started to hit this mark pretty quickly. When people have the freedom to make their own decisions, they can surprise you.

And instead of undermining franchisees and store managers, corporate started to actually help them out. One thing we did was nearly double our national marketing budget so that we could get our name and our unique promise—Better Ingredients. Better Pizza.—out to more and more people. A lot of our new marketing campaigns sought to build our brand by using me in new and unique ways. It turned out that a lot of viewers thought I was a paid actor in the late 1990s and the early-to-mid 2000s. So we tried a new tack, starting with the "Papa's In The House" campaign. The marketing campaigns we run to this day are in a similar vein. They're some of the most effective we've ever had.

Papa's in the House ad campaign

This is only a partial list of all the changes we made starting in late 2008 and early 2009. It would take a second book to list them all and describe their impact. But suffice it to say, the more we did, the brighter things got.

Today, Papa John's is stronger than it has ever been. Our profitability is at an all-time high. Our stock is up six-fold since 2009. The board has a great understanding of our business and has really grown to understand the way I think. The Executive Leadership Team members are unified in their pursuit of excellence and their desire to utilize the principles that I've outlined in this book. Our team member satisfaction has never been higher and we've been named one of the Top 25 Places to Work in Kentucky for the third consecutive year. We're opening stores left and right—we hit store #5,000 this year. Our pizza scores and customer service have never been better. And here's the truly crazy thing: there's still so much more we can do to improve. At Papa John's, the sky's the limit.

Awards for Top 25 Places to Work in Kentucky

Here's my point: the results will blow your mind when you put the Head Coach model into action. You just have to have the courage to see it through. It's easy to give up when the going gets tough, but a Head Coach realizes that the right thing is always worth doing, no matter how hard it is. In fact, I've found that the harder thing to do is usually the right thing to do. If you can stick to your guns during the hard times, you can make it through anything. You'll also be stronger for it in the long run. As I said in Chapter Six, a Head Coach refuses to lose.

● ● ● ● ●

Here's the most important thing that's happening at Papa John's today. We've faced our fair share of hard times and dark times, as I've told you. There's never a question of whether or not we will face another storm—we will. The question is whether we will be prepared to navigate through it, using the guiding principles that have brought Papa John's this far.

I believe the answer to that question is a resounding "Yes!" I realized several years ago that we needed to start *training* the Papa John's team to recognize what a Head Coach was. You have to know what good is if you ever hope to practice it and make it a reality.

Developing this training program has easily been one of the best things that's happened in all of Papa John's history. In 2011, I started meeting with some of our team members to sketch out what a training program would look like. I've spent the better part of the last five years fleshing this out. By the end of 2011 we determined that we wanted to call it "Go Left: A Culture of Intrapreneurship." When you go left, you take the harder road of the Head Coach. The other option is to take the easier road to Kingship. We've put together hundreds of pages of training materials and created an entire syllabus that explains what this means and how it plays out in practice.

After years of development, refinement and improvement, we're now rolling out this program to our entire system. We started in 2013 with the Executive Leadership Team. In 2016, we began rolling it out to department heads and managers across the organization. My vision is for every Papa John's team member to go through this Go Left training. And we'll continue to improve it so that it resonates with as many people as possible.

I can't overemphasize just how important this is. Papa John's 30-plus-year story is the story of ups and downs, highs and lows, peaks and valleys. When we reached those peaks, it's because we were Head Coaches who knew that we had to Go Left. When we wandered into those valleys, it's because we forgot the principles that made us so successful. We lost our focus. We started operating within the Kingship model. We forgot that our job is to make the world a better place. It is undeniable that the company suffered when these problems manifested themselves. Now I want to do everything in my power to make sure we never repeat the mistakes of the past.

The best way to do that is to give every Papa John's team member the tools and the knowledge they need to do what's right—to be Head Coaches who Go Left. I've said throughout this book that we're in the people business more than we're in the pizza business. Now we're even better than that. With the results we've had utilizing the Head Coach model and the Go Left program, I believe that Papa John's has transformed into a people company that happens to sell pizza.

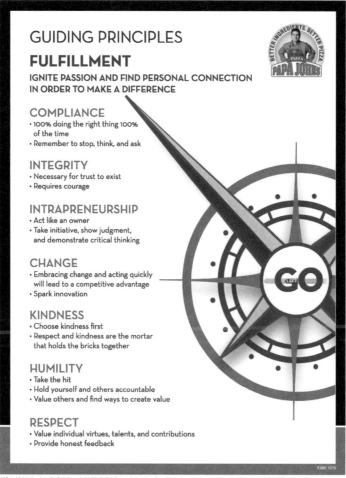

Go Left Guiding Principles

Following these principles won't be easy—it certainly hasn't been easy at Papa John's. But it's what we needed to do. We've faced our fair share of crises over the years. Yet we've always come out stronger because we turn back to the principles and the practices that guided us in the broom closet more than 30 years ago. We'll face more crises in the years to come—I have no doubt of that. I also know that if we remember to Go Left, we'll always get back to making the traditional, superior-quality Papa John's pizzas.

I've spent the majority of my life working to make that vision a reality. People often ask me why, after all these years, I still work so hard, day in and day out. My answer is simple. You never know, maybe someday I'll get it right.

CONCLUSION: WHAT'S NEXT

Thank you for reading my book. I guess you could say this is the end of the beginning, as the future holds much more for the Papa John's story.

I believe that Papa John's shows what's possible when a business is built on a solid, principled foundation. Even before I made the first Papa John's pizza in a broom closet in the back of a bar in 1984—32 years ago—I knew that I wanted to run a good business and earn a good profit. I knew that even before I made my first pizza at all, which was 40 years ago at Rocky's Sub Pub. For as long as I can remember, I wanted to follow the example set by my Dad and my Papaw, the two most important men in my life. In their own ways, they taught me that a good business improves people's lives and communities.

That is what we have always tried to do, one traditional, superior-quality Papa John's pizza at a time. Papa John's is my life's work.

It has definitely been a bumpy ride. But we've always held on to ourselves, persevered through the hard times and come out the other side stronger. Looking at how bad things were at times and at how good things are today, I can't help but feel a sense of pride in what we've accomplished. Today, our team operates one of the largest and most admired pizza companies in the entire world. Papa John's has been on fire since the dark years ended in late 2008 (take a look at the charts on the next page). We have 5,000 stores, our stock value has soared, our culture is booming and our pizza quality is great and still getting better year by year. "Better Ingredients. Better Pizza." has never been more true for us.

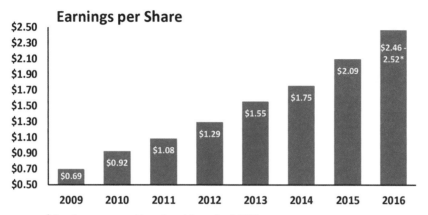

Earnings per Share

Year	EPS
2009	$0.69
2010	$0.92
2011	$1.08
2012	$1.29
2013	$1.55
2014	$1.75
2015	$2.09
2016	$2.46 – 2.52*

* Based on company guidance issued November 1, 2016
2009 and 2010 are presented on a non-GAAP basis for comparability purposes

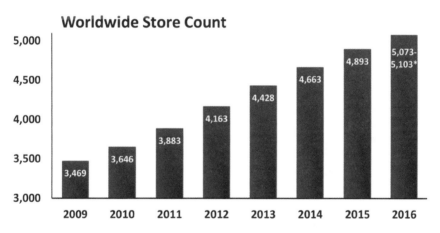

Worldwide Store Count

Year	Stores
2009	3,469
2010	3,646
2011	3,883
2012	4,163
2013	4,428
2014	4,663
2015	4,893
2016	5,073 – 5,103*

* Based on company guidance issued February 23, 2016

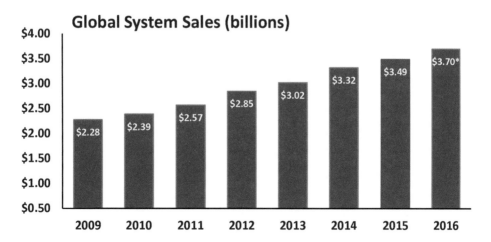

Global System Sales (billions)

Year	Sales
2009	$2.28
2010	$2.39
2011	$2.57
2012	$2.85
2013	$3.02
2014	$3.32
2015	$3.49
2016	$3.70*

* Based on company investor presentation dated September 26, 2016

But it's also increasingly clear to me that it isn't enough. That's why we're expanding our motto to "Better Ingredients. Better Pizza. *Better People*." As I've said throughout this book, people are ultimately much more important to us than pizza. Our team members, our franchisees, our suppliers, our shareholders and our customers are all like teammates to me. Papa John's wouldn't be where it is today without them. As I walk through the halls, visit stores, check in with suppliers and give my team members high-fives, I can't help but marvel at what we've built together.

One of the biggest challenges we face is that knowledge and data double every year. If we hope to make sense of it—and use it most effectively to improve the world around us—then it's critical that we collaborate, challenge each other, and share our thoughts on the opportunities that lie ahead. How can we figure out 'what's next', and how can we be the first to it?

It's because of our people that I believe that Papa John's best days are ahead of us. It goes without saying that we'll run into tough times—it's never a question of whether a storm is coming, but when the storm will hit and how you handle it. Yet we have never been better prepared for whatever will come our way. We will make the hard choices, and we will make them quickly. We will be Head Coaches, and we will Go Left.

I only briefly outlined how we turned Papa John's around in the previous chapter. But the truth is that it would take a lot longer to explain how we got from where we were at the end of 2008 to where we are today. Since then, we have maintained the two frameworks that were key to Papa John's early success: our business model and our customer experience matrix. But we have also strengthened Papa John's and made its foundation even sturdier by building the framework of *culture*—the framework of Go Left. The combination of these three crucial frameworks is responsible for our non-stop growth, employee satisfaction, customer satisfaction, and continued success.

Though we have accomplished much since the days of the broom closet, I still have goals for myself and my team. My primary goal is to continue improving at being a Head Coach who chooses to Go Left, and that my team members do the same thing on a daily basis, whatever form it may take. If we do this, we'll surprise ourselves with what's possible at Papa John's.

I'm sure you have goals as well, and after reading this book, I hope that becoming a Head Coach is now one of them. I firmly believe that if more people seek to wake up every day, Go Left, and practice the Head Coach model, then our world will be a better place. The story of Papa John's proves that the decisions we all make on a day-to-day basis can transform our own lives, our communities, and even society as a whole. If this book can change even one or two lives for the better, then I'll consider it a success.

I can't wait to hear your stories about how you apply the Head Coach model in your life or business. Please share your experiences with me at headcoach@papajohns.com. I hope to learn from you, just as I hope you've learned from me. Who knows—you may even make an appearance in my next book!